ON MENTAL GROWTH

ON MENTAL GROWTH

Bion's Ideas that Transform Psychoanalytical Clinical Practice

Lia Pistiner de Cortiñas

Originally published in Spanish in 2011 as
Sobre el crecimiento mental: las ideas de Bion que transforman la clinica psicoanalitca by Editorial Biebel, Buenos Aires

First published in English in 2017 by
Karnac Books Ltd
118 Finchley Road, London NW3 5HT

Copyright © 2017 to Lia Pistiner de Cortiñas.

The right of Lia Pistiner de Cortiñas to be identified as the author of this work has been asserted in accordance with §§77 and 78 of the Copyright Design and Patents Act 1988.

All rights reserved. No part of this publication may be reproduced, stored in a retrieval system, or transmitted, in any form or by any means, electronic, mechanical, photocopying, recording, or otherwise, without the prior written permission of the publisher.

British Library Cataloguing in Publication Data

A C.I.P. for this book is available from the British Library

ISBN 978 1 78220 380 3

Edited, designed and produced by The Studio Publishing Services Ltd
www.publishingservicesuk.co.uk
email: studio@publishingservicesuk.co.uk

www.karnacbooks.com

CONTENTS

ACKNOWLEDGEMENTS   vii

ABOUT THE AUTHOR   ix

PREFACE by Lawrence J. Brown   xi

FOREWORD by Arnaldo Chuster   xv

INTRODUCTION
The ultrasensorial and infrasensorial spectrum: xvii
the extension of the psychoanalytical map of the mind

CHAPTER ONE
Bion: the thinker and his work   1

CHAPTER TWO
Differentiation between the psychotic and the non-psychotic   13
parts of the personality

CHAPTER THREE
Projective identification: realistic, communicative,   27
and hypertrophic modalities

CHAPTER FOUR
An illustration of the ideas in Chapter Three used
as clinical material through the film *Pi* — 39

CHAPTER FIVE
The origin and nature of thinking — 59

CHAPTER SIX
Illustration of the ideas about the origin and nature
of thought using the film *Twelve Angry Men* — 71

CHAPTER SEVEN
Learning from Experience: alpha function and reverie — 95

CHAPTER EIGHT
The matrix functions of thinking:
myths, dreams, and models — 111

CHAPTER NINE
The function of dreams and myths as instruments
with which to investigate mental life — 121

CHAPTER TEN
A theory of knowing–dreaming–thinking:
emotional links and the container–contained relationship — 133

CHAPTER ELEVEN
Transformations — 151

CHAPTER TWELVE
The difference between reparation and transformation — 161

CHAPTER THIRTEEN
Tropisms and mental growth — 165

NOTE — 183

REFERENCES — 185

INDEX — 189

ACKNOWLEDGEMENTS

I want to thank all my students of the Bion seminars and especially Marta Lilliecreutz, Maria Pistani, and Maria Pollitzer, students and colleagues who, for many years, have been part of a study group in which we have a creative dialogue that contributes to our mental growth.

*To my husband, Jorge, and to my children,
Julian, Luciano, and Eugenia*

ABOUT THE AUTHOR

Lía Pistiner de Cortiñas is a training analyst, a full member of the Argentine Psychoanalytical Society (SAP), and a fellow of the International Psychoanalytical Association (IPA). She is a professor at the Faculty of Psychology, Buenos Aires University, and runs seminars on Bion and the Theory of the Psychoanalytic Technique at the University Institute of Mental Health (IUSAM) of APDEBA (Buenos Aires Psychoanalytic Association). She is the author of *The Aesthetic Dimension of the Mind: Variations on a Theme of Bion,* and *Autismo: Una Perspectiva Psicoanalitica,* and has contributed to numerous other publications.

PREFACE

The great civilisations of antiquity have nearly always arisen in the fertile cradles of life-giving rivers: the Nile and its bountiful delta, the generative soil of the Tigris-Euphrates, and the lush Indus valley all gave nurture to early communities from which impressive empires grew. In the psychoanalytic world, the River Plate, which separates Argentina from Uruguay, has been the site of an impressive analytic tradition that has contributed in significant ways to our profession. The cultural ambience of the Argentine Psychoanalytic Association (APA), which was formed in 1942, was one that combined psychoanalysis with input from Gestalt and social psychology, the study of group phenomena, philosophy, and literature, Kurt Lewin's ideas on the field, some familiarity with the writings of Harry Stack Sullivan, together with Kleinian notions of primitive object relations, giving the institute a broad intellectual tradition from which to draw.

Many influential writers and their ideas arose from this polyglot of influences in the River Plate region and have had an impact on psychoanalytic theory and practice in important ways. Racker's groundbreaking studies of countertransference remain fresh and relevant seventy years later; the 2008 publication in English of Willy and Madeleine Baranger's (1968) classic paper, "The analytic situation as a

xii PREFACE

dynamic field", can be credited with launching the notion of field theory in Italy and more recently in the USA, and Jose Bleger's writing about the analytic setting continues to foster further exploration of this concept. However, these are only a few of the many original ideas that have sprouted in this rich analytic climate. This brings us to the contributions of Lia Pistiner de Cortiñas.

Dr Pistiner de Cortiñas is a leading figure in the contemporary Argentine and Latin American psychoanalytic scene. A graduate of APDEBA in Buenos Aires and a faculty member as well as a supervising and training analyst there, she is a much respected child and adult psychoanalyst who also lectures internationally. She has been trained largely in the Kleinian tradition and has become a significant figure in propounding the work of Wilfred Bion. In addition, as a child analyst, Dr Pistiner de Cortiñas has studied and written about the work of Frances Tustin, applying her theories to the treatment of disturbed children. She has published widely in Spanish and, in recent years, has had her work translated into English. Her first book in English, *The Aesthetic Dimension of the Mind: Variations on a Theme of Bion*, published in 2007 by Karnac, developed the implicit theory of aesthetics in Bion's work and elaborated those ideas in important ways. In his comments about that book, James Grotstein said, "This work constitutes an outstanding piece of Bion scholarship and interpretation. One comes away from it with a deep appreciation for the author's dreaming of Bion's work and for the light she has shone on many of Bion's more recondite themes".

Pistiner de Cortiñas' current book, *On Mental Growth: Bion's Ideas that Transform Psychoanalytic Practice*, represents a return to some of Bion's basic concepts, which are then reconsidered from the perspective of mental growth. This is a timely and much needed task because it draws the reader's attention to an implicit, but not always appreciated, aspect of Bion's thinking—his emphasis on mental growth. It has been rewarding to those who study Bion's work in depth to see his ideas proliferate to a much wider analytic audience; however, it is also frustrating to some students of Bion to see that authors frequently appear to cherry-pick his concepts without fully understanding the meaning of those ideas. For example, many contemporary psychoanalytic authors write about their use of reverie without understanding that one's reverie is an *in vivo* transformation of an unconscious process in the analyst that requires further self-reflection in order to

PREFACE xiii

understand the meaning of that reverie within the immediacy of the clinical hour. In this book, Pistiner de Cortiñas helps us revisit Bion's original usage of his unique theories. For example, when discussing the nature of alpha function and the importance of dreaming, she cites Bion's alimentary model of dreaming in which the dream "mentally digests" affective experience, *but also* tells us that, "'Dreaming' is part of the process of digesting the truth". By introducing the notion of the "truth", Pistiner de Cortiñas is reminding the reader of Bion's emphasis on the truth and how it nourishes the growing psyche, which brings to mind Bion's statement in *Cogitations* (1992) that "the true dream *is* felt as life promoting". Thus, by underscoring the relationship between dreaming and "digesting the truth", she is linking this book's theme of mental growth with coming to know emotional truth as a required nutriment in the development of the mind.

Although "digesting the truth" enables mental growth, Pistiner de Cortiñas reminds us that this process is not always a welcome experience for the developing individual, since that growth might also signal catastrophe for many patients. In this connection, Pistiner de Cortiñas aptly quotes Bion: "Of all the hated possibilities, mental growth and maturing are the most feared and hated" (Bion, 1979, p. 53).

The classic Greek concept of *entelechy* (see Grotstein, 2009) refers to the realisation of one's potential as a principle that guides development and implicit in this idea is the notion that there resides within the person a sort of blueprint of the self that is subsequently realised, an assumption that underlies Freud's outline of psychosexual evolution. Elaborating on Bion's concept of "O," the ultimate reality that is unknowable, Pistiner de Cortiñas offers that

> Mental growth refers, on the one hand, to "catastrophic change" and becoming one with oneself . . . as an ongoing but simultaneously discontinuous process with the quality of a mutation. On the other hand, this growth also refers to the formulation of different levels of abstractions, with varying degrees of complexity, and to the elasticity of use.

I am reminded of an Asperger's boy I analysed, whose fifth birthday was approaching: in one session I naïvely said that it was special to reach that age and that more exciting events awaited him as he grew older. He broke down and wept deeply, saying that he feared no one, including his parents and himself, would know the older him and he would, therefore, cease to exist. I had failed to appreciate how growing up in his mind was a catastrophe that he hoped to avert.

Pistiner de Cortiñas also introduces us to some of Bion's less well-known concepts of subthalamic terrors, the embryonic mind, and tropisms. In postulating these concepts, Bion moved our exploration of the early states of mind to the vague stirrings of inchoate experience that underpin the infantile mind. The embryonic mind, in Pistiner de Cortiñas' view, is "the hypothesis of somatic anticipation of what will later be transformed into emotions" (p. 166) and is rooted in experiences that may be prenatal in origin or linked to tropisms unique to humans. Just as plants may be "equipped" with a tropism that draws them to the light, so humans, too, are primed to seek out receptive objects that are able to absorb and also transform the earliest projective identifications. Pistiner de Cortiñas takes Bion's ideas about these earliest phenomena further and considers these as primordial modes of linking that are involved in the formation of a container.

Thus far, my remarks have been primarily about the carefully thought out theoretical ideas which Pistiner de Cortiñas proposes, but it is important to add that the concepts discussed in this book are illustrated with many clinical examples. These include presentation of her work with patients and also discussions of poetry and film that further enrich this volume. The reader will surely come away with a deepened understanding of Bion from Pistiner de Cortiñas' scholarly elaboration of his work from the perspective of the growth of the mind.

Lawrence J. Brown
Newton Centre, Massachusetts

FOREWORD

Psychoanalysis owes to Bion some of its most profound and original moments. He took it to its limits and sometimes beyond them, and also he highlighted more than anybody its limitations and potential, establishing a dialogue with other human disciplines such as mathematics and philosophy, literature, poetry, arts, and science in general. This dialogue generated stimulants and innovative questions for psychoanalytic practice that changed psychoanalytic technique forever.

Even more, this amplitude, together with an intuition through which he was anticipating questions that were beyond his time, which did not have yet a theoretical frame in which to lodge them, made Bion an author whose work was very difficult to read. He is an author whose writings do not speak of things that are commonplace, but one who wrote for psychoanalysts, often overestimating their knowledge, as if he expected of them a culture and wisdom that a psychoanalytic training patently cannot give.

Lia Pistiner de Cortiñas is internationally known as an author who studies Bion profoundly, having a solid experience and acknowledged capability to communicate Bion's ideas. This book once more demonstrates these qualities.

Pistiner de Cortiñas presents Bion's ideas, starting with the historic influences that allow us to see the context where the author's ideas come from. She then goes on to elucidate Bion's significant legacy of the differentiation between the psychotic and non-psychotic parts of the personality and its evolution, step by step, in Bion's writings through the years. This differentiation establishes a new model that produces important modifications in the already established concept of projective identification and also generates significant new concepts. Pistiner de Cortiñas illustrates these changes, providing us with an agreeable read filled with perceptive illustrations.

In the final chapter, Pistiner de Cortiñas addresses questions related to the primitive mind, which Bion tackled in an original way based on the concept of tropism.

Arnaldo Chuster
Rio de Janeiro

INTRODUCTION

The ultrasensorial and infrasensorial spectrum: the extension of the psychoanalytical map of the mind

"The most beautiful thing we can experience is the mysterious. It is the source of all true art and all science. He to whom this emotion is a stranger, who can no longer pause to wonder and stand rapt in awe, is as good as dead: his eyes are closed.

(Einstein, 1931)

"MAN: When the mind ± has been mapped, the investigations may reveal variations in the various patterns which it displays. The important thing may not be, as the psycho-analysts suppose, only revelations in illness or diseases, but patterns indiscernible in the domain in which Bio ± exist (life and death; animate and inanimate) because the mind spans too an inadequate spectrum of reality. Who can free mathematics from fetters exposed by its genetic links with sense? Who can find a Cartesian system which will again transform mathematics in ways analogous to the expansion of arithmetic effected by imaginary numbers, irrational numbers, Cartesian coordinates freeing geometry from Euclid by opening up the domain of algebraic deductive systems; the fumbling infancy of psychoanalysis from the domain of sensuality based mind?"

(Bion, 1991, p. 130)

Wilfred Bion is a post-Kleinian author who developed innovative ideas in the psychoanalytical field, opening up possibilities for a psychoanalytical approach to phenomena that, until then, had neither been much understood nor investigated. His ideas provide us with a means for a psychoanalytical approach to severely disturbed patients. Most psychoanalytical treatments nowadays develop in borderline spaces that confront the analyst with clinical problems that, for a long time, remained beyond the possibilities of approach and treatment; now we need to try to understand them, not only to be able to act in a therapeutic way, but also because developments within psychoanalytic research, such as those of Bion, has put forward new ideas that extend our knowledge and, therefore, our field of action. One of the aims of this book is to provide theoretical and clinical tools, taking as a starting point the innovative ideas Bion introduced, to address what could be called "the current problems of psychoanalysis", although it means a lot more than that, as I shall go on to develop in the following chapters.

One of his most important contributions was to place psychoanalytical theory and practice in a new dimension that, none the less, retains the most valuable aspects of Freud's and Klein's contributions while, at the same time, seeing them from a different perspective.

Studying his work contributes new instruments to psychoanalytical clinical practice, both for investigation in the session as well as for the possibility of elaboration afterwards, through the exercise that he proposes using the Grid. An interesting question is if we can consider the Grid an instrument equivalent to a Cartesian system that will help us to transform and extend psychoanalysis.

Bion conceives the mind as an expanding universe, which is also evolving; he considers psychoanalysis as a powerful and disruptive idea that is difficult to accommodate, so a container has to be created. The originality of his ideas, the richness of his hypotheses, and the new models he puts forward need an open-minded approach: "without memory, without desire and without understanding".

The psychoanalytical hypothesis that he proposes stimulates a new attitude in the analyst, an attitude open to new ways of thinking in psychoanalysis. The disposition to approach clinical observation "without memory, without desire and without understanding" implies a technical tool for the development of intuition and a disposition to open up to what is new and changing in the patient–

analyst relationship. It helps to put the mind in a state open to discovery.

Approaching his ideas presents difficulties that are due, on the one hand, to the complexity of his hypotheses and, on the other, to his style of exposing them. The reading I propose takes into account these difficulties, and aims to counter them with a methodology that operates through an alternation between abstract concepts and models for thinking or "digesting" these concepts. The chapters in which I develop more abstract notions are followed by a psychoanalytic approach to films such as *Pi*, *Twelve Angry Men*, and *Wild Strawberries*, which I use as if they were clinical illustrations.

Freud extended the map of the mind and our conception of it, including the unconscious. Klein moved forward towards the understanding of the emotional life of infants. My intention in this book is to take Bion's suggestion that psychoanalysis, as far as we know it thus far, might be no more than a stripe on a tiger, or such a rudimentary instrument as the white stick carried by the blind man, which, to some extent, extends his field of perception, but still leaves him groping in the dark. Bion's ideas added more than a stripe to that tiger. We owe to this author—among other things—the psychoanalytical investigation and understanding of the function of thinking and, towards the end of his contributions, the idea that the challenge of a psychoanalytical treatment is not only getting to know oneself but also achieving mental growth, which implies becoming oneself, becoming one with oneself.

Bion's hypotheses transform psychoanalytical clinical work through a revolutionary change of perspective in psychoanalysis, a transformation from the medical model of cure towards a model of evolution, development, and mental growth. Through the tools that Bion's hypotheses provide us, I propose to work through these ideas that explore beyond the borders of classical psychoanalysis, using the resources of these new conceptions. Alpha function, emotional experience, catastrophic change, and emotional turbulence are some of these Bionian hypotheses that already herald the originality of his contributions.

Psychoanalysis has disclosed the dimension of our ignorance through the discovery of the unconscious functioning of the mind, and also that our impressive logical constructions might be rational appearances in the service of dark and primitive emotional drives. The actual crisis of psychoanalysis in this twenty-first century poses questions that still need to be formulated.

Bion's perspective is that the mind is still in an embryonic and rudimentary stage of development and that, up to now, psychoanalysts, in their explorations, have not been able to get further than trying to map the nature of the mind.

However, new hypotheses, ideas developed by psychoanalytic authors such as Klein, Winnicott, Lacan, Bion, and others, have contributed to extending the map of the mind, including the understanding of infant emotional functioning, the psychosomatic, the borderline, psychotic functioning, group phenomena, etc.

Bion's proposition is that we need to extend our understanding of the mind towards what he terms protomental, prenatal phenomena and towards the mysterious transformations in hallucinosis (Bion, 1965). He also explores, and contributes to our understanding of, psychoanalytical intuition and its psychoanalytical use and evolution towards mental growth. His hypothesis that it is not enough to have thoughts, that we also need the development of an apparatus for thinking, and the idea that thoughts can also be used for manipulation or be evacuated, etc., opens up new clinical perspectives. I want to stress some of his ideas which add to these new clinical perspectives: he puts forward the disturbing idea of "thoughts without a thinker" and he draws our attention to the fact that, in our practice, we do not always encounter in our patients a mind capable of thinking, or, at least, we have to be aware of that and not take it for granted that the patient is thinking.

The evolution of psychoanalysis needs to include these phenomena through a development similar to that of quantum physics, which means creating instruments, such as radio telescopes or electronic microscopes, which will give access to the ultra- and infrasensorial phenomena that Bion calls protomental, prenatal, thalamic, or subthalamic. Here, I am referring to those emotional experiences and psychological phenomena that cannot be apprehended by the senses; they are beyond the sensorial field. Bearing in mind the transformations in the conception of psychoanalysis, I also suggest a context for the development and use of those clinical tools: this context is mental growth.

Bion's ideas have often been considered a contribution to psychoanalytic theory and, thus, frequently the fact is overlooked that in his work we find very important technical contributions, such as his recommendation to listen to the patient "without memory, without desire, without understanding", his hypothesis of projective identification as a "normal" primitive means of communication, the container–contained function, reverie, etc. The complexity of his ideas makes it sometimes difficult to be aware of these clinical contributions. His clinical seminars and his lectures, which are framed in a more accessible language, help us to discover these technical recommendations and ideas, particularly if we can associate them with our own clinical practice. My understanding and evolution have their roots in my clinical experience as a psychoanalyst, through many years of practice, and the understanding extends towards "a memory of the future" in the transformation through contact with Bion's ideas and the emotional experience of each session, in each turbulent step towards becoming a psychoanalyst. Mental growth is inherent and a significant part of that experience.

Bion said that the difference between a philosopher and a psychoanalyst is that the latter has to meet the following day with a patient. This meeting implies an emotional experience for both partners of the analytical pair. The transformations are not only those of the patient. The psychoanalytic situation is now conceived as the meeting of two people who have a dialogue in a room, and what happens in this meeting inevitably includes emotional turbulence. Why turbulence? Because, considering Bion's ideas, psychoanalysis can be conceived as a discipline and a technique for making "the best of a bad job", that is, an emotional experience in which mental pain, the search for truth, and mental growth cannot be absent. In one of his final papers, he writes, "When two personalities meet an emotional storm is created" (Bion, 1979, p. 321).

The conception of the infant's projective realistic identification as a means of primitive communication—complemented with the idea of maternal reverie that detoxifies and transforms the infant's raw emotions into something tolerable that his personality can now assimilate—is one of his hypotheses that transforms psychoanalytical clinical practice. In its evolution towards the hypotheses of alpha function, dreamwork alpha, and the container–contained relationship, the psychoanalytical relationship acquires a new perspective. We perceive the change of paradigm not only in the transformation of the medical model of cure towards a model that includes mental growth, but also in the notion of the development of the personality. Mental growth is defined as a-temporal and catastrophic (which does not mean an actual catastrophe, but a sudden change, such as a major geographical disruption: for example, when the Andes Mountains emerged).

We shall see in Chapter Nine that reparation and transformations are two different notions. Reparation, in Klein's theory, implies a previous attack; transformations are not related to attack but to evolution, although that evolution might be towards creative transformations and mental growth or towards deterioration, as in transformations in hallucinosis.

From a psychoanalytic vertex, evolution does not mean to look towards the past; the only time in which we live is the present, and, in the personality, past and future are included by means of different disguises that depend on different emotional states. In his developing towards becoming a human being, the infant depends on maternal reverie; it is through the mother's reverie that the infant's anxieties acquire meaning. Without reverie, the danger is of a transformation into a nameless terror. The patient needs the analyst's alpha function, to transform his emotional experiences, his unbearable anxieties; the analyst mediates between the patient and his emotions, metabolising them and giving them a meaning. Once they have been detoxified, the patient can receive these emotions again and assimilate them as a part of his personality. This is how the patient's personality and his emotions can evolve.

The patient does not only receive the contents of the interpretation, the patient also identifies, and takes in through introjection, the alpha function of the analyst and can develop his capacity for thinking and becoming himself, just as the infant introjects the alpha function of the maternal reverie.

Both members of the analytical pair are engaged in this psychoanalytic task. The relation of the mother's mind and the infant's mind is conceived as a link that allows—if everything goes well—both to grow. So, psychoanalysis also can be conceived as a link that changes both members of the analytical pair. It is possible that the change and growth in the analyst will demand more personal analysis for him, not because the previous one has failed, but because the evolution of the personality opens up new problems that demand a new and deeper understanding.

This new understanding of psychoanalysis implies that it aims not only to rectify the wrong solutions of the emotional problems that the patient developed and crystallised during his life, but also the need to find new, more appropriate methods and new spaces through the development of mental functions and reliance on two central items: learning from experience and finding a place inside where it is possible to exist and feel real. Learning from experience, as we shall describe in this book, implies alpha function and the matrix functions for thinking, to allow the development of a capability to "dream". This new meaning of "dreaming" is described throughout the different chapters of the book: facts have no meaning; they need to be "dreamed" to acquire one. Finding a place inside where one can exist and feel real implies getting rid of the primitive superego that usurps the place of the ego and of reverie, and it means also developing tolerance for catastrophic change, which makes evolution towards mental growth possible. This is how I understand mental growth.

Bion's ideas have a high theoretical and abstract level, but, as we shall see, all of his hypotheses have a clinical connection. His psychoanalytical understanding of the disturbances of the function of thinking and of the development of thoughts, as well as his notions of the container–contained relationship and the PS↔D oscillation, to mention but a few, provide new tools for psychoanalytic clinical practice.

The Copernican revolution he introduces in psychoanalysis is implied in the evolution of his ideas towards the conceptions of catastrophic change, transformations, and at-one-ment. The hypothesis of catastrophic change challenges the idea of genetic continuity, the concept of transformations is, at least, an observational theory for clinical psychoanalytical practice, and at-one-ment means becoming one with oneself, a mental state difficult to achieve because, in one way or another, it implies not only change, crisis, and evolution, but being alone with oneself without the "protection" of any god or superego who "knows" everything. These three ideas, which contain the core of Bion's evolution of thinking, lead us to a new conception of analysis, not only as a process that aims to develop a disposition of knowing oneself, but also a disposition to be in at-one-ment with what one is becoming.

Among Bion's technical recommendations, maybe one of the most controversial is "without memory, without desire, without understanding". Even if it is very much related to Freud's free-floating attention and to what he wrote to Lou Andreas Salomé about blinding oneself artificially, "without memory, without desire . . .", as a technical instrument it is a development that provides a tool for the psychoanalyst to "dream the session" and "dream the patient". It also extends the idea of approaching the unconscious and favours intuition about what is happening in the emotional atmosphere of the session. It means facing our ignorance, our dislike of the unknown, and, therefore, dealing with our tendency to saturate with what we already know, to avoid the new facts and notions that we do not know, and what is evolving in each session. The analyst needs to develop a mental discipline in order to forget what he already knows about the patient and approach each session as if it were the first one. This is the negative capacity, "that is, when a man is capable of being in uncertainties, mysteries, doubts, without any irritable reaching after fact and reason". Bion's quotation from Keats refers to a capability that is associated with the mental discipline of "without memory, without desire, without understanding" (Bion, 1970, p. 124).

Before ending this introduction, I want to stress that, although Bion's formulations introduce a radical transformation in psychoanalytical clinical practice, some of his ideas are inspired by an ever-renewed dialogue with Freud's and Klein's conceptions and, in this catastrophic change, the invariant is the psychoanalytical idea—albeit with transformations—that we meet again in the new system of the Bionian clinic.

This book is part of a more ambitious project, so I approach the final themes here in a rather synthetic way. The book deals most of all with the first part of Bion's ideas, where I emphasise the technical significance of "dreaming" the session, of "dreaming" the patient, and the construction of models as a polyvalent technical resource, which, in turn, is illustrated by films used as if they were a kind of clinical material. The final chapter also contains some thoughts about tropisms and their transformations, which is a very valuable hypothesis as a tool for observation of the primitive states of mind and their evolution.

In a second part of my project, I hope to develop the ideas of catastrophic change, transformations, and at-one-ment, which meant a turning point in Bion's ideas and an evolution from the aim of knowing oneself towards becoming in at-one-ment.

"sobre a nudez forte da verdade o manto diáfano da fantasia"
Eça de Queirós.

O poeta é fingidor
Finge tao completamente
Que chega a fingir que é dor
A dor que deveras sente.

E os que leem o que screve,
Na dor lida sentem bem,
Nao as dores que dle teve,
Ma só a que eles nao tem

E assim nas calhas de roda
Gira, a entreter a razao
Esse comboio de corda
Que se chama o coraçao

Fernando Pessoa

CHAPTER ONE

Bion: the thinker and his work

To approach the ideas of an author as original and complex as Bion, it is worthwhile knowing what life experiences and influences contributed to the development of his personality and of his ideas.

Two autobiographies provide us with Bion's personal perspective: *A Long Week-End* and *All My Sins Remembered* (Bion, 1982, 1985). Due to his death, the latter book remained unfinished and it was his widow, Francesca Bion, who added some letters that Bion wrote to her and to their children. She wanted to show another side of Bion, and she subtitled the book: *The Other Side of Genius*. She wanted to temper the impression of sombre sadness that she thought the autobiography showed and to display some aspects of Bion's "other side".

The beginning of Bion's life was shaped by the contrast between two different worlds and cultures—those of India and England. He was born in 1897 in Muttra, India, where his father was a British engineer who specialised in irrigation matters. He had a sister who was three years younger. His early childhood experiences of living in India and Hindu culture remained engraved in his memory, impressions that he shows in different ways in his writings and in his quotations from the *Bhagavad-Gita*. When he was eight years old, he was sent to a boarding school in England, as was customary then in the British colonies, and never returned to India, a country he loved very much. He had planned a trip to Bombay, but died before this could be accomplished.

The years of public primary school encompassed much suffering. One can imagine how inexplicable and disastrous an eight-year-old child must have found the change of circumstances that deprived him of his parents, his home, and the warmth of the Indian sun, as he was left in a strange country with a climate that must have seemed awful, and surrounded by disagreeable children who were sometimes cruel. It was three long years before he saw his mother again. In his autobiography, there is a poignant image of their parting when she left him at the school in London: he watched her hat intermittently appearing over the top of the hedge and then disappearing as she walked away. These experiences, later transformed by analysis, helped him to develop a deep understanding of the primitive states of mind and the sufferings of the human being.

However, by the time he went to high school, he had adapted and he felt that he could learn from, and enjoy, the experience. In his autobiography, he speaks also about the friends he made then. He seems to have thought that his physical strength and his athletic prowess were of great help in overcoming those potentially catastrophic changes, a concept that we know he defined and developed later on. When he was up at Oxford, he was captain of both the rugby and the water polo teams.

In 1915, when he finished high school, the First World War had started and he wanted to enlist in the army. In his autobiography, he describes ironically how he was turned down because of his "round baby face" and how he had to make use of certain contacts in order to be accepted. He was assigned to the Royal Tank Regiment and sent to France, where he was on active service in the trenches and the dreadful battles there until the end of the war. The First World War was a cruel one, full of horror because of the very high number of deaths. From these experiences, Bion learnt much about life and about the primitive states of mind of the human being, which the stark facts of the war revealed to him. Although he often says that he saw himself as a coward, he also learnt that being afraid of dying means wanting to live. Recognising this allowed him, years later, when practising as a psychoanalyst, to go deeper in the understanding of catastrophic anxieties, which he called "nameless dread". When, during the war, he received the Distinguished Service Order (DSO) medal and the L'ordre National de la Légion d'Honneur, he also learnt that he should not believe in what the medals stood for, because if he believed that he was a hero, he would act like one and that would be a death sentence.

The war experiences inspired in him a model for analytical work and, in *Experiences in Groups* (1961), he wrote that contact with reality requires a certain internal discipline, which also demands participation in an external discipline, which, in turn, depends on two factors: (a) the presence of an enemy (mental illness in the analytical situation) and (b) the presence of an "officer" (the analyst) who is aware of his own difficulties, respects the integrity of his men, and is not afraid either of being loved or of being hated.

When the war ended he was already twenty-six years old, and he felt that he and many of his companions who had been in the war had remained mentally disturbed and were in a very different condition to the youngsters who were now beginning university. He went up to Oxford to study History and the years he spent there gave him valuable impressions that stayed with him all his life. He felt enriched by the conversations he had with the philosopher Paton, and he was later able to integrate much of what he learnt in Oxford into his psychoanalytical experiences.

In his work, he uses in a very free way the ideas of different philosophers, which he transformed through his experience as a psychoanalyst. He says that a philosopher and an analyst investigate matters that are common to both of them, the difference being that an analyst has to meet a patient the following day. This fact allows the analyst to think about the contributions of philosophy to psychoanalysis as well as considering the resistance to it through psychoanalysts remaining at a theoretical level to avoid the disturbing experience of making contact with the patient.

When he came down from Oxford, he taught at his old school for two years. Already knowing that his main interest was psychoanalysis, he studied medicine at University College London. Since obtaining a position on the faculty was difficult at that time, he prudently avoided revealing that interest in the admission interview, and instead he mentioned his sporting achievements at Oxford. His ironic comment about the "key" that opened up his access to the university shows his ideas about the difference between wisdom and shrewdness.

4 ON MENTAL GROWTH

The impressions and experiences of those years, that is, from 1924 to 1930, were very vivid and lasting. He admired Wilfred Trotter, who was not only a remarkable surgeon, but was also the author of *Instincts of the Herd in Peace and in War* (1916), a book that Freud referred to in *Group Psychology and the Analysis of the Ego* (1921c). His ideas would have an important influence on Bion's interest in the behaviour and mental functioning of groups. Trotter's book was published during the First World War, when its horrors revealed to Trotter and to Bion himself the stupidity of the leaders of the nations and of the armies.

Bion develops a model for the relationship of the analyst and the patient: he makes the observation that Trotter knew how to listen to his patients, very different from the attitude of another surgeon who disdained what the patient could say and describe about his illness. Bion says that it was said of Trotter that when he did a skin graft it "took", while those that the other surgeon did failed. This model speaks of the need for the analyst to listen to his patient, who is the only companion he has in the session and who is also the one who has lived with himself the most.

Trotter made observations that remind us very much of Bion's later ideas. He speaks of the human being's "resistance" to new ideas, the submission to tradition and the power of the "governing model", the power of the same class whose members were insensible to experience, closed to new ideas, and obsessed with being satisfied with things as they are, and who did not want to run any risk by opening up to new ideas, resisting "courageously" against suffering the dreadful pains of "thought and thinking". Many of these observations—and his own war experiences—influenced Bion's psychoanalytical ideas about the danger for mental growth and maturity of "reverence" for leaders. Bion's ideas about the primitive groupishness and the difficulties of keeping an open mind, a mind of his own, are inspired by those experiences.

After getting his medical degree, Bion worked at the Tavistock Clinic. Following an experience with a therapist whose method was to tell him to "look into the past" (whom he humorously called Dr Feel: "feel it in the past"), in 1938 Bion started analysis with John Rickman, an analyst he describes as having an independent mind. In that analysis, for the first time, he felt a true psychoanalytical contact. The contrast between these two experiences illustrates what Bion later wrote about the difference between speaking about psychoanalysis and doing psychoanalysis. The analysis with Rickman ended when both worked together as colleagues in hospitals during the Second World War.

During that war, Bion worked as a psychiatric officer in hospitals, in contact with soldiers that came back traumatised from the battle-front. Having had his own experiences during the First World War as a soldier, he could now relate to this with his professional experience as a psychoanalyst.

It was during that experience as a psychiatric officer that he began on his "experiences in groups", which he continued after the war at the Tavistock Clinic. At that time, Bion developed his very original ideas and terminology. His observations of group phenomena led him to describe groupishness as something that becomes obvious in a group when it comes together, but is something that exists in all of us human beings because we are gregarious animals, or political animals, as Aristotle said.

Bion observed two kinds of functioning in the groups that co-existed: one level is that which he named the W group (working group), while the other level he called the BA (basic assumption) group. The functioning of BA is a kind of automatic relationship, in which the emotions of the group combine as valences, akin to the combining of chemical substances. He described three types of function at the level of primitive emotions: (1) the basic assumption of dependence that reveres a god–leader; (2) the basic assumption of fight or flight; (3) the basic assumption of pairing, which could be described as an emotional state of waiting for a Messiah, with the condition that he should never be born.

The functioning of the BA group is hostile to the passing of time and contact with reality and it cannot learn from experience. It is the task of the work group—besides the specific task for which they come together—to deal with and contain the BA, so that what is implied in BA is not transformed into action and does not prevent contact with reality and the realisation of the specific task. It is my opinion that the BA refers to primitive situations regarding the survival of our species, which might have been useful at some stage in the process of evolution, but, in the present day, are emotional states that lack contact with reality. Being automatic reactions, they do not require each member of the group to think, and do not involve the responsibility and solidarity

6 ON MENTAL GROWTH

that are needed for the functioning of a working group. The relationships at the level of BA lead to mental starvation of the leader and the group and, what is more, Bion says that, in his experience, he could see that when he refused to be the leader, the one usually selected was the most mentally ill member of the group. He warns that we should beware of the charismatic leader.

Here, I am describing these two levels of functioning, which coexist in different ways in all groups and, bearing in mind the ideas that Bion developed later about the container–contained relationship, what we need to observe is whether or not the work group can contain the BA, that is, how the container–contained relationship between these two levels of functioning can be seen.

Later on, we will see these ideas about two levels of functioning transformed, when Bion is working with psychotic patients and developing a theory about thinking and the development of thoughts.

After this brief consideration about *Experiences in Groups*, I come back to his experiences in life. At the beginning of the war, he married a well-known actress, Betty Jardine, who died giving birth to their daughter, Parthenope (Parthenope is the Greek name for Naples). So, at the end of the war, Bion was left in mourning, with a baby to take care of, little money, and no fixed income.

All My Sins Remembered, the title of the second part of his autobiography, refers to this loss: it is a quotation from Hamlet, in which he says to Ophelia: "Nymph, in your orisons / Be all my sins remembered". Hamlet is speaking of his feelings of guilt, and Bion felt guilty because he could not be with his wife when she gave birth. The part of the autobiography that narrates that period of his life is very moving and contains, perhaps, the more sombre aspect mentioned by Francesca Bion; it also has some passages in which, with a certain irony, he describes how he was acquiring some moments of insight.

When the war came to an end, Bion returned to the Tavistock Clinic, where—making use of his experiences during the war—he worked with different kinds of groups and developed his observations on this matter. He also started his psychoanalytical training and his analysis with Melanie Klein.

In those years, influenced by Klein's ideas on anxieties, defences, and early object relationships, some analysts began working with psychotic patients using a psychoanalytic setting. Among those analysts, the most well known are Herbert Rosenfeld and Hanna Segal.

Bion also began to work with psychotic patients and, from 1950, the year in which he presented his paper "The imaginary twin" to become a member of the British Psychoanalytical Society, he began publishing papers on the language and thinking of schizophrenics in which were the seeds of the ideas he developed later on, in another seven papers, which gave birth to a psychoanalytical theory of the function of thinking and its disturbances. In 1967, these papers were published in a book titled *Second Thoughts*. Being faithful to his idea of offering more than one perspective, or vertex, as he called it later, Bion left his papers in their original version and, at the end of the book, he added a chapter with comments in which he detailed his current perspectives on what he had written before from the point of view of the theories he had been developing.

In 1951, he meets Francesca, who becomes his second wife, collaborates with him throughout the rest of his life, and with whom he had a son, Julian, and a daughter, Nicola. Absorbed as he was by his dedication to psychoanalysis and with the writing of the seven papers I have already mentioned between 1952 and 1957, his book, *Experiences in Groups*, was not published until 1961. It was his most successful book and interest in these papers on groups continues to the present day. In Klein's opinion, working with groups was not compatible with psychoanalytical work. She had little faith in some of Bion's psychoanalytic theories, although she finally recognised their validity. Bion, in turn, never considered the work with groups to be divorced from psychoanalysis. The evidence of his perspective is the subtitle to his book *Attention and Interpretation* (1970), *A Scientific Approach to Insight in Psycho-Analysis and Groups*, which refers to insight in individual and group analysis. In this book, he puts forward a new perspective: the relationship between the mystic (the new idea), the Establishment, and the group.

In the Introduction to *Experiences in Groups*, he wrote,

> I am impressed, as a practising psychoanalyst, by the fact that the psychoanalytic approach, through the individual, and the approach these papers describe, through the group, are dealing with different facets of the same phenomena. The two methods provide the practitioner with rudimentary binocular vision. (Bion, 1961, p. 8)

Something he says in that Introduction provides an answer to the frequently repeated question, "Why did you stop working with groups?" He was already absorbed by psychoanalytical practice while he continued working with groups, but, in the end, he realised that, at least for him, the work with two parallel methods would not benefit the group, the individual, or the analyst.

Bion was convinced of the fundamental importance of the Kleinian hypothesis of projective identification and the alternation between the paranoid–schizoid and the depressive positions. In some of the chapters of this book, we shall see what changes he made to those concepts, modifications that are new clinical instruments for psychoanalytical practice.

In 1967, Bion was invited to work for two weeks in Los Angeles, USA, where some analysts were interested in Klein's theories and wanted to invite a Kleinian analyst to come to California to work with them. Moving to California offered Bion a free space in which to work and develop his ideas, a freedom that he felt he lacked in the Kleinian group. In a lecture she gave in Canada, Francesca Bion says that Bion had experienced for a long time the feeling of being "fenced in". As he expressed it, he felt the risk of being "sunk by medals and honours". He was already a famous psychoanalyst and he had been twice President of the British Psychoanalytical Society, as well as of other important institutions.

Introduction to Bion's ideas

In *Second Thoughts*, Bion wrote,

> This view that psycho-analytical papers are to be treated as experiences which affect the development of the reader will not be subscribed to by all psycho-analysts. I do not contend that it is a matter of conscious choice determined by the reader's wishes, but that certain books, like certain works of art, rouse powerful feelings and *stimulate growth* willy-nilly. As everyone knows, this was so with Freud. (Bion, 1967, my italics)

That is also the case with Bion, a complex author who was interested in philosophy, mathematics, literature, etc.. and who could combine them with his psychoanalytic ideas, giving them a new meaning.

I have mentioned before the singularity of Bion's style of writing: it was disturbing and it also left seeds of ideas that stimulated the reader to develop his own.

For pedagogical reasons, but also to show the evolution and the changes that Bion introduced, we can divide his work into three parts, which do not necessarily correspond to a chronological criterion.

The first part contains what we could call the foundational nucleus of his ideas, which are contained in four books:

1. *Learning from Experience* (1962a).
2. *Elements of Psycho-analysis* (1963).
3. *Transformations*, whose subtitle is *Change from Learning to Growth* (1965).
4. *Attention and Interpretation* (1970).

These four books contain developments and changes at a conceptual level and an innovative contribution to the theory of psychoanalytical technique. They are a contribution to understanding both the earlier and later parts of his work. They are deep and complex and require an open-minded reader, who, if he of she is able to tolerate the experience of not understanding and the consequent frustration, might find it rewarding because it means discovering a stimulus which could well help his or her thinking to evolve and mature.

In my experience, each time I read his works—as happens also with Freud and other great psychoanalytical authors—the reading stimulates developments and changes. As has already been mentioned, these four books and *Experiences in Groups,* and the very original ideas that we find there, acquire a new dimension when seen in the light of his later work. Also, before those four books, there are his articles, later gathered together in *Second Thoughts* (1967). His growing experience with psychotic patients, treated with the psychoanalytical method and the changes of perspectives in his psychoanalytical practice, produced these scientific papers through the 1950s, When they were published as a collection in *Second Thoughts*, he added comments revising the earlier ideas he had put forward and reflecting on them from a new vertex: that of his later evolution. Thus, he provides the reader with binocular vision. These first papers contain original ideas, albeit written in a more Kleinian language than in his later books, and in them he started to find his own way of expressing these new developments.

These papers, written when he was trying to understand psychotic functioning, are: "The imaginary twin" (1950); "Notes on the theory

10   ON MENTAL GROWTH

of schizophrenia" (1954); "The development of schizophrenic thought" (1956); "The differentiation of the psychotic from the non-psychotic personalities" (1957); "On hallucination" (1958a); "On arrogance" (1958b); "Attacks on linking" (1959); "A theory of thinking" (1962b). Later, we shall look in more detail at "The differentiation of the psychotic from the non-psychotic personalities".

His later papers—which he wrote after those that I have identified as the "foundational nucleus"—develop new ideas. "Caesura" is a paper in which he puts forward imaginative conjectures such as the prenatal aspects of the mind, which, in turn, have implications for psychoanalytical technique. Reading these new contributions, one recognises the deep changes he proposes, and how he conceived psychoanalysis not only as a cure, but also as a means for the development of the potential of the personality. His paper "The Grid", published together with "Caesura" in 1977, contains a development of ideas that have already appeared in *Elements of Psycho-analysis*. With "The Grid", Bion is trying to provide an instrument for the analyst, so that he can exercise his psychoanalytic thinking outside the session, as the musician reflects on his playing before or after a concert. In this book, we find that he uses myths in the context of thinking about the clinical practice. In this way, he is able to illustrate new technical ideas about using dream thoughts and myths in clinical practice. He also extends the meaning of "dreaming" and dream-thoughts. This is a theme that is approached in this book and that is illustrated through the film by the Swedish director, Ingmar Bergman, *Wild Strawberries*, which we shall use as if it were clinical material.

We also have the good fortune that his clinical seminars and the supervisions he gave in Brazil, Rome, Buenos Aires, and New York have been published. There, we find a more colloquial style of writing, although with ideas that are no less complex than the difficult formulations of the four foundational books already mentioned. This explosion of ideas is complemented with his last four lectures: "Emotional turbulence" (1976a); "On a quotation from Freud" (1976b); "Evidence" (1976c); "Making the best of a bad job" (1979), that once more contain deep psychoanalytical and clinical thinking which invites the reader to develop his own ideas. These papers are reproduced in *A Memoir of the Future*, first published as a trilogy that is constructed in a way that could be described as similar to a musical opus. From the conceptual point of view, it is an important work because of its implications and the direction in which these can evolve. The title contains a paradox and, in my opinion, the three volumes reveal, in turn, more paradoxes. Psycoanalysis is about investigating the paradoxes of the human personality and its infinite states of mind.

In California, Bion begins to write, at the same time as his autobiography, *The Dream*, the first volume of *A Memoir of the Future*. It was published in 1975, followed by the second volume, *The Past Presented*, in 1977, and the third, *The Dawn of Oblivion*, in 1979. The three volumes were later combined in one volume, published in 1991 in accordance with the wishes of Francesca Bion. This masterwork, which stirs up emotions and is also quite disturbing, is written in different keys, as in music, and uses dialogues. It is a fictional presentation, which takes a dramatic and paradoxical form, of experiences of life, of Bion's psychoanalytical ideas, expressed by different characters who represent the various mental states, of different aspects of the personality, of different moments of man's evolution, of theoretical ideas, etc. It is a book written in a psychoanalytical science-fiction key that, at the same time, allows us to think of those fictional characters as incarnations of emotional experiences and of scientific ideas, with their psychoanalytical connotations. In the Epilogue, Bion writes,

> All my life I have been imprisoned, frustrated, dogged by common-sense, reason, memories, desires and—the greatest bug-bear of all—understanding and being understood. This is an attempt to express my rebellion, to say "Good-bye" to all that. It is my wish, I now realize doomed to failure, to write a book unspoiled by any tincture of common-sense, reason, etc. (see above). So although I would write 'Abandon Hope all ye who expect to find facts—scientific, aesthetic or religious—in this book, I cannot claim to have succeeded. All these will, I fear, be seen to have left their traces, vestiges, ghosts hidden within these words; even sanity, like "cheerfulness" will creep in. (p. 579)

This brief synthesis of his work is intended to provide the reader with a panoramic vision, as from a bird's eye view, of what he wrote and published in life. After his death, Francesca Bion published *Cogitations* (1992), a book that details the "cooking pot effect" of his ideas, a kind of diary of ideas that he kept for twenty years. In that book, we find traces of the evolution of certain concepts, such as his developments of the notion of common sense and the theory of "dreamwork alpha", an idea he uses to effect a transformational development of Freud's theory of dreams and dreaming (Freud, 1900a). This book shows his ideas in progress, while he was "digesting" them, which later took on a more synthetic and condensed form in his published books. If we compare this book with his published work, we see that there his hypotheses are less difficult to understand and that they also allow us to trace the evolution of his thinking.

CHAPTER TWO

Differentiation between the psychotic and the non-psychotic parts of the personality

The title of this chapter is based on Bion's paper of a similar title (Bion, 1967[1957], p. 43) in which he develops an idea that has its source in the beginning of psychoanalysis. Since the discovery of the unconscious, it is not possible to conceive the human personality as an undivided totality. As Freud goes further in his psychoanalytical understandings, new developments arise that contribute to the conception of the human personality as divided into different parts. *The Ego and the Id* (Freud, 1923b) introduces the idea of the division of the personality into id, ego, and superego, a divided personality in conflict with the different parts and with reality. In describing the mechanism of the splitting of the ego, the paper "Fetishism" (Freud, 1927e) also provides a milestone in this process of understanding the functioning of the human personality as divided into different parts, with some divisions that are pathological. That mechanism (the one described in "Fetishism") avoids conflict: in this kind of splitting, a part of the ego is in contact with reality and another part disavows it, both parts coexisting in the same personality.

Klein, in turn, developed the ideas of the splitting of the object and of the ego: the phantasied sadistic attacks on the breast, the idea of the paranoid–schizoid and depressive positions, and that of projective identification, etc. All these ideas inspired Bionian developments.

In the 1950s, psychoanalysts showed a remarkable interest in psychosis. Klein's investigation, her ideas on the development of infant's psychic functioning, and the adaptation of the psychoanalytical method to child analysis without changing its essence but only the means of communication, introducing the technique of playing, stimulated and made possible this interest.

At that time, the analysts that followed Klein's ideas—Bion included—were beginning to treat psychotic patients with the psychoanalytical method, which implies using the same technique and the same setting, but demands that greater attention is paid not only to what the patient says, but also to what he does. Psychoanalytical observation now includes how the patient uses verbal language and is also interested in problems with the development of symbols and symbolisation, the systems of notation, the development of the function of thinking and of thoughts, the use of ambiguity, the meaning, the characteristics of silences, the musical aspect of language in contrast with the lexical aspect, etc.

At the same time, the significant papers of Heimann (1950) and Racker (1948, 1953) on countertransference were published, considering it not merely as an obstacle, but as an instrument that the analyst can use through the observation and understanding of his own mental and emotional states in the session. This proved to be a significant technical tool, most of all with patients in whom the psychotic part of the personality predominates.

The papers gathered in *Second Thoughts* (Bion, 1967) show this extension of the observational field towards discerning imperceptible trembling, registering the characteristics of a glance, or the misunderstandings in the use of language, all data to which the analyst adds an observation of his own internal functioning—of his own emotional and mental states—evidenced by registering associations with what the patient said six months before, or with a phrase, apparently incoherent and without meaning, that he repeats over several years, etc. Bion observes these dissociations over a long period: a patient says something that sounds like: "No ice cream"; he repeats it six months later and so on over a number of years, until, one day, Bion hears it as "No—I scream". When he hears it in that way, Bion can make an interpretation of the relation of the patient to the breast.

This powerful capability for observation is one of the sources of Bion's originality, who, at the time that he wrote these papers, was still struggling to find a new conceptual frame that would allow him to articulate in a significant way all these new observations. So, although we find in these papers a theoretical frame that does not reveal so evidently the originality of his ideas, it is in the clinical material that we find an opening to new fields and to the observation in the consulting room of new phenomena. Although Bion's terminology at that time seems to refer to schizoid patients, in these papers we find theoretical developments and new clinical tools: for example, when he describes the analysis of patients with different degrees of disturbances that, from a clinical perspective, are not obviously psychotic.

It is from these investigations that Bion introduces revolutionary ideas about psychotic functioning and approaching it through the psychoanalytical method. One of the most disturbing of these ideas states that in every human being there coexist, to different degrees, a psychotic and a non-psychotic part of the personality.

This innovative idea is a significant development for psychoanalytical practice, leading towards thinking that when the psychotic part of the personality predominates, it is necessary first to approach that type of functioning before being able to deal with neurotic problems.

The paper "Differentiation of the psychotic from the non-psychotic personalities" (1957) continues the exploration described in the earlier paper, "The development of schizophrenic thought" (1956), in which we can see how Bion is finding original and creative ideas, even if these are still expressed in Kleinian terminology. This paper deals with verbal language and thought, which implies a process of abstraction and depressive integration, while, in "Differentiation", he approaches preverbal functioning and its disturbances. As we shall see later on, Bion describes the functioning of the psychotic part of the personality as characterised by hatred towards external and internal reality. In this paper, he says that he will not deal with the environmental factor; for that we will have to wait until his formulation of maternal reverie (Chapter Nine in *Second Thoughts*).

In the 1957 paper, we find him dealing with the disturbances of symbolisation processes at a level previous to verbal language. This investigation will lead him afterwards to formulate a central modification of the theory of dreams and dreaming, in which he develops the notion of alpha function.

16   ON MENTAL GROWTH

In this paper, he starts his research on the embryonic germs of thoughts: he explores preverbal thought, ideography, or ideograms, as a kind of thinking—one that Freud called unconscious—that establishes the relations between consciousness and the sense impressions, all of which allows the development of mental functions such as attention, memory, etc. Bion is interested in the disturbances due to the attacks on this early development, not yet verbal, but at the level of images, that are the matrix of thinking. He will call these seed ideas "the furniture of dreams", a name that seems both poetic and mysterious. We will have to wait for his later books and for *Cogitations* in order to understand this revolutionary investigation of the preverbal precursors of symbolisation and to appreciate how this embryonic matrix develops, how its development is disturbed, and what Bion means when he speaks of "dreaming the reality".

In the first paragraph of the paper, he formulates his central hypothesis: that the differentiation between the psychotic and non-psychotic part of the personality depends on attacks that generate fragmentation of minute particles (a kind of pulverisation) of that part of the personality that relates to the capability of being aware of internal and external reality, and the violent evacuation of these fragments. Concerning contact with reality, Bion differentiates between the mental state of a rudimentary consciousness that perceives but is not aware of what it perceives, and being aware. Awareness is a kind of evolved consciousness related to the development of the reality principle and the mental functions associated with this development.

As I have already stated, this paper develops the disturbing idea that psychotic and non-psychotic functioning coexist in every personality. The neurotic aspects are obscured when the psychotic mechanisms predominate. As reality cannot be destroyed, what are attacked are the perceptual apparatus and the ego functions capable of linking the sense and emotional impressions with the consciousness that is able to be aware of what it perceives. This awareness implies making a differentiation between the "thing" and its sense impression (the "no thing").

We shall come back to these ideas later on. Let us look again at Freud's and Klein's hypotheses, which Bion takes as a starting point for his developments, and what the changes and innovations he proposes are. To start with, Bion takes Freud's description of the mental functions that develop due to the demands of the reality principle. In

"Formulations on the two principles of mental functioning" (1911b), Freud describes how consciousness—defined as the sense organ for the apprehension of psychological qualities—begins to link not only with the perception of pain and pleasure, but also with the impressions that the sense organs receive from the external world. This process is associated with the development of the mental functions that make contact with reality possible: attention, that, from time to time, takes samples of the external world, meeting half way with stimulus, a system of notation or memory, which registers what attention takes in, judgement, which makes it possible to differentiate whether an idea is true or false, and action, which implies a motor discharge that allows the modification of reality and not merely one that aims to rid the mental apparatus of stimuli, etc. A central hypothesis of Bion's paper is that these are the functions that will be attacked.

The model that Bion uses is Klein's idea of the sadistic attacks on the breast, but he goes a step further in relation to Klein's concept of splitting (the kind of fragmentation to which I referred before, that is, a fragmentation into minute particles), and he says that the attacks are not directed towards an object, but towards the ego functions that enable thinking and being aware. As we cannot escape from the facts of reality, the psychotic part of the personality attacks those functions that enable being aware of the facts through the minute fragmentation of the functions of the apparatus that is in contact with external and internal reality. Bion will introduce an important modification related to the reality principle: he posits that it exists from the beginning of life, although still in a rudimentary form, together with the pleasure principle: the question is how it is used—to evade reality or to modify it. The patient never completely loses contact with reality, although this fact can be masked by psychotic functioning. This modification anticipates the differentiation between shrewdness and wisdom. In the psychotic part of the personality, the reality principle is used shrewdly to evade it. A shrewd evasion of reality is possible. Wisdom helps to tolerate reality as it is and to avoid trying to transform it through making it into what one wishes it to be.

The other modification that Bion introduces is the hypothesis that that retreat from reality is an illusion, not a fact, and that this illusion is maintained through the deployment of projective identification towards the mental functions that Freud describes as developing due to the demands of the reality principle.

18   ON MENTAL GROWTH

The psychotic patient, or the psychotic part of the personality, when it prevails, registers the psychic reality and feels it to be persecutory. Its hostility to the mental functions that allow the patient to make contact with external reality also militates against contact with psychic reality. This is related to the patient's hostility towards dreams or his incapability to dream, as we will see later on. The hatred of emotions and everything that stimulates pain also means that the patient cannot connect with pleasure. He that avoids suffering pain cannot experience pleasure either, because he has attacked the functions that allow him to connect with psychic and external reality. In his later works, Bion develops the idea that a way of avoiding contact with reality is splitting or attacking the emotions.

We have already said that he takes from the idea of the phantasied sadistic attacks on the breast, and also the notion of envy. In agreement with the Kleinian conception of instincts, he postulates that, in the psychotic part of the personality, the destructive impulse prevails so that even love is transformed into sadism.

As he goes on developing his ideas, Bion uses the idea of instincts less frequently. In *Learning from Experience*, he says that instincts are not facts that can be observed; they are a theoretical hypothesis. In turn, we will see him develop the idea of links, which can be observed in clinical practice in the relationship of the patient with the analyst. Emotions are links; Bion also describes negative emotions, or anti-emotions, as Meltzer (1973) calls them, which imply attacks on linking. Linking is a function and it is this that is attacked.

I want to stress again this theoretical change: the transformation of the Kleinian idea of the sadistic attacks on the breast into the innovative hypothesis that the attacks are directed against the mental functions that make contact with internal and external reality. Bion does not posit a differentiation between internal and external reality in terms of making contact.

This idea that the mental functions are damaged leads us towards the central clinical problem: the damaged mental equipment cannot think the problems the patient needs to solve, so this equipment is what needs to be repaired first. These ideas imply also the development of a different technical approach: emotional problems have to be formulated before being solved. Klein's hypothesis is that each emotional experience has an unconscious phantasy that underlies it, although she considered a pathological paranoid–schizoid position.

Later on, we see how Bion develops the hypothesis that, in the psychoanalytical treatment of psychotic patients, the disturbances of the function of thinking is what needs to be investigated and is what has to be repaired and even developed.

In the 1957 paper, Bion takes the Kleinian model of splitting, but the splitting that he is describing is not the natural splitting that Klein described for the paranoid–schizoid position, the one that, at the beginning of life, organises the world into a good and a bad object and a good and bad ego. When the splitting concerns the psychotic part of the personality, we are dealing with attacks that split the ego functions into minute particles. When the patient gets rid of the apparatus that is aware of the external and internal reality, he is now in a mental state in which he is neither awake nor asleep. He cannot be unconscious and neither can he be conscious. This description will be better understood with Bion's further developments where, as we shall see, he postulates the need to develop a mental function—alpha function—in order to achieve an evolved consciousness, capable of awareness and, at the same time, related to, and also separated from, an unconscious by a contact-barrier. Psychotic functioning is not related to an unconscious or to repression. From Klein, he also takes the notion of projective identification, but with some substantial modifications that I mention here only briefly because, in the following chapter, I develop this issue further.

In her paper "Notes on some schizoid mechanisms" (1946), Klein introduces the idea of projective identification as an omnipotent phantasy of getting rid of parts of the personality—aspects that are either felt as good or those felt as bad. The content of the phantasy is of getting rid of these parts and transferring them, through projective identification, into the object. In Klein's formulation, this object is the inside of the mother's body. As we know, Klein conceived the inside of the mother's body as the scenario of the unconscious phantasy.

This Kleinian conception has two characteristics that I describe below, and then I approach the changes that Bion introduced.

1. Klein conceives projective identification as an omnipotent phantasy, a means of getting rid of some aspect of the personality.
2. This conception is related to the idea of an object with an inside, which she conceives as a three-dimensional space into which these parts of the personality can be introduced or from where

20   ON MENTAL GROWTH

they can be ejected, and projective identification aims to protect a good part of the personality or to get rid of a bad part and/or to control the object. As often happens with aesthetic transformations, in the film *Being John Malkovich* (Jonze, 1999), we can see a very good illustration of the confused consequences of projective identification.

I now describe the modifications of the notion of projective identification that Bion introduced, which are not explicit in the paper we are considering, but we need to describe these conceptual changes now in order to follow the development of Bion's ideas. Bion was not eager to start theoretical controversies, which he thought were sterile and also because he was aware that the controversies at that time between Klein and Anna Freud had made the Kleinian group very sensitive about disagreements, so Bion, in my opinion, developed his own ideas without making it too explicit what changes he was introducing. I believe that Bion introduced these theoretical changes based on his experiences in groups and on his clinical insights in his practice with psychotic patients. He conceives of projective identification not only as an omnipotent phantasy, but also as a primitive and realistic means of communication, which means that it is not only an omnipotent phantasy but can also produce real reactions in the object. The infant, through his screams, movements, etc., conveys his feelings and anxieties to the mother through a projective identification that is realistic and communicative; the mother with reverie receives and transforms it into something the infant can take back and assimilate into his personality.

In this paper, Bion says that he will not deal with the environment, but, in his further developments, he discovers and describes the function of maternal reverie, and the concept of projective identification will evolve towards a conception of a relationship between the contained—the infant's projective identification in search of a container that can lodge, transform, and give it a meaning—and a container, the mother's mind through her reverie function. So, in its evolution, the concept of projective identification is transformed into a mental function: the container–contained relationship, to which we will refer later on.

So far, we have been describing the infant's projective identification; now, we will see what happens in psychotic functioning. Bion says that minute fragments—the consequence of a minute splitting due to the attacks against the apparatus that makes contact with internal and external reality—are evacuated through a hypertrophied projective identification that is massive and excessive in its omnipotence. Here is the second modification of the Kleinian concept: it does not concern the interior of an object; in the hypertrophied projective identification, what happens is an explosion of particles that are scattered in an infinite, astronomical space that is not three dimensional, but has all the terrifying characteristics of a vast and infinite space, such as astronomical space. It also can be an implosion, as Bion describes in another model, that of the surgical shock: the patient bleeds into his own blood vessels. A catatonic patient would be a good illustration of this kind of implosion. The patient feels imprisoned in his own mental state from which he cannot escape because he lacks the apparatus that makes contact with reality. Bion is describing, in an innovative way, the claustrophobic anxieties stirred up by, and related to, the lack of instruments to develop a potential space for psychic reality. Not being able to construct this kind of space is associated with the difficulty of making a differentiation between a mental image or an idea and the "thing in itself", a differentiation between the "thing" and the "no thing" (ideas and symbols are what Bion called "no things").

The evacuated fragments surround the patient in a menacing way. These fragments are like bizarre planetary objects that surround the patient. These bizarre objects are composed of aspects of the personality (bits of ego, of superego, of mental functions) contained or containing—encircled or encircling—external objects. Later on, Bion refers to beta elements, but there is a differentiation that must be made between the infant's beta elements—which Meltzer (1973) calls beta virginal or *betes*—and the psychotic beta elements that can be understood as the bizarre objects which Bion describes in this paper. These objects are conjoined with parts of the ego, parts of the superego, etc., put together in a bizarre manner and are conscious, which differs from an object of this kind that can appear in a dream or in a surrealistic vision.

Having said that, the patient lives in a world that is not a world of dreams; it is a world of things that usually belong to the "furniture of dreams". Instead of using the sense impressions to shape dreamlike figures to express emotional experiences, these bizarre objects

22   ON MENTAL GROWTH

conjoined with remainders of the personality—bits of ego and super-ego—are very concrete, haunting the patient. So, in an example that Bion gives, if the patient projects his sense of sight on a gramophone, which is an apparatus that plays sounds, the patient will feel that the gramophone is looking at him. The patient tries to use these objects for thinking; if they are words, they are felt as things and are the result of symbolic equations (Segal, 1957).

In the very interesting and difficult clinical material of this paper we can see Bion and the patient in a dialogue in which the analyst can relate the word "nothing" to an idea that is a "no thing". For the patient, very concretely, an idea is a "no thing". This clinical material is also very interesting because it is one of the few opportunities we have to see Bion working with a patient and approaching the question of the need to repair the patient's ego functions. In this paper, he says that the neurotic part of the personality needs to approach a conflict of emotions (such as the Oedipus conflict), but the psychotic part needs to repair the instruments and the ego functions before being able to resolve the neurotic conflict.

Later on in his work, he describes the flaws in maternal reverie as a factor in the evacuation of objects that are not appropriate, that do not allow for the metabolisation of raw emotions. The analyst also has a function in terms of the psychotic part of the personality, which implies helping the patient to repair these functions. The splitting and evacuation of parts of the personality is a vicious circle: in this paper, Bion refers to the hypertrophy of projective identification, but only when he formulates the notion of alpha function does he have the elements to think which are the developments that lead to a harmonious functioning of projective and introjective identification and which are those that lead towards hypertrophy. In the psychotic part of the personality, the mind functions like a sieve.

In this paper, he describes the incapacity to introject; the place of the introjective function is taken by a projective identification in reverse: what has been identified by projection comes back through the same space from which it has been evacuated and with the same violence. For the patient who has made a projective identification through his eyes, as the patient in the clinical example does, when that which was projected returns, he says, "I cannot see". In turn, Bion makes the following interpretation: ". . . you feel that you have lost your sight and your ability to talk to your mother and to me, when you got rid of these abilities evacuating them in order to avoid pain" (Bion, 1957, p. 56). Bion says here that

> The non-psychotic personality was concerned with a neurotic problem, that is a problem centred on the resolution of a conflict of ideas and emotions to which the operation of the ego had given rise. But the psychotic personality was concerned with the problem of repair of the ego, and the clue to this lay in the fear that he had lost his sight. (Bion, 1957, p. 56)

Without mental resources, mental problems cannot be solved.

We can see here that Bion, in this analysis, is approaching the reparation of the function of contact with reality, that is, the capability to see, and not a neurotic conflict. While the neurotic personality represses, the psychotic personality resorts to projective identification. In the psychotic part of the personality, there are no means to develop an inner space for psychic reality. And if there is no space for ideograms and for dreams and phantasies and they are, thus, evacuated, the psychological and emotional problems cannot be solved because, without dreams and phantasies, the emotional experience cannot be formulated or represented. As I said before, what happens is a projective identification in reverse: what was identified by projection returns, with the same violence and through the same space from where it was evacuated. When attacking the functions that could help him deal with his problems, the patient feels imprisoned in his own mental state. These functions need to be repaired. I stress this idea, so significant in the clinical practice, that if the instruments are not repaired, the patient lacks the mental equipment that he needs to be able to think about, and deal with, his problems.

I now refer to two issues that open a new perspective for considering psychotic functioning and psychoanalytical practice: the idea of psychotic anxiety and psychotic transference.

Psychotic anxiety

In this paper, Bion describes this kind of anxiety as a catastrophic anxiety, as the fear of an impending annihilation. This description has clinical implications. In these catastrophic feelings, the patient feels the threat of an impending annihilation: that means that we are dealing

24   ON MENTAL GROWTH

with an anxiety in which the notion of time and space does not exist. When a mother tries to bring relief to her infant, she often says, "It will go away soon", which includes a notion of time. When Bion continues to develop his ideas, he will say that notion of space develops from the tolerance of the space where the breast was and is no more, and that the notion of time develops from the tolerance of the time when the breast was and is no longer. This construction implies a tolerance of absence, in the past because the object is no longer there, and, in the future, because it is still not there. Constructing time and space coordinates is fundamental for mental equipment that is ready to be in contact with reality. In our clinical practice, we can see very often that the patient finds a way to relieve his mental pain when he can include a perspective of time.

Psychotic transference

The kind of object relationship is described by Bion in a very interesting way, which allows it to be related to what, later on, he conceptualises as prenatal states of mind. He says that the object relationships are precipitate, premature, and fragile. On the one hand, we can conceive the premature as embryonic, but, in this conception, it also means a relation between the task the personality has to deal with and the maturity it has to perform it. Many people might have good cognitive development but lack an equivalent emotional maturity, which implies a gap that makes it impossible for these people to face an evolution without suffering some kind of emotional crisis. Prematurity, thinness, and tenacity are characteristics of the psychotic transference. The idea of thinness is associated to the transference movement from linear to planar—always two dimensional in my opinion—depending on the anxieties that prevail in the patient. It is a line without breadth or a plane without depth, where all emotional states are reflected without any discrimination: it could be the noise of the street, the buzz of a fly, or a serious and important fact of the patient's life. All project the same reflection on this line or plane. All are observed by the patient and none is more important than another. There is an oscillation in which linear transference turns into planar, and *vice versa*, and both lack depth. This, in turn, leads from a restriction of the relationship towards its amplification through projective identification and then towards a new restriction. This two dimensionality has the same effect as monocular vision; it lacks depth, in contrast with binocular vision. Bion often uses binocular vision as a model: for example, the conscious–unconscious vision. The result is a vicious circle from which the patient cannot escape by himself. When the patient widens his relationship, two phenomena come about: (a) projective identification with the analyst becomes hyperactive, with the consequent confused states, because the projective identification with such characteristics does not allow the patient to be aware of the difference between him and the analyst; (b) mental activities of others through which an impulse or emotion tries to express itself are attacked and mutilated. We have already seen, in Bion's clinical illustration, what happens with the sight of the patient.

The patient, wanting to escape from the confused states of mind and haunted by the mutilated functions that he has identified through projective identification, returns to a restricted, linear relationship. Transference is again invested with anodyne, superficial, and devitalised characteristics. One of the difficulties that the psychoanalyst experiences if he allows his intuition to languish, stimulated by the atmosphere generated in his consulting room, is that psychoanalytical intuition is replaced by the theories he has learnt. If this is transformed into habit, the effect on the psychoanalyst's intuition is disastrous. As we can see, this is a very powerful clinical description of the transference movements that allows for the evocation and visualisation of many clinical experiences from this vertex. With the theory of alpha function, one can see these transference movements as a disturbance of the projective–introjective process.

In ending this chapter, I want to make two comments.

1. To understand in some depth the ideas to which I have been referring, Bion's paper has to be read while attempting to tolerate not understanding and going on with the reading despite this. Bion thought that this was good clinical training in listening to the patient without "memory, without desire and without understanding". Furthermore, the reader needs to be able to forget what he has read, because this helps to develop not only tolerance of frustration, but also the capability to find associations in our own experience. Psychoanalytic papers need to be read and "forgotten" so that, when reading them once again, they can

stimulate an evolution of the ideas therein. We have also to keep in mind that only the best papers stimulate a "resistant" reading, because they bring innovative ideas that demand that we open up our already known system. This resistant reading—clinging to what we already know—is a substitute for the experience of reading and opening up to new ideas, as theoretical "armour" does not allow the experience of vivid contact with the patient and with what is happening in the session. A good antidote to this kind of reading is the question without answer.

2. The reader should avoid being tempted to try to assimilate Bion's concepts with previously known theories. This kind of assimilation is always premature and it leads to saturation of the vertex of observation with already known concepts, and so we come back to the theoretical armour. A psychoanalytic paper, such as the one we are considering in this chapter, is an experience that affects the development of the reader. It has nothing to do with a conscious choice, but with the fact that there are some books, as well as some works of art, that stimulate both powerful feelings and mental growth in those who read them (Bion, 1967).

CHAPTER THREE

Projective identification: realistic, communicative, and hypertrophic modalities

In Chapter Two, we explored the concepts that Bion develops in his paper, "Differentiation of the psychotic from the non-psychotic personalities". In this chapter, we are going to explore two concepts that will help us to understand this differentiation: the first is projective identification and the second is the notion of link and attacks on linking.

In the previous chapter, we also considered the difference between Klein's and Bion's ideas regarding projective identification. I would like to expand on Klein's ideas by including her paper "On identification" (1955), in which she illustrates projective identification and its consequences for the personality through Julien Green's novel *Si j'etais vous . . . [If I Were You]* (1947). The novel's plot centres on the main character, Fabian Espezel, who is unhappy with his life and would prefer to be someone else. The Devil offers him a deal: he will be given the opportunity to penetrate other people's personalities in exchange for his soul. Fabian accepts: the Devil tells him to write down his name and keep it in his pocket. Why, what for? Throughout the novel, we see how, as Fabian gets into other personalities and then gets out, he starts losing parts of his own personality, until he does not know who he is, as he loses parts of himself, of his identity, through his successive incursions into other personalities.

28   ON MENTAL GROWTH

I want to refer to Klein's paper to borrow the idea that this omnipotent phantasy, which underlies intrusive projective identification, carries the consequence of losing aspects of one's own personality and, therefore, affects the sense of identity. We see it as the novel unfolds, since, after Fabian Espezel's intrusion into different personalities, he ends up not knowing who he is and barely remembers that he has the paper with his name on it in the pocket of his trousers.

As we saw in the previous chapter, Bion's experiences in treating groups and analysing patients with a prevailing psychotic part of the personality led him to consider that projective identification was not just an omnipotent phantasy in the patient's mind. We shall approach this change through the following quotation from Bion:

> Melanie said that patients have omnipotent phantasies, that they split off parts of the personality and project them into the breast. She meant what he said and I think that was correct—as far as it went. What I am not sure about it that it is *only* an omnipotent phantasy. I have experienced the situation in which the patient can arouse in me feelings which have a simple explanation. You could say, "Anybody would know why the patient makes you feel like that; you need to have more analysis". I think that the patient does something to the analyst and the analyst does something to the patient; it is not just an omnipotent phantasy. (Bion, 1980, p. 14)

Personality does not exist only in the anatomy, which is what our sensory perception would have us believe (Bion, 1962a). Projective identification extends the personality beyond the limits of anatomy. In the group's functioning—at the basic assumptions level—communication takes place mostly through crossed projective identifications, like valences in chemistry. This is different from the mechanisms present at the work group level, which imply contact with reality, co-operation, and a separate mind. We are members of a herd species, a "political animal", as Aristotle said. Even if we are isolated, this condition of "groupishness" is part of us.

Analyst and patient form a group, one that is not exempt from the group dynamics of basic assumptions, and the analyst must cultivate a discipline to keep a separate mind with capacity for thinking. It is the discipline of "no memory, no desire and no understanding", which we mentioned in the previous chapter.

One of the models that Bion uses is the following: the analyst's task is analogous to that of a general in a war, who must retain his capability for thinking while the bombs fall.

Taking into account what we have said previously, we see that, unlike Klein, Bion conceived projective identification not only as an omnipotent phantasy, but as equivalent to an action that produces real effects in the receiver. As he went further in his investigation, most of all in his practice, and continued evolving his ideas, he understood that projective identification was a realistic kind of primitive communication.

Klein wrote about excessive projective identification; Bion defined excessive as related to omnipotence. His clinical experience made him understand that the principle of reality coexists with the pleasure principle right from the beginning of life. However, the psychotic part of the personality uses contact with reality to evade that reality.

Some of Bion's clinical material illustrates this idea: for example, the patient who attacks the analyst's capacity to think, making statements or asking questions that aim to disable that capacity: "How does the lift know where to go if two buttons are pressed at the same time?" says the patient. We can consider that, through this question, the non-psychotic part is trying to collaborate so that the analyst can understand the nature of the problem, while the psychotic part is attacking the analyst's capacity to think. As often happens in psychoanalysis, clinical research also contributed, with the understanding that projective identification could become hypertrophied and excessive in its omnipotence if there were serious flaws in the mother–infant primary relationship. We shall see later on how the idea of projective identification developed into the notion of a container–contained relationship.

In another clinical illustration, Bion says that one of his patients told him that he, the analyst, was unable to tolerate "that". Psychoanalytical research led Bion to understand that "that" was projective identification as a means of primitive communication. The patient had introjected an object hostile towards projective identification as a primitive means of communication, a hostile object with which he was identified. In *Cogitations* (1992), Bion describes how what is communicated—when there is hostility as much from the object as from he who is making the projective identification—remains trapped in the means of communication.

30   ON MENTAL GROWTH

In the paper "On arrogance" in *Second Thoughts* (1967), he starts developing the hypothesis of projective identification as a primitive means of communication, and the disastrous consequences for a personality that is growing and maturing when this kind of communication is denied and, thus, is not received and transformed. One of the consequences is that projective identification, which is equivalent to an action (because the mind is working like a muscle), becomes hypertrophied.

Later on, in *Learning from Experience* (1962a), Bion conceptualises the idea as a container–contained relationship, which acquires a different level of generalisation and enables an understanding of the relationship between a realistic and communicative projective identification of the infant (contained) and his need to be received and transformed into thought by a mental function of the mother (container). This function is what we now know as the reverie function, which we examine later on.

Projective identification can be seen as content in search of a cotainer, exploring like a probe, and if it finds a receptive container to give it meaning, it can be transformed into thought and, therefore, be used to think, as we mentioned regarding the infant.

Meaning is an important factor in the capacity to tolerate the relationship between the thing and the no-thing, and this implies developing a symbolisation process. Bion illustrates this by stating that the infant who is afraid of dying and projects this fear into the mother, can receive in return a meaning, in which case he will develop a capacity for thought: the fear of dying means a desire to live. If the projective identification is rejected, he feels that meaning has been taken away and what he receives in turn is a "nameless dread". The infant is left at the mercy of his extreme, catastrophic anxieties, and, putting it in adult terms, he feels that the meaning has been violently taken away. In the infant's primitive world, the absence of meaning does not exist; if his anxieties are not received and transformed, he feels that meaning has been destroyed, and so has the breast, which is experienced as the source from where all meaning emerges. Projective identifications then become more violent and omnipotent. We can understand this in terms of a small child having a tantrum: if the child is contained by an adult who is not upset by the child's catastrophic anxiety, the child will calm down; if the child is scolded angrily or left alone with his tantrum, he becomes increasingly violent and out of control.

The absence of a receptive container leads to a hypertrophied projective identification which can be found in the psychotic part of the personality. The "object hostile to projective identification" can be conceptualised as a negative container, expelling instead of receiving. When there is a predominance of co-operation and a tendency towards growth—or, in instinctive terms, the life instinct prevails—in an analysis, the infant part and the psychotic part of the personality search for an object with whom this primitive form of communication is possible. If it finds one, as the infant may find containment in the breast, this enables the patient to explore aspects of his or her own personality in the object in a less terrifying way. An adult who is not terrified by the infant's catastrophic fears acts as a receptive container and transforms this primitive form of communication into thought.

Projective identification not transformed into thought stays trapped in the vehicle of communication itself and becomes parasitical, be it language, action, or thought. In the same way, the organs of perception used in reverse for hallucinations are not receptive to stimuli or apt for their functions as vehicles of communication—language or thought. Instead of receiving, they become emaciated and evacuative. Speaking can become evacuative; even telling dreams can become evacuative. One of my patients used to bring many dreams to her sessions, but I realised that she was telling them as if they were a screen behind which her authentic self was hiding.

To illustrate this idea, I will once again make use of one of Bion's clinical vignettes: while analysing a patient who stammered, he discovered through the noises the patient was making that, apparently, two organs were fighting over the patient's capacity to express himself through language: on the one hand, the mouth to communicate, while, on the other, the anus to evacuate. The outcome was the stammering.

From this perspective, we may understand thought and language disorders in their different modalities, not only used for communication. The reintrojection and assimilation of the emotional experiences then becomes disturbed, and what might appear to be communication, such as words, is being used in an evacuative and/or provocative manner. Later on, we examine the role of maternal reverie and the analyst's alpha function to establish or re-establish a harmonious relationship between projection and introjection.

Now I want to come back to the development of preverbal thought and its vicissitudes, to understand how intolerance of this embryonic

32   ON MENTAL GROWTH

thought might affect its development, even before the emergence of verbal thought. Regarding the significance of visual aspects, in "The imaginary twin" (1950), Bion suggests that if he were to observe the manifestations of his patient in the consulting room in terms of the analysis with a child who uses playing as a means of communication, he would consider the "two eye men" as a representation of parts of his body, possibly his two eyes, meant to be harmonised into binocular vision. In his clinical records, it is made clear that the patient had already brought material regarding eyes and eyesight several times. Bion makes what, in my opinion, is an important conjecture from a theoretical and technical viewpoint: that the capability to personify fragments of the personality is, in a sense, analogous to the ability to form symbols, a capability that Klein highlighted.

In the clinical material of the patients he analyses, he finds that the emergence of a visual potency throughout the analysis represented the birth of a new capacity to explore the environment. It was possible to show the patients that the analysis was being perceived as an addition to the equipment of the personality for exploration of the environment, and was also reactivating emotions associated with very early psychological developments, which had a similar effect in increasing this capacity. The three patients seemed to feel that the problem had always been there, but that the fact that it could be revealed depended on developing the capability to be aware of it. Through this description, we can understand that, in these patients, the analyst did not have to deal with repressed material, which the patient can become aware of and have an insight into once the obstacle, the repression, is removed. These patients were conscious of the content, but it was a rudimentary consciousness. Only when the capacity for being aware developed did an evolved consciousness appear, bringing the capability of becoming aware and understanding.

Bion also established a relationship between (a) the increasing capability for awareness brought on by psychological development; (b) the phenomena discovered by this increased capability; (c) the physiological development of eyes and sight, associated with the psychological development that reveals the relationship between the parents in the external world.

In the three cases analysed by Bion, he had the impression that the patient felt that eyesight produced problems of mastery of a new sensory organ, similar to the psychological consequences and implications when teeth were coming out, as described by Klein. This had its equivalent in his conjecture that the development of the psyche, together with the development of visual ability, implies the appearance of the oedipal situation. So, Bion puts forward the question of whether psychological development is linked with the development of eye control towards binocular vision, in the same way that developmental problems linked to oral aggression coexist with the emergence of teeth. If this is so, then it raises the question of whether these psychological developments towards the early oedipal complex emerge in the first months of an individual's life. These observations are also very interesting in considering the problem of strabismus.

The ideogram, linked to eyesight and which Bion conjectures as an embryonic thought, develops before verbal thought that is related to hearing. These ideogram particles of thought depend on a balanced ability for introjection and projection of objects, a process that requires the development of awareness. This awareness depends on the non-psychotic part of the personality that, through the patient's introjection, leads towards the development of what Freud calls unconscious thought; thoughts focused on the relationship between objects.

Bion suggests that this unconscious thought, which establishes or apprehends the relationships between objects, is responsible for the awareness that is linked to sense impressions. If we take into account that one of the patient's aims is to rid himself from the capacity to be aware of reality through projective identification and splitting (minute fragmentation), it is clear that maximum disconnection can be achieved by directing these destructive attacks towards the link, and towards linking.

If the patient realises that ideograms connect sense impressions with consciousness, if he cannot tolerate ideograms, one alternative is to evacuate them. The consequence of this evacuation is that instead of the patient generating an inner representational, potential space to "dream" reality, he finds himself surrounded by particles of these ideograms, as if they were things—what Bion calls the "furniture of dreams". The pieces of this "furniture of dreams" are experienced by the patient as actual things in themselves. To illustrate this, I am going to use the case of a patient who could not tolerate mirrors because she actually "saw" in them something that terrified her. We could say that what she "saw" was a dream that the patient could not dream; actually

34 ON MENTAL GROWTH

seeing it in the mirror means that it cannot have a meaning, or have an interpretation—it is a hallucination. At the end of the chapter, the reader will find comments on the film *Pi*, directed by Darren Aronofsky, through which I illustrate these ideas.

Coming back to the ideograms, I want to differentiate between two situations with different clinical implications.

1. We can find an absence of ideograms. These are patients with literal speech, in the style of "calling a spade a spade". Patients in such a mental state cannot receive an interpretation of the meaning of what they are saying, since they lack the internal space for psychic reality. Their emotions are at a protomental, or prenatal, level, so they have not achieved psychic birth and their fate is often neuro-vegetative or muscular evacuation. This is what Bion called protomental, or prenatal, aspects of the mind. They can appear as psychosomatic or soma–psychotic disorders and/or violent or impulsive actions or hyperkinesis. These are evacuative forms at a somatic or muscular level, in which even speech can be used as a muscular evacuation. These situations require the analyst's mind to act as a "painter", to "dream" what the patient cannot dream; the analyst is faced with the task of helping the patient not only to repair mental functions, but also to help him to develop them through what Bion will call the alpha function.

2. We can be in the presence of ideograms that, if tolerated, will be transformed into ideas or, on the contrary, if they do not find an adequate container, will be evacuated. In this latter case, part of the analytical task will imply the construction of a container for the patient, who needs to become aware through observation of the problem of this mechanism of evacuation, awareness that implies, as I said, the construction through analysis of a container function receptive to the emerging ideograms.

Attacks on linking

I now come back to the idea in item (3), above, which refers to a significant clinical observation that Bion made: if the patient's aim is to evade reality, the most economical way of doing this is to attack the links with both internal or external reality and the function of linking.

Later on in his work, Bion defines psychoanalysis as a science of relationships, and not of the related objects. The objects are anchors for the relationships. These ideas have illustrious predecessors. When Freud discovered transference, psychoanalysis became a science of relationships. This was furthered by Klein's contributions on the positions and her hypothesis that object relationships are present from the beginning of life.

Bion introduced the significant idea that the attack is not aimed at the objects but at the links. As he states in *Cogitation*, breast and penis are not names of things or objects, but of links, and they are the prototype of all relationships.

It is easy to observe attacks on the link between two objects during therapy, since patient and analyst establish a relationship and do so through verbal communication. This is what the evolving creative relationship depends on, and, therefore, it will be possible to observe attacks on this relationship.

Analysis also enables the observation of different attacks on anything that has a linking function, including that which can carry out the function of communication, whether intrapsychic, as with dreams and thinking, or with another person. Bion calls them private and public communication, or publication.

In several clinical cases described in "Attacks on linking" (1959), Bion presents communication as a link and how this linking function is attacked, and he also describes the consequences of these attacks for the personality. I have already mentioned the stammering patient and the stammer. Bion, in that case, considered stammering to be evidence of intolerance of the use of verbal language as a means of communicating with the group: in other words, intolerance of publication. He also uses the myth of Babel to illustrate the idea of a god who is hostile to co-operation and, therefore, creates a confusion of languages. This hostile god is considered by Bion to be a primitive and hostile superego, usurping the functions of the ego. We shall develop this idea later on when we consider the problem of curiosity and the disposition to know.

Another clinical manifestation is insomnia: being unable to sleep for fear of dreaming. Bion mentions a patient who could not differentiate his ideograms from things in themselves, and so, in him, evacuation prevailed; he felt that, in dreaming, his mind was actually draining away.

36   ON MENTAL GROWTH

Unlike the patient who could not dream, Bion understands dreaming as an intrapsychic communication and metabolisation of emotional experiences. This patient also perceived good interpretations being transformed into urine through consistent and minute fragmentation, and that they drained away as urine.

In this analysis, Bion discovered that for his patient, sleeping was equal to an irreparable de-mentalization. These ideas gain in depth and understanding when Bion develops and uses his own terminology to introduce the idea of flaws in the container or in the container–contained relationship.

Here, we find the beginnings of the idea that to be awake refers to a conscious mental state and to be asleep is related to an unconscious one. If these mental states are disturbed, the patient cannot be asleep or awake. Being awake and able to think implies a consciousness capable of being aware, which is different from a rudimentary, truncated consciousness. We see that a new hypothesis begins to develop among these ideas, that of the conscious–unconscious relationship and how the unconscious emerges.

We will understand this idea better when we come to *Learning from Experience* (1962a). For now, let us try to follow Bion when, in the clinical material of his paper "Differentiation of the psychotic and the non-psychotic personalities" (1957), he describes how the patient reveals his neurotic conflicts when he can tolerate being aware of the fact that there is a reality outside of himself, a reality that it is independent of him. This comes up when the patient refers to the weekend. The patient, who has been able to repair some of his ego functions, of his mental equipment, can connect with an inner reality and speak about his feelings: this is what he says to Bion, *I hate you*, when he connects with external reality represented by the awareness of the weekend separation. We can see that the patient's links with himself and his emotions are being repaired, and also the link with the analyst as a separate person and not as a part of himself, as a twin.

Finally, I stress once again that what Bion introduces in his paper "Attacks on linking", such as attacks on links and linking, due to jealousy, and manifested in minute fragmentation and projective identification. Later, in *Learning from Experience* (1962a), he will develop these as flaws in the container–contained relationship and a hypertrophied projective identification due to those flaws. Then he considers the container–contained relationship as a conceptual tool to investigate different aspects of that relationship, the relationships that stimulate mental growth, and those that lead to deterioration. These ideas are powerful tools for clinical practice: sometimes a patient feels overwhelmed and, in turn, overwhelms us with his material, so, in following Bion's ideas, instead of interpreting the content of what he is saying, we can say that the patient has no container for the emotional experiences he is trying to convey to the analyst. First, the patient needs to develop a container before taking the next step, which is to be able to understand these emotional experiences.

CHAPTER FOUR

An illustration of the ideas in Chapter Three used as clinical material through the film *Pi*

The film's title refers to an irrational number, and here we use the film to illustrate some aspects of what Bion describes as the psychotic part of the personality.

Pi (Aronofsky, 1998) was made in black and white, despite the fact that colour was an option. A conjecture about why it was filmed in monochrome is that black and white could be taken as an illustration of the extreme contrasts of mental functioning. The tempo of the score to the film is remarkably fast, underlining the accelerated and over-whelming functioning of the mind of the main character, Max, who does not find a good enough container for his overwhelming anxiety.

The film begins with the credits superimposed on images of brains, neurons, and dendrites, lists, numbers, a Möebius strip, and, finally, a sun that fades into a screen of absolute black. As we will soon find out, the sun blinds when looked at without protection. We see half of Max's face, the main character, a mathematician from the University of Columbia.

Max is continually making personal notes that include the time of day. The first note in the film, timed at 9.15, says that when he was a little child, his mother told him not to stare at the sun. So once, when he was six, he did. The doctors did not know if his eyes would ever heal. He was terrified, alone in that darkness. Slowly, daylight crept in through the bandages and he could see.

We can interpret this statement about his mother's warning either as a caring action that Max omnipotently challenges, or as a rule that forbids curiosity, which Max disobeys and is punished for. In any case, we can think that looking at the sun directly implies a lack of mediation, a challenge to omnipotency, and this is blinding. We hear Max saying this while we watch him washing off the blood streaming from his nose—later, we find out that this happens to him in each episode of migraine he has. The headaches seem to be an implosion due to not being able to contain what he "sees". The blood also represents the lack of a container.

Max looks through the peephole of the door of his apartment and, seeing the empty staircase, leaves after opening several locks. Again, we see sight being used as a defence against intense paranoid anxieties, also illustrated by the locks. His withdrawal into himself and feeling surrounded by a world full of persecutors is a kind of blindness. He uses sight for projective identification, instead of using it to receive visual impressions.

On the other side of the door is Jenna, a Chinese girl, who asks him, calculator in hand: "How much is 322 by 49?". Max answers immediately: 158,102. And, as they go down the stairs, the girl asks him a similar question, the answer to which is 3.181818, and we hear him mumbling one-eight, one-eight, as in an infinite repetition. The girl seems to use Max as if he were a toy, a mechanical thing, an extension of her calculator, an inanimate object. But the instantaneous calculations also show Max's amazing mathematical skill and his capability for abstraction, something that seems to have been used as an escape from extremely intense anxieties.

Bion differentiates between abstraction that is achieved through the PS↔D function (an oscillation between states of dispersion and harmonisation through the discovery of the selected fact) and abstraction achieved through avoiding or despoiling the meaning of the emotional experience. The abstraction arrived by despoiling the meaning as a defence against anxieties is not the same as an abstraction achieved through the matrix functions of thinking: the container–contained relationship and the oscillation between states of dispersion and integration, through discovering the selected fact. This second modality of achieving abstraction is characterised by successive

AN ILLUSTRATION OF THE IDEAS IN CHAPTER THREE   41

synthesis in a spiral form; it is a process of transformations, a process from which one does not "obtain" anything. This means that when abstraction is achieved as an escape from intense anxieties, this process differs from achieving abstraction through tolerating dispersion and the anxieties it generates until it encounters constancy and harmonisation through the discovery of the selected fact. Tolerance of the achieved harmonisation implies tolerating the point of integration, that which was harmonised, and leaving out the other possibilities. It also entails tolerating the fact that this harmonisation is never definitive, but that the achieved constant conjunction can be accessed when evolution makes it necessary to face new experiences.

In the scene in which Max goes out on the street, we realise that he lives in Chinatown.

In the film, we hear him list his personal notes, marking the time. At 12.45, he makes a personal note where he restates his assumptions: (1) mathematics is the language of nature; (2) everything that surrounds us can be represented and understood through numbers.

Max seems to live in a world in which he needs to reduce everything to numbers thus obviating the difference between animated and inanimate objects. Does this kind of reduction not show an omnipotent manifestation, an arrogant characteristic of the psychotic part of the personality? Bion describes an enforced splitting as a defence against emotional conflicts emerging from the relationship with a living object. Dissociation between the material (milk) and the emotional experience (feeding from a breast) enables the infant to continue breastfeeding in order to survive, but the price of this enforced splitting is thast it will determine a peculiar outlook and a peculiar kind of relationship with the world. How different from Mandelbrot's (the creator of fractal geometry) poetic wording who said that a cloud cannot be measured with a circle or a mountain with a cone, you need to invent a new geometry."

(3) Max says that if you make a graph with the numbers of any system, patterns emerge. Therefore, there are patterns everywhere in nature. He enumerates the evidence: the cycles of disease epidemics, the waxing and waning of caribou populations, sun spot cycles, the rise and fall of the Nile. Max is aware of constant conjunctions, what he calls patterns, but when he says that models are in nature he has a concrete thought in which he seems to confuse models—which are thoughts—with "the thing in itself" that he calls nature. Besides, we

42 ON MENTAL GROWTH

can see his intolerance of not being able to encompass everything and so, immediately, at the same, accelerated breathless pace, follows the question: so what about the Stock Market? he describes it as a natural organism, as millions of hands at work, as billions of minds. He says that it is a vast network screaming with life. And his hypothesis is that within the Stock Market there is a pattern as well. What he says sounds quite delusional using mathematics.

As he says all this, we see the leaves of a plantain moved by the breeze against the sunlit sky. The plantain, or its leaves, has a pattern, which may be "measurable" through fractal geometry. But Max cannot seem to tolerate the animate–inanimate distinction or the relationship between infinite and finite possibilities, the finitude of human beings. We see the contrast in the film's final scene, which shows Max and Jenna; Jenna is persisting with her mathematical questions and Max is apparently connected with the beauty of the plantain's leaves, moved by the breeze, having put an end to his delusions and also to his migraines.

An earlier scene takes place in his apartment with the maxi-computer. The phone rings: it is Marcy Dawson, a representative of a mega-company. Max looks out through the keyhole. He stays inside his apartment while the landlady is cleaning the stairs; when she leaves, he opens the locks and runs into Davi, a Hindu neighbour, who tidies up his hair and insists that he accept the cookies she has baked for him.

Davi represents a human relationship of a maternal kind that Max cannot accept because of his isolation. This is why he lives with Euclid, his computer, an inanimate object that seems to be an extension of his brain.

In the next scene, Max is in a café. He makes a new note where he states the hour, 16:25, and the results: that Euclid predicts anomalies in the Stock Market. Max is approached by Lenny Meyer, a young orthodox Jew, who speaks to him about Kabbalah and the ceremony of the teffilin. Lenny is also interested in him, but Max replies reticently. We see the dark circle of his coffee cup, into which he pours a drop of milk where he again sees spiral figures of white against black. In everything that he connects together, in everything he does, he is searching for the patterns or rules, even in his cup of coffee, as a manifestation of his delusion. Suddenly, the camera focuses on his hand, which has begun to shake again; these are the early stages of a migraine attack. The migraine attack represents the lack of a transformational container for his delusions.

Then we see him in his apartment, overwhelmed by pain, praying to God: "Please let it be mild." This prayer is an expression of the search for a container that he does not find. Then he makes another personal note where he states the hour, 17:55, and that it is the second attack in he has suffered in twenty-four hours. He states that he took a dose of medicine and then goes on with a long list of medicines, plus a subcutaneous injection. We see the shot, done with an instrument that resembles a gun and which leaves a dark circle in his arm. His face runs with sweat. He massages his right temple. We hear noises on the soundtrack; he seems in pain and holds his head with both hands. He stares at the door. We see the locks slowly open from outside, the door handle turns, and the door moves until it suddenly opens fully. Is it the first hallucination? Or was the first one when he looked at the sun? The screen goes absolutely white.

Does the colour white represent a hallucination? The emotions he tries to evade through mathematics and rationalisation reappear at a somatic level. So he oscillates between hallucination and somato–psychotic manifestations.

In the next scene, we see him on the bathroom floor under the sink. We can imagine his feelings of helplessness and terror. The phone rings once more. It is Marcy Dawson again, wanting to meet him. Max, again responding to his paranoid anxieties, asks her how she got his number. "At the University of Columbia", Marcy answers. Once again he goes from a feeling of helplessness to one of persecution. He is next seen entering the closet, or some sort of small space. He takes a book from the shelf and the camera shows him from the inside framed between two books, reading while he is standing. Is he trying to escape the feelings of terror, helplessness, and persecution through his intellectual quest to find patterns or rules?

He calls on Sol Robeson, his former university lecturer. They play "Go" with shiny white and black pieces. The camera focuses on Max's face to show his tics, tics which can also be considered as motor evacuation, typical of the psychotic part of the personality, coexisting with intellectual, non-psychotic aspects that can think.

Sol says that he should "stop thinking" and "just feel and use his intuition" and he also asks Max if he was able to connect with his reading. "How did it go with *Hamlet*?" Max replies, "I haven't started

44 ON MENTAL GROWTH

it yet." Sol: "It's been a month since I gave it to you." Max continues to isolate himself in his search for patterns and says, "I'm so close," Sol again tries to connect him with something else, something alive; he asks Max if he saw "his new fish". Sol says that he named him Icarus (in Greek mythology, Icarus made wax wings in order to fly, but when he came too close to the sun, his wings melted and he fell to earth), wanting to make Max understand that he is under the spell of a delusion. He continues by saying that he spent forty years looking for patterns in pi and found nothing. Sol is trying protect Max: he draws his attention to living things such as the fish, he expresses his concern that Max will fall like Icarus, but Max cannot hear.

In the next scene, Max again makes a personal note in which he states that Sol died a little when he stopped his research in spite of being so close. However, Sol seems to be using his experience to help Max abandon his defensive abstraction from any human contact, but Max cannot read Hamlet or connect with intuition. We are once again shown the circle of his cup with the milky spirals, the spirals that obsess him in his search for a pattern. In the next scene, he is in a subway carriage and he is asking how he could stop believing that there is a pattern, an ordered shape behind those numbers, because he needs order to prevent his mind from feeling as he cannot deal with emotions. He aims to discover the simplicity of the circle under the never-ending series of numbers. Max looks for an order within mathematics as a defence against his catastrophic anxiety and the mental chaos that contact with other human beings stimulates in him. At the other end of the carriage, a man in a dark suit is sitting motionless. Suddenly, he begins singing a silly, loud love song that includes the line, "My baby only has eyes for me". When Max looks at the seat again, it is empty. Was it a hallucination?

The scene now shifts to Chinatown. He is once again speaking with Lenny Meyer, who tells him that he works with the Torah. Lenny becomes excited when he finds out that Max is a mathematician. He tells him, "Hebrew is pure mathematics", and he gives him examples of letters, such as Aleph, Bet, which are part of the words father, mother, and son and have a numerical equivalent: the triangular oedipal relationship turned into numbers. He carries out a numerological demonstration and concludes, "Some believe that it is a code sent by God." We can use Lenny's words to consider the difference between a representational space, where ideas are represented by numbers but the numbers are not "things", and the use of numbers for omnipotent beliefs: the code sent by God. Later on in the film, we see to what fanatical extremes these beliefs are taken. But when Max is faced with the numbers mentioned by Lenny, he quickly replies, "The Fibonacci numbers." (Fibonacci was a thirteenth-century Italian mathematician.) Max refers to the golden spiral, the golden ratio. (This is the division of a segment in extreme and mean ratio, present in many elements of nature, such as the spirals in molluscs or the leaves of trees. It is a proportion which many people find subjectively harmonious.) It is interesting to see the appearance of plantain leaves in the film, particularly in the film's final scene, where Max seems at last to be at peace with himself, having been freed from his mind.

The answer Max gives to Lenny seems to come from the scientific part of his personality, but we already see that Max is also looking for omnipotent perfection by trying to encompass everything within scientific knowledge or mathematics. He cannot tolerate the relationship between man's finite possibilities and the infinite. There is also some arrogance in Max—indeed, Bion described arrogance, curiosity, and stupidity as traits of the psychotic part of the personality. Max leaves the bar and he writes down what he does or thinks in an obsessive manner, stating the hour at which each note is made. My conjecture is that he tries to deal with his anxieties though obsessive defence mechanisms. I quote from the film some of Max's notes to show examples of these obsessive mechanisms, which have a maniacal quality.

13.26 hours. He says that he restates his assumptions. (He repeats the same three as at the beginning.)

22.18 hours. He presses "Enter" on the computer's keyboard. We see the maxi-computer and a continuous strip that turns on lights that indicate small numbers. He presses "Print". "Shit!" There is a short-circuit and the power goes out.

In the next note, at 22.28 hours, he says that he got ridiculous answers, that Euclid predicts that some stocks will fall to 6½ points the following day. They have never been below 40!

He looks very disturbed as, with gloved hands and a surgical mask that give him the air of a surgeon, he accesses the top of his computer. He drills inside it and pulls out a piece of glass. It is interesting that he uses a drill to enter the machine, which represents an extension of his brain, and what he will later do with the drill regarding his own brain at the end of the film. He finds an ant, a living object, inside the

46   ON MENTAL GROWTH

computer. He tries to catch it with his gloved finger. He discovers that there is a sticky substance, which he stretches between two fingers. Something animate has come out of the machine. Later, we see him explore the substance of his own brain while hallucinating. We can see in this sequence that Max seems unable to tell the difference between his brain, his thoughts, and an instrument such as the computer. The psychic part of the personality prevails. As an aside, I should mention that many science fiction films include the fantasy of machines, being animate objects, being more perfect than men. Hal, the computer in *2001—A Space Odyssey*, says that only human beings make mistakes.

We can conjecture that Max is already losing the notion of the difference between inside and outside. Max continues taking notes obsessively but he now refers to the result of the headache treatments that failed: he notes them in a seemingly endless list, while he looks at the list of numbers printed out by the computer. This confusion regarding inside–outside shows up here as a correlation between the list of migraine treatments (both psychological and pharmacological) and the list of numbers printed by the computer. The computer has no reverie, it is an inanimate object, but the psychotic part of Max's personality, which prevails, cannot tolerate the care and reverie that his professor, Sol, is trying to give him.

In the next sequence, he is again playing "Go" with Sol. He tells him that Euclid crashed. Sol becomes interested, and asks Max for the string of numbers that Max threw out, and adds that, while investigating pi, he had some viruses that brought down his computer systems. He points at the fish that he has named Archimedes. He tells the story of Archimedes of Syracuse, who did not sleep for months while trying to find the answer to the King's demand: to find a method of telling whether a golden crown was solid or hollow without breaking it. Archimedes' wife, tired of sharing the bed with her sleepless husband, suggested that he take a bath to relax and rest. When he entered the water, he saw its level rise in a way that was proportional to his body's volume and discovered the way to determine volume and density by linking weight with volume. Excited by his discovery, he ran naked through the streets of Syracuse, shouting "Eureka!", until he reached the Royal palace. Sol says that the moral of this tale is: "Rest, Max, otherwise there'll be no order, only chaos. Go home, Max, and take a bath." With this story, Sol is referring to the need for human contact as a necessary element in the resolution of a problem;

AN ILLUSTRATION OF THE IDEAS IN CHAPTER THREE   47

this link with a caring person enables the solution that brings order. Sol says that Archimedes could not sleep, and therefore could not dream. When he could rest, he could "dream" the problem and solve it.

> The attacks [that we see in Max] on the linking function of emotion lead to an excessive prominence of the psychotic part of the personality, of links that appear to be logical, almost mathematical, but never emotionally reasonable. (Bion, 1984[1959], p. 109)

In the next scene of the film, at a subway station, Max is sitting on a bench and sees a man in a dark suit in front of him. Then we see him travelling in a carriage with the same dark-suited character reading the paper. He is the same man we saw in the scene where we heard the song, so it is once again a hallucination. When Max notices the headlines saying that there was a crash in the Stock Market, he asks for the paper and is stupefied to read that AAR stocks closed at 6½ points, *as the computer had predicted.* He gets off and follows the man down the subway corridors. Again, we are not sure whether or not this is a hallucination. He runs into Marcy Dawson, the representative of a mega-corporation, who is looking for him. He runs away. The camera focuses on Asian and Western faces through the streets of Chinatown. Max confirms the stock numbers in a newspaper at the supermarket. He runs home to the rubbish bin, where he had thrown the computer's string of numbers, and desperately tries to find it while his mistrustful landlady looks on. Frustrated, he kicks the metallic basket and then runs into Lenny Meyer, and goes with him to the temple, escaping his landlady's accusatory gaze. He allows the tefillin to be put on him and repeats a prayer in Hebrew, amazed to find out that the number 216 is the pattern of the Torah.

He goes back to Sol Robeson's home. He tells him excitedly that it is the same number. Sol answers that it is pure coincidence. But Max lets him know that Euclid's predictions turned out to be correct; he says that something is happening and that it has to do with this number. Sol answers, "Max, look at the empty 'Go' board. Although, when it's empty, it appears simple and in order, the possibilities of the game are infinite. Two 'Go' games are not alike; they are similar to snowflakes. The 'Go' board is a strange, complex and chaotic world. It cannot be easily summed up in math[s]." Max says that maybe there

48   ON MENTAL GROWTH

is an order underlying every "Go" game. Sol answers that it is madness to connect a virus he had to one that Max might have had and to religious rubbish.

Sol is arguing the scientific method *vs.* the omnipotent and omniscient method. Max cannot tolerate the finite–infinite relationship, because he is looking for a perfect "key", the one that excludes chance and uncertainty. My conjecture is that uncertainty increases Max's paranoid anxieties.

The discovery of quantum physics and Heisenberg's uncertainty principle and the theory of relativity changed the way in which physics views the world. If, with Newton's physics, the world functioned as neatly as a clock, whose clockmaker was ultimately God, now the model of the Universe is like a dolphin in its unpredictable movements. There is also a discussion within "hard" sciences regarding chance. Einstein used to say that God does not play dice. Some scientists and science philosophers, who accept chance, argue over whether chance is epistemological, that is to say, if it is a problem about which we need to know more, or if it is ontological. There are two formulations in physics regarding light: one is the particle theory, and the other, Maxwell's, is that it moves as waves. Both seem valid. Bion took this as a model to state that there are moments of dispersion in mental states, and moments of integration, and if you can tolerate the moments of dispersion with patience and the moments of integration with security, you can develop thoughts and thinking.

I will now continue examining the film, using it as if it were clinical material to illustrate Bion's ideas.

In the next scene, Max is once again at the subway station, alone as always. We hear in the background the powerful sound of accelerated heartbeats; it is a new migraine attack. Max hits his head. The pain produces despair, and he has no resources with which to face it. He is alone and terrified of people. He seems to be losing his capability to discriminate between inside and outside. He sees again the same character in the subway. The camera zooms in on his right hand, from where a stream of blood is dripping on to the ground. At this point, the hypothesis that this is a new hallucination is more likely. Max shouts at the man and runs after him, down the subway stairs. The man has disappeared. He returns to the station and bends down to see the blood and the drops that form a line on the ground, which ends near him. There is invariance in the living substance that he finds in

AN ILLUSTRATION OF THE IDEAS IN CHAPTER THREE   49

Euclid (the computer named after a Greek mathematician), the blood and brain as living substances: they are related to life, with the finitude that seems intolerable to Max. He cannot understand it, or give it meaning. He does not search for meaning. He hides in numbers, as a defence mechanism, looking there for the regularities that will calm his catastrophic anxieties.

Now, in the next scene, he sees a human brain. He stabs it with the tip of his pen; we hear a high-pitched noise and the train lights converge on him, until they fade into a blank screen. It is a new hallucination. In the hallucination, the sensory organs work in reverse; they do not receive stimuli, they project them.

Next, we see Max curled up sleeping on the bench of a subway carriage. An inspector wakes him and tells him he is at the last stop: "Coney Island".

Now we see him at the seashore, his figure against a background of sparkling lights reflecting in the water. He picks up a seashell, the empty shell of a mollusc; the light brings out its pearly, spiral-shaped glow (remember the golden ratio and that Max's only interest is finding patterns). This scene ends with another view of the glittering sea: we do not see the brilliant dots as numbers in the computer any more, but the points of refraction of sunlight in the moving water. The camera shows nature; Max can only look for regularities that calm him, which, in my hypothesis, might be a substitute for the regularity of the rhythm of breastfeeding, of the coming back of the breast, or else another option is to hallucinate it.

In the next scene, we see him at his computer once again. He examines with the microscope the sticky substance that he found when he opened the top of the computer. When amplified by the lens, it is seen to be *spiral*-shaped. He phones Lenny. They meet. Lenny asks Max to help the Hasidic Jews who study the Torah and want to find something related to what is written there. Max is not interested in religion; he tells Lenny about Pythagoras, the mathematician who lived in Athens in 500 BC. (Pythagoras was—besides being a great mathematician—a member, or possibly the leader, of a religious sect which believed in reincarnation and that the Universe was, concretely, made of numbers. We can see how abstraction can be used to generate a theorem, in this case the Pythagorean theorem, and to give support to religious beliefs.) Pythagoras's theory posits that the Universe is made up of numbers. One of his main contributions was the golden ratio:

50   ON MENTAL GROWTH

there is a balance between the length and width of a object so that, when you cut out a square, you are left with a rectangle of the same proportion but smaller, and so on to infinity. Leonardo discovered the perfection of the golden ratio and, in one of his designs, inscribed it on the human body. In the film, we see a copy of this famous drawing, on which Max draws a spiral, the golden spiral that is found in whirlpools, in tornadoes, and in the shape of the Milky Way.

We then see the whirlpool of milk in the coffee once again. Pythagoras, Leonardo, the coffee, everything is viewed by Max from the same psychotic perspective; he is searching for the governing pattern in order to alleviate the chaos of his mind, but this method avoids the emotional conflict of facing the living object and leads to despair and impotence.

Bion speaks of an enforced splitting in which there is a dissociation of the emotional link with the breast and the link with the milk. He says that to avoid emotional conflict, the infant stops sucking; however, the threat of starvation makes him return to the breast, but with a dissociation between the emotional link and the material milk. In our culture, we can see this kind of splitting in people who seem only to value and acquire material goods.

To return to using the film as an illustration of the psychotic part of the personality, in the film there is a second version of the childhood memory. Max says that when he looked at the sun, he closed his eyes and could see clearly. He understood then that the Universe is made of spirals; everything he touches is infused with the spiral. The first version of the memory is of a breakdown, of a psychic catastrophe, and this second one is an attempt to escape or to find a way out of this painful mental state.

Max calls Marcy from a public phone and they reach an agreement: he will get the chip for his computer and in exchange he will give them stock predictions.

He meets Lenny once again, who asks him to "find the number". Max asks him, "What is the number 216?" and Lenny answers, "I don't know. I want you to find that out."

Utilising all his paranoid precautions, Max receives the briefcase with the chip. He instals it in the computer. "Happy birthday, Euclid", he says to his computer, with whom he has a warmer relationship than with human beings. He begins to see Hebrew letters alternating with strings of numbers that take up the entire screen. He presses

"Enter". He seems to have another migraine because he puts a hand-ful of medical capsules in his mouth. The computer and the new chip did not provide containment. We hear voices and his hand shakes. He is having another migraine attack, which is always preceded by an aura. He has a convulsion, as if having an epileptic attack.

In the last part of his work, Bion speaks about psychosomatic phenomena and plays with the expression, calling it soma–psychic, or soma–psychotic, as if showing two faces of the same coin. The possi-bility of having two observational viewpoints contrasts with the observations made by Max from a single viewpoint: it is a defensive observation where abstract intellectualisation and this single perspec-tive are defences against emotional conflict. In *Cogitations*, Bion refers to tropisms. As we shall see in more detail in the final chapter, trop-isms are defined as seekers of an object. He conjectures that what pre-dominates in a patient who wants analysis is the tropism of creation, and what he is looking for is an object that can receive his projective identifications. In other words, an object that can receive, contain, and transform the raw emotional experiences communicated through projective identification. Tropisms need to be transformed by the object (a similar notion to that of transformation through reverie); if the object cannot transform the tropisms, they continue to be disturb-ing, now lodged in the communication organ, because neither the object, the infant, nor the patient accepts them. We can find an illus-tration of these hypotheses in Max's hallucinations.

My own psychoanalytical experience with some psychosomatic and autistic patients enable me to present the hypothesis that there is another destination for non-transformed tropisms: the neuro-vegeta-tive system, which Bion desribes as protomental in *Experiences in Groups*. Max's terrible migraines could be thought of as phenomena at a protomental, psychosomatic level, without psychic transformation, since his defensive system is inadequate to transform them into feel-ings that he can be aware of and thoughts that can be thought.

Continuing with the film as a clinical illustration, Max talks about the hour, seeming obsessed. As he is constantly looking for a once and for all "solution", he has very little capability of being patient and no tolerance of frustration. In a sense, he is like an infant without a mother whose reverie can help him develop a capacity for waiting, which mitigates the pain of frustration and uncertainty. Max seems always to operate at a frenetic pace, seeking to calm his anxiety. This

52   ON MENTAL GROWTH

is how we see him in the next sequence, but now he is having a breakdown.

He screams. He gives himself an injection. He lifts his hand to his right temple. He cuts his hair. We hear chaotic background noises. He bangs his head again and again against the bathroom mirror, seeming to be in despair. The mirror breaks. He is very disturbed, and cannot find an adequate container. He continues desperately trying to calm the pain but it is useless. He does not even consider the idea of asking another human being for help. He injects himself directly in the temple. We see him now on the bathroom floor. The screen alternates light with darkness, from total blackout to blank white, and we hear the beating heart as the ominous background noise. He writes the number 314, which increases in size until the screen returns to total blankness and then blackout.

Now we see his Indian neighbour taking care of him as he lies on the floor. The landlady shows up, shouting and demanding that he leaves. Max throws them all out and locks the door. Once again he isolates himself from all human contact. The phone rings. He just says, "Only God is perfect." We see number sequences again.

In the next scene we see Max with his shaved head covered by a woollen cap. The phone rings endlessly again and again, but he does not pick it up. He looks at his shaved head in the mirror. We can suppose that his psychotic deterioration is advancing. We see him once again at Sol's house and he reproaches him: "You lied to me". Sol says, "Yes, I gave up before I pinpointed it, but . . . just before the computer crashed, they become aware of their own structure. The computer has a sense of its own silicon nature and it prints out its ingredients." They argue fiercely. Max says, "It's a door, Sol." Sol answers, "A door to a cliff." Max: "You retreated to your 'Go' and books and goldfish." Sol: "Go home, get out!"

We can see this discussion as being between a part of the personality that is more connected to reality and caring, with maternal functions (such as the mother who told him not to look at the sun without protection) represented by Sol, and a more psychotic part, represented by Max. If these discussions were part of a dream, we could consider that Sol also makes a statement belonging to the psychotic part: the part which, as I mentioned before, appears in many science fiction films—the machine becoming human. However, it could also be seen as a way to explain the psychotic "breakdown" as intolerance of the

AN ILLUSTRATION OF THE IDEAS IN CHAPTER THREE   53

development of awareness in the human being, an evolution in the capability of being aware, to which psychoanalysis has undoubtedly contributed.

In the film, we see Max again in the deserted corridors of the subway. On the street, a young man photographs him. Max runs after him and shouts, "Leave me alone", as he opens the young man's camera and removes the film. The young man says, "I'm a student doing a class assignment." As the subway is the place where he had his hallucinations, we can wonder if this is not a new hallucination. When projective identification becomes hypertrophied, paranoid anxieties increase.

Marcy and her two thugs find him and start chasing him. Max runs and hides. Finally, Marcy finds him and shouts, "The market is going to crash!" Max says, "I didn't do anything!" Marcy says, "Give me the rest of the code!" One of the thugs points a gun to his head. Lenny saves him by putting him in a car. Lenny also demands the number again. Max says, "I have it in my head." Lenny asks him if he would give the Hasidic Jews the number.

In the next scene, we see a human brain again, but this time it is in the bathroom. Ants are crawling over the lavatory. Max hits it violently with a hammer, screaming. It is another hallucination. The bathroom seems to be another place linked to hallucinations, where the migraine attacks increase the feelings of helplessness.

Then Max is standing in front of a black cloth that has Hebrew symbols on it. He is surrounded by Lenny and his fellow Hasidic rabbis. In the centre stands the Chief Rabbi, with a long white beard (which is visibly fake). They shout, "You have to give us the number! 2000 years ago, the Romans destroyed our temple, and, with it, our most sacred secret: the Earthly residence of our God, the Ark of the Tabernacle with the Ten Commandments. Only on Yom Kippur, on the Day of Atonement, the holiest day of the year, the High Priest could enter the precinct and intone the true name of God, and if he was pure, we would have a prosperous year, one year closer to the Messianic age." They go on, saying that he had to utter a single word, the true name of God, made up of 216 letters. It is the key to the Messianic age. "We have been looking for that key ever since." Max asks, "Is that the number that's in my head? I have seen God." The Chief Rabbi shouts at him, "No, not you, you are not pure!" All the rabbis shout at him and mistreat him. Max says, "I received the

54   ON MENTAL GROWTH

message. It's just a number. I know you have written down all the possible combinations with 216 digits. And where has it gotten you? The number is nothing. It's the meaning. I've got it and I understand it, it's the spiral" [the golden ratio]. It seems as if Max's defiance is born out of omnipotence.

In the film, we see numbers on the screen again, 7 to 16, and others in an accelerating succession. Max sees all the possible designs of the spiral.

In the next scene, Max goes to Sol's house. Instead of his teacher, a young woman opens the door and tells him that Sol has had a second stroke (we understand that he has died from this brain haemorrhage). Max is in the room where they always met. He looks at the fish in the tank and at Sol's notebook. There is a final, loose page. He takes it, folds it, and puts it in his pocket. He looks at the "Go" board and sees that all the chips, both black and white, are arranged to form the beginning of a spiral. The death of Sol, the only human being with whom Max communicated, represents the challenge of having to face a mourning process. Max lacks the mental equipment for this.

We now see him back in his apartment, rocking back and forth like an autistic child. "No! No!" he screams. He has another seizure. He breaks the computer, screaming; this is the prelude to the scene in which he drills into his head.

In a "dreamlike" sequence, we see him silhouetted in black against a white background. He says "8 . . . 9 . . .", breathing slowly. We hear: "Number, Max, number. Stay with me, Max. My God, Max!" He burns the paper with Sol's notes. He cannot deal with the mourning. In a brief shot, he is hugging a brunette woman. Could it be his mother?

He penetrates his temple with the drill, which enters his head. The screen goes from white to absolute black. We see a final explosion.

We can surmise a psychotic explosion due to a severe flaw in the container–contained relationship: Max cannot overcome either his sense of feeling helpless, abandoned, or his anxieties, increased by Sol's death. The scenes of hallucination in the subway often follow his visits to Sol. Every time he has problem with his computer, the migraine returns. We can interpret the migraines as an implosion.

We can also think of the blank white screen as an absence of nuances and the blackout as blindness. We can suppose that staring at the sun is a defying act of omnipotence, typical of the psychotic part of the personality. The defiance could be, in this case, aimed at maternal

AN ILLUSTRATION OF THE IDEAS IN CHAPTER THREE   55

caring. However, we could also consider whether this is actual caring or a prohibition issued without explanation. The first statement of what his mother says still contains some contact with reality: he almost went blind and the results of omnipotently defying maternal caring are migraine and isolation. The follow-up to this defiantly omnipotent attitude is the refusal of the care provided by Davi, his Indian neighbour, or Sol, his teacher. But we might also surmise a child who has developed a system in which he isolates himself from human contact, from emotional links, because he has no container, so he cannot bear it.

Sol tries to pass on to him his life experience: he tells him about Icarus (from Greek mythology) and his attempt to reach the sun with the inadequate means of wax wings; he speaks to him about Hamlet, about intuition, about Archimedes and his wife. But Max cannot listen to him and every time he defies Sol he ends up with a hallucination. Sol speaks at a metaphoric level, of models which preserve a quality very close to experience: Icarus, Hamlet, Archimedes . . . but Max, who seems to have highly abstract intellectual processing at a mathematical level, cannot use this to think and work through emotional experiences. These experiences seem beyond his capacity to assimilate, to "digest", and so they remain as "undigested" facts at the level of hallucinations and a powerful somatic symptom: the chronic migraines.

Euclid, the computer, functions as an inanimate extension of Max's brain. But Euclid also "collapses", and something living emerges from the machine. Sol speaks to him about machines that become self-aware. Pi is an irrational number that seems to provide evidence of the fact that it is impossible to reach perfection and explain everything through numbers; perfection is something that is a manifestation of the omnipotence of the psychotic part of the personality. The Greeks believed in the rational perfection of numbers until they discovered the square root of 2. They then spoke of irrational numbers.

Max tolerates the relationship with Jenna because it is based entirely on her apparent interest in mathematics; for her, Max is a kind of a toy, like her calculator. He does not tolerate emotional relationships, represented by the care and concern of his Indian neighbour. He is easy prey for Marcy's voracity, who wants to use him as a machine that will provide the formula for unlimited wealth, and for the fanatical Jewish sect, who also use Max without consideration for him as a human being and who give numbers a messianic quality. Both Marcy

56   ON MENTAL GROWTH

and the sect represent different manifestations of the psychotic part of the personality; they deal with Max as if he were an inanimate object. Max is neither greedy nor a religious fanatic. He falls prey to these two groups because he wants to be the one to reveal all the world's mysteries. The title of the film, the name of the irrational number pi, can also be considered a reference to humankind's ambition to rationalise everything that escapes rationality.

Max oscillates between implosions, isolation, paranoid anxieties, and hallucinatory explosions. In order to reach his omnipotent perfection, but also to find a pattern to soothe his mental chaos, he lets himself be used as an object by Marcy and Lenny. The things that could rescue him—this other logic of intuition and emotion of which Sol speaks—is beyond his reach. This is what leads him to drill into his head, and, with that, he finally acquires the ability to smile and to see the beauty of the plantain trees against the sky without having to find order in it.

In the film's final scene, Max is in the park, wearing a woollen cap, and seems to be calm (unlike his previous frenetic self) and not thinking about anything in particular. Jenna is sitting next to him, and asks him, "How much is 255 by 183?" Max replies, "I don't know" with a faint smile—it is the first time in the film that we see him smile, and also the first time that he seems to have feelings. Jenna tells him, "I know: 46,665." She continues with her insatiable questions, as if Max were a calculator: "758 divided by 238?" Max instead watches the plantain leaves moving in the breeze. Has he given up mathematics? He seems finally to be at peace with himself.

In contrast to Max, who is using mathematics as a defence against psychotic anxieties, I want to end with some words about a mathematician who was the main creator of fractal geometry: Mandelbrot. Fractals are geometric structures that combine irregularity and structure.

Benoît Mandelbrot and fractals

The "father of fractals" was born in Warsaw in 1924. His parents, of Lithuanian Jewish descent, were forced to move to Paris in 1936 due to the serious political and social situation of Poland at the time, and thanks, of course, to their liberal professions (his mother was a dentist

AN ILLUSTRATION OF THE IDEAS IN CHAPTER THREE   57

and his father a salesman). His mathematical inclination was not accidental; Benoît's uncle, the mathematician Szolem Mandelbrojt, taught at the Collège de France. Anticipating events linked to the Second World War, the family escaped towards southern France, settling in the city of Tulle. There they lived for several years, until Paris was liberated by the Allied forces. Benoît decided to study, and applied to enter the École Normale and the École Polytechnique. He was admitted thanks to his best asset: his geometrical intuition. He began at the Normale, leaving it soon for the Polytechnique. As the main creator of fractal geometry, having coined the term in 1975, he published his book *Fractal Geometry of Nature* in 1982, in which he explained his investigations in the field. The book demonstrated the impact of this discipline on the perception and interpretation of natural objects. Fractal geometry is distinguished by its more abstract approach to dimension than that of conventional geometry. In many cases, fractals can be generated by a recursive or iterative process capable of producing similar structures independently of their specific scale.

I have the impression that this definition of fractals could well apply to a way of perceiving human personalities.

Stochastic fractals are linked to chaos theory, and the word "stochastic" refers to a system that works, above all, through chance. The word comes from the Greek στοχαστικός, meaning "skilful in guessing". The known laws of cause and effect do not explain in a definitive way how the phenomenon works; the explanation is probabilistic. I find these considerations interesting because I think that Bion's ideas introduce a stochastic and conjectural factor into psychoanalysis, which is one of the features of his theoretical system that transformed psychoanalytical practice. We can see the importance of these models in how he extended the function of dreams and dreaming, etc.

CHAPTER FIVE

The origin and nature of thinking

Emotional experience: link

In this chapter, we examine a term that Bion made increasing use of in his work: emotional experience. This term is related to the idea of links because emotions are links.

While, in Freud, the core of his theoretical developments is the hypothesis of drives or instincts and, in Klein, the heart of her theory is the idea of positions and partial and total object relations, in Bion, these terms practically disappear and we find the terms "emotional experience" and "links". This does not mean that Bion rejects the drive or object relations hypothesis, but the context and emphasis in which they appear is different.

In *Learning from Experience* (1962a), he speaks about drives from the vertex of clinical practice; he does so making a differentiation between primary and secondary qualities, and in the context of differentiating between hypothesis of a theoretical kind and those that refer to observable phenomena.

Drives are a theoretical, non-observable hypothesis; emotional experiences and links can be observed. This does not mean, as I said, that Bion questions the drive theory, although, in *Cogitations* (1992) he

60 ON MENTAL GROWTH

introduces a different term, tropisms, which he mentions little and explains less in what was published during his lifetime (see Chapter Nine of this volume). Bion is deeply interested in the practice of psychoanalysis and in developing a theory that fits with the observation of clinical facts. He does not leave out the hypothesis of object relations, but writes that when psychoanalysts use the terms breast and penis, these names do not refer to anatomy, but to a relationship, a link. Bion is trying to find a terminology that enables communication with the patient, most of all with patients with disturbances in their symbolisation process, without causing confusion between the object—the thing—and the relationship to which the object's name refers.

As for object relations, Bion says,

> The conception of the part-object as analogous to an anatomical structure, encouraged by the patient's employment of concrete images as units of thought, is misleading because the part-object relationship is not with the anatomical structures only but with the function, not with the anatomy but with physiology, not with the breast but with feeding, poisoning, loving, hating. (Bion, 1967, p. 102)

These considerations, which are consistent with Bion's investigation of the development of thinking and its disturbances, also require a hypothesis concerning an apparatus for thinking.

Later on, I discuss the development of this apparatus. Now, however, I want to approach the problem by describing Bion's introduction of this new concept that he calls link. This is what will be established or attacked.

> I employ the term "link" because I wish to discuss the patient's relationship with a function rather than with the object that subserves a function; my concern is not only with the breast, or penis, or verbal thought, but with their function of providing the link between two objects. (Bion, 1967, p. 102)

Let us now come back for a moment to the term emotional experience, to define it, first of all, as encompassing all human links. This might be too broad a definition, so we are going to narrow it down—taking into account the developments in *Learning from Experience*—to every relationship which can be included in the field of learning. We can immediately realise its connection with curiosity. Now, every

THE ORIGIN AND NATURE OF THINKING   61

learning process takes place within an emotional experience. This does not mean that the term describes the nature of the link we call emotional experience. Links may be positive or negative, despoiling (meaning that they show a relationship with an emotional quality), positive, such as the disposition to know, as well as links which show an attack on linking, a –K link, a misunderstanding. The term "experience" indicates that the link undergoes a transformation that can be observed and "emotional" is the name for the implicit or visible emotions that impregnate the relationship. I am now going to propose some examples of emotional experiences to contribute to the understanding of this notion.

- Reading a book.
- Talking with a friend.
- Dreaming, remembering a dream.
- Having a child.

Curiosity: the disposition to know

While, for Freud, knowledge is the consequence of a sublimation of the child's curiosity about sexuality and is, therefore, a transformation of the libido, the instinctual energy, for Klein, curiosity, as a key factor in the development of personality, is related to an epistemophilic instinct, and, for Bion, knowledge, or, more precisely, the disposition to know, becomes an emotional link.

In the previous chapter, we described projective identification as a kind of primitive communication and how Bion discovered, in very disturbed patients, the functioning of an object that is hostile to this primitive communication. In the evolution of Bion's ideas, this notion will later be transformed into the container–contained relationship.

Bion's evolution led him to investigate myths which he considered as preconceptions, and also, as Freud did with the Oedipus myth, he approaches these myths from a psychoanalytic perspective but taking other elements of a particular myth to formulate curiosity, the disposition to know as a link, and the attacks on linking. In what follows, I show the illustration in myths of an object that is hostile to the disposition to know.

62   ON MENTAL GROWTH

Freud took some elements from the myth of Oedipus in order to understand a pattern: that of incest and parricide. Bion took other elements of the same myth to investigate the link with knowing and curiosity. The enigma presented by the Sphinx represents mankind's curiosity directed towards itself. In the myth, this enigma is presented by a monster (the Sphinx, illustrating a bizarre object) and the relationship with enquiry is represented by Tiresias, who has gone blind due to his seeing snakes in coitus, and who tells Oedipus not to investigate. Oedipus, in turn, stubbornly continues his investigation: when is this stubbornness arrogance and when is it determination to know the truth? Bion differentiated between pride, in which there is respect for growth and life, from arrogance. Arrogance is a characteristic of the psychotic part of the personality.

The myth of Eden is interesting for psychoanalysis in that it shows God planting the tree of knowledge. Thus, God stimulates curiosity and also forbids the eating of its fruits: curiosity becomes a sin. In this context, this kind of curiosity, arrogance, and stupidity are features of the psychotic part of the personality.

In the myth of Babel, God punishes, with the confusion of languages, the construction of the tower that would make it possible to reach Him and explore the nature of Divinity; this confusion prevents communication and, therefore, co-operation. The process of active misunderstanding in some patients obviously obstructs the necessary co-operation between analyst and patient. Analytical communication is a link. The Divinity in this myth represents the unconscious.

These three myths show, as an invariant, a God hostile towards the disposition to know and its instrument, curiosity. Bion describes this God hostile to the disposition to know as a "moral conscience without morality".

The thinking function

What follows requires the complementary reading of Chapter Nine of *Second Thoughts*. Its title is "A theory of thinking", as a reference to the thinking function. This chapter is, on the one hand, the result of Bion's investigations through the years in which he worked with psychotic patients, and, on the other hand, what he presents here is the seed of the developments in *Learning from Experience*, which is almost contemporary to this paper. In this chapter, it is the first time that he introduces his revolutionary ideas regarding the thinking function from a psychoanalytical perspective. Bion differentiates his theory from a philosophical system, saying that philosophers and psychoanalysts deal with the same problems, with the difference that the psychoanalyst has to meet with a patient the following day. He also stresses the clinical implications of his ideas, saying that the relationship with a philosophical system is the same as the one between pure and applied mathematics.

I shall now synthesise the innovative contributions introduced by Bion, and then develop some of these ideas.

1. He extends the concept of partial object relations and its transformation towards the notion of mental functions.
2. He presents the concept of linking and link as that which is established or attacked when there is an attempt to destroy the capacity for thought and emotions.
3. He takes from the Oedipus myth the elements of curiosity and arrogance in the enquiry as being hostile towards the disposition to know, and as part of what he will later call the Oedipal preconception, part of the ego's mental equipment for making contact with reality, which implies recognising otherness and the third.
4. He considers the link between the infant's mind and the mother's mind as the prototype of the link that generates learning. This conception is the first to discover the function of the human environment in the introjection–projection process in the frame of a container–contained relationship and in the development of the capacity for thought.
5. He gives a meaning to Klein's idea of "excessive projective identification", as excessive in its omnipotence and omniscience, linking it to a hatred of emotions which is undistinguishable from hatred of life itself.
6. By taking Freud's concept of consciousness in its operational definition of a "sense organ for the apprehension of psychic qualities", Bion can also differentiate between a rudimentary consciousness which perceives but does not understand, and what I call an evolved consciousness, capable of perceiving and being aware of what it perceives.

7. He provides an innovative view of omnipotence, which, in the field of knowledge, works as omniscience and materialises in a "moral conscience without morality". This latter substitutes a scientific approach to reality, which distinguishes between true and false, for a dictatorial statement of something being morally good or bad.

8. He presents a truly revolutionary idea from an epistemological standpoint: thoughts are previous to thinking and stimulate the development of an apparatus to think them.

9. Finally, the crucial and important suggestion that Bion makes about the mental apparatus feeding on truth in the same way that the body needs food as a nutrient. Lies are poison for the mind.

Development of the function of thinking and its obstacles

The epistemological revolution brought about by Bion with regard to thought is the inversion of the idea that "thinking" generates thoughts. His hypothesis is that thoughts are prior to thinking and that these thoughts stimulate the development of an apparatus to think them. He says that it is convenient to consider thinking as dependent on two mental developments: one is the development of thoughts, and the other is the development of an apparatus to think them; he provisionally names this apparatus "thinking". This thinking is a development imposed on the psyche by the pressure of thoughts. Disorders can emerge in relation to either of these developments (thoughts or the apparatus to think them). This has very profound implications for clinical practice, and is associated to other, very disturbing, ideas of Bion's, such as "thoughts without a thinker".

In what is a foreshadowing of an aspect of The Grid, Bion describes and classifies "thoughts" according to the degree of their development, in progressive levels of complexity and abstraction. I want to draw the reader's attention to the fact that the names he chooses are based on a model of human conception, using terms such as "mating". This is how he differentiates preconceptions from conceptions and concepts. The name he uses refers to the link with unconscious phantasies and its transformation.

Conceptions originate in the mating of a preconception and a realisation. This has the advantage of combining two meanings: materialisation through experience, and becoming aware of the experience.

In this text, Bion defines preconceptions as what Kant understands as an "empty thought" and also as innate expectations that can mate with a limited number of experiences. As an example, the infant's mouth has the innate expectation of a breast. The conception will emerge if there is tolerance of frustration, of the difference between the expectation of the breast and the real experience of finding the breast, being breastfed, with which this expectation mates. This breast will obviously not be equal to the expectation. If the infant can tolerate the difference between the expected breast and the real one from which it feeds, it will form a conception. Bion gives the name of positive realisation to this mating between preconception (the expectation of a breast) and the experience of feeding from a real breast. Conception is then formed by the realisation of the emotional experience of meeting with the breast, and being *aware* of that experience. *Thoughts*, on the other hand, develop from the mating of a preconception (the expectation of a breast) with a negative realisation, a no-breast (an absent breast). If the infant tolerates the frustrated expectations of meeting a breast, that is, if it tolerates a no-breast (absent breast) and the realisation of this experience, it will develop a thought. This conception of the development of thoughts through tolerance of a no-breast has important implications throughout Bion's work.

Bion sees concepts as another step in the increasing evolving complexity of the capability for abstraction. A concept implies giving a name to a conception.

Maternal reverie

In this paper, Bion introduces a new concept with unimaginable implications, which he formulates throughout his work and that he will complement with the notion of alpha function in *Learning from Experience*. This concept is maternal reverie.

The methods of facing and modifying mental pain or of evading it reflect in the vicissitudes of the mental equipment. The aptitude for discovering and for giving meaning to the emotional experience depends on reverie, that "natural" capacity of the mother's mind to accept, receive, and transform a kind of preverbal primitive communication, the realistic projective identification. Avoiding panic while receiving what the infant communicates in an atmosphere of urgency

66   ON MENTAL GROWTH

and catastrophe acts as a modulator of mental pain and as a condition that this communication can be transformed in a "dream" or a "dream thought". In this way, the infant receives and can reintroject a part of its personality wrapped in a tolerable emotion, analogous to a protective atmosphere. If this communication fails, what the infant receives is a nameless dread and this increases its state of helplessness and the precariousness of the apparatus to face mental pain. Winnicott, Bion, Money Kyrle, and Bick, among other psychoanalytical authors, have stressed the function of the mother as a thinking object and the notion that maternal mental–emotional containment builds a support structure of meaning, the scaffolding for primitive childhood experiences. The absence of this support structure, especially in preverbal experiences, leaves the child at the mercy of mental states that remain in the turbulent void of no meaning. A long deprivation of the maternal capacities of holding and meaning transform a relatively benign void into a virulent nothingness, or can degenerate into chaotic states which, in extreme cases, affect the central nervous system, such as Spitz described as marasmus (Spitz, 1968).

The notion of maternal reverie introduces—from a psychoanalytical vertex—the function of the human environment in the infant's cognitive and emotional development. We are no longer speaking only about a good breast as the ego's core, as Klein did, but also of a thinking breast that thinks—digests, detoxifies—the emotional experiences that the infant cannot metabolise alone. Reverie is a function and also a factor of the psychoanalytical function of the personality. It is a mediating function between projective and introjective processes through which the infant, the human being, builds his picture of the world, external and internal. It is reverie that makes reintrojection processes possible, transforming raw emotions, which Bion describes in *Cogitations* as an erosive liquid, into something tolerable that the personality can assimilate. The reverie function is the condition for reintrojection in as much as it transforms these crude emotions into a "dream" or a "dream thought". When this function fails, reintrojection becomes a "nightmare" or a nameless dread, without a container to withstand the erosion, with the characteristics of confusion between the sensory and the emotional experience that creates a disturbance within the projective–introjective movement. Dreamlike thoughts make the process of introjection and assimilation possible because, using the digestive model, it transforms heteronymous proteins into "proteins" that the mind can assimilate. "We are such stuff as dreams are made on", as Shakespeare has Prospero say in *The Tempest*.

The maternal reverie harvests the sensations that the infant conveys through realistic projective identification and gives them a meaning, so through reverie they are transformed and the infant receives them as something now made tolerable which he can now incorporate as a part of his personality. Failure in reverie implies that the infant feels, in adult terms, that meaning has been taken away and what is returned is a nameless dread. The infant has no notion of absence and cannot conceive the absence of meaning; this is experienced as if the meaning and the breast, as the source of meaning, have been destroyed. The tasks that maternal reverie leaves unfinished fall upon the infant's rudimentary consciousness. The capability for reverie is a prerequisite for the development of a consciousness capable of tolerating facts, which I have referred to as an evolved consciousness.

Moral conscience without morality

The consequence of failure of maternal reverie is that instead of an evolved consciousness, which can perceive and be aware of what it perceives, what develops is a moral conscience without morality, which Bion describes in other works as a super-superego, which usurps the functions of the ego in its contact with reality, and which substitutes a scientific approach, however rudimentary, attempting to distinguish falsehood from truth, for a dictatorial determination of what is morally good and morally bad. This can be illustrated in the relationship between Galileo and the Cardinal, as described by Brecht in his book *Life of Galileo*: while Galileo invites the Cardinal to look through the telescope to prove his hypothesis, the Cardinal answers that first he needs to discuss whether it is good or bad to use that instrument.

Breakdowns in maternal reverie and the substitution of reverie— which the infant, in turn, incorporates as a function if all goes well— for this moral conscience without morality stimulates the development of an apparatus for a hypertrophied projective identification, instead of stimulating the development of an apparatus for thinking. This is better understood once Bion presents the notion of the container–contained in *Learning from Experience*.

Some final considerations

Psychic reality, which is what we can think of as the psychoanalytic object, was conceived as "real" by Freud, who first gave it this status in the letter to Fliess, in which he wrote "my hysterical patients lie" (1897), and who, through his discoveries, aimed to develop the instruments and techniques to approach and investigate it. When Bion began to treat psychotic patients, he discovered thought and communication disorders.

Freud discovered a method for understanding conscious psychic phenomena, postulating its relationship with the universe of unconscious phenomena. Bion realised that, in order to understand the disturbances of thought and communication in severely disturbed patients, we need to postulate the investigation of the relationship between a finite and an infinite universe. Thoughts are a restriction to infinity. A thought implies tolerating the fact that it is precisely that one and not one of the infinite number that could be. Thoughts and thinking imply a decision and a choice between what belongs to that thought and what is left out of it. Thoughts must have both a saturated and an unsaturated part to avoid being crystallised and to continue evolving. Thoughts provide instruments to mitigate frustration as long as certain limitations are tolerated. Then the personality can develop thoughts as instruments that help to deal with mental pain instead of evading it.

When we approach psychic reality as a non-sensory reality, we enter the realm of emotions without specifically associated sense qualities; in other words, anxiety has no taste, no colour, no sound, no smell, etc. We might ask with what emotions are perceived. In a much later text, *Attention and Interpretation* (1970), Bion writes that emotions are apprehended through intuition. Senses present material to the personality that must be worked through in order to develop what Freud called "the consciousness linked to sense impressions" (1900a, p. 615) so that they may be transformed into sense and then psychic data. It is difficult to think that sense data, as it is commonly understood, can provide valuable data when the object of the senses is an emotional experience. As we saw with anxiety, there is no sensory data that is directly linked to psychic qualities, such as is the case with actual objects from the outside world, which are seen, heard, smelled, etc.

THE ORIGIN AND NATURE OF THINKING   69

Bion suggests that thinking is something that has been forced by the demands of reality and the predominance of the principle of reality over an apparatus that is inadequate for that purpose. A modern analogy of this problem is provided by the fact that the demands of reality not only stimulated the discovery of psychoanalysis, but also led to the deflection of verbal thought from its original function of providing a restriction to motor discharge, towards tasks of self-knowledge (such as a psychoanalytical treatment) for which that apparatus is not adequately equipped. This inadequacy for self-knowledge means that this mental apparatus has to undergo drastic changes.

Bion conjectures that such an apparatus exists, and it had to, and still has to, adapt to the new tasks involved in fulfilling the demands of reality by developing the capacity for thought. The apparatus that had to, and still has to go through this adaptation, is the one that originally dealt with sense impressions related to the alimentary channel. This is why Bion uses this model and speaks of the digestion of emotional experiences. These ideas have deep implications for clinical practice.

In the next chapter, we examine the notion of alpha function and go deeper into Bion's ideas on the nature and development of the function of thinking and on the disposition to actively know and actively disavow.

CHAPTER SIX

Illustration of the ideas about the origin and nature of thought using the film *Twelve Angry Men*

I use this film to illustrate some of Bion's ideas regarding the factors that allow thoughts to develop, and what are the obstacles to that development.

The film is from the year 1957, the first work of fiction directed by Sidney Lumet. There is another, later version but I prefer this one for several reasons, one of which is Henry Fonda's magnificent performance.

The theme presented by the film: over six days, twelve men who make up a jury have heard the testimonies and evidence concerning a murder. The accused is a seventeen-year-old boy; the crime he is accused of is having murdered his father by stabbing him in the chest.

The judge tells them that they have to discuss the case, and reach a verdict of guilty or innocent based on these criteria; the verdict must be unanimous in order to be valid. If they have a "reasonable doubt", the verdict is innocent; if the verdict is guilty, the sentence will be the electric chair, without any option to appeal. They have to differentiate fact from fantasy and discuss the case according to the facts. This is not an easy task, since the evidence comes from witness testimonies about what happened. The position of the Thinker—the character played by Henry Fonda—is to differentiate possibilities from proven

72   ON MENTAL GROWTH

facts. That requires the introduction of doubt in the dimension of thought. We will see later what the "evidence" is on which the witnesses based their testimony. In each of them, perception and its alteration due to emotional factors play a significant role.

During the film, it is made clear that if they do not reach a unanimous decision, they can address the judge and the trial will be annulled. In that case, a new trial would be carried out with another jury. When the members of the jury leave the room to start their deliberation, the film cuts to the face of the accused young man. It is a pathetic, perplexed face with a terrified look; he realises that his life is in the hands of these men.

The weather is an important aspect of the film. There is an unbearable, sweltering heat; the forecast is for one of the hottest days of the year. The jury is locked in a small room in which the fans do not work. There is an anxious wish for rain to bring relief. Through these elements, the director attempts to convey an atmosphere of enclosure and claustrophobia. This atmosphere could be meant to illustrate the confinement felt by those who cannot tolerate the implications and responsibilities of thinking. The members of the jury do not perceive thinking as an instrument that precedes an appropriate action, they experience it as a restriction to movement in a supposedly infinite universe; they tend to use action as a substitute for thought.

The jury room has a bathroom and windows. It is in the bathroom where personal relationships are established, as well as the place where intimidation, threats, and references to personal lives take place. It is in this place where the different characters start to acquire identity and become individuals.

After the words from the judge and the view of the accused boy's pathetic face, the next scene shows the twelve men coming into the jury room, with many of them already beginning to show signs of feeling confied and claustrophobic. This confinement is not only physical, but also refers to the realm of thought: they have to think and make a decision. However, as a group, they are operating on the principle of basic assumptions. The feeling of confinement in the realm of thinking and wishing to escape from it is part of this problem. In order to be able to think, you need to have training in the exchange of ideas and a mind that can be receptive to the thoughts of another person. All thoughts imply a restriction: thoughts without a thinker belong to infinite mental space; thoughts that have been thought, thoughts that

ILLUSTRATION OF THE IDEAS ABOUT THE ORIGIN AND NATURE OF THOUGHT 73

intersect with the mind of the thinker, define a finite space, even if only temporarily.

In this case, the frustration stems partially from tolerance, or lack of it, of the fact that the evidence is derived only from the senses. The situation requires the capability to make imaginative conjectures about what has not yet been stated, of what has not yet been thought.

Thinking also necessitates the development of a separate mind for the individual to be able to resist the attraction of the primitive group mechanisms of basic assumptions and contain them through the functioning of the work group mechanisms. This implies tolerance of feelings of being alone and the maturity to assume responsibility as an individual required to fulfil a task, with the co-operation of the group. This is illustrated in the film through the character played by Henry Fonda, whom I have named "the Thinker". To be able to resist the basic assumption group dynamic means feeling separated from that which, our being gregarious animals, leads us to assume is the vital foundation of survival.

Thinking has emotional implications. The film shows how, in a trial, eleven members of the jury did not think. Neither did the prosecuting and defence lawyers. Therefore, this trial shows us how "thinking" can be deeply inhibited when unconscious motivations or undigested emotions disturb the jurors. The Thinker says that if he had been the accused, he would have wanted to have a different lawyer and that lawyers can be incompetent.

The "facts"

At midnight, a fight is heard in a first-floor apartment that is directly opposite an elevated railway. A witness, an elderly half-paralysed man who lives in the apartment below, has his window open and through it hears, "I'll kill you!", the noises of a fight, and a falling body. He gets up and goes to his apartment door and sees the boy fleeing.

A woman who lives in an apartment opposite suffers from insomnia and cannot sleep; she gets up and looks through a window and sees the boy kill his father through the windows of an empty, unlit train that is passing.

She starts to shout and the police arrive.

74   ON MENTAL GROWTH

The murder is discovered. The father, a man with a very bad record, has a knife in his chest.

Three hours later, the son returns and receives the information that his father has been murdered. He is questioned (while in shock?) by the police in the room next to where his father's body lies. He says that he went to the cinema but cannot remember the names of the actors or the title of the film he saw. He has no witnesses to attest to his alibi. There are witnesses who saw him with a blade identical to the one used by the killer. He says he lost it through a hole in his trousers. The knife is considered unusual because of its ornamentation. Some friends say he showed off with the knife that same night. He had been physically punished by his father countless times, thus providing an assumed motive, and witnesses heard a fight that same night. The boy claims he left for the cinema at 23.30 hours.

Two witnesses testify against the boy: the first is the paraplegic man who heard the boy's voice saying, "I'll kill you" to his father, and heard the noise of the body falling. On hearing this commotion, he went to his door and saw the boy fleeing down the stairs. The second is the elderly, insomniac woman who lives opposite to where the crime took place and saw the crime through the windows of a train passing with its lights out. She claims it was the boy, and that she recognised him.

Here, I raise the question of reasonable doubt, regarding which it is worth remembering the concept of negative capability. In *Attention and Interpretation* (1970, p. 125), Bion proposes an "uncertainty principle" for psychoanalysis; he calls it negative capability and takes it from a quotation of Keats who says,

> . . . at once it struck me what quality went to form a Man of Achievement, especially in Literature, and which Shakespeare possessed so enormously—I mean Negative Capability, that is, when a man is capable of being in uncertainties, mysteries, doubts, without any irritable reaching after fact and reason . . .

We need to keep in mind that the judge tells the members of the jury that if they have a reasonable doubt, they have to vote innocent— which does not mean that the boy is actually innocent. If they are sure that it was the boy who committed the murder, they should declare him guilty, and that verdict in this case would mean a sentence of execution without an option to appeal.

ILLUSTRATION OF THE IDEAS ABOUT THE ORIGIN AND NATURE OF THOUGHT   75

When they enter the jury room, we can see that the Thinker goes to the window, not because he has any feeling of confinement, but because he is concerned and engrossed in something. We can assume that he is thinking while he looks through the window. The camera shows him lost in thought, in contrast with the movements, actions, and compulsive talking of the other members of the jury. He could also be realising his responsibility and experiencing a deep pain because of that heavy burden.

He goes to the window in other scenes of the film, such as when he seems to be thinking about having to decide tactically and strategically in which moment to show a knife he has purchased, and also when he needs to clear up his doubts about the guilt of the accused. Is he trying to find a strategy, determining what he will do independently of what the others do? The answer to finding a strategy that can enable him to be listened to by the others seems to be simply to have faith in the possibility of examining the problem through dialogue. His proposition is to have conversations about the problem, and not to speculate; he proposes just to talk. *Speaking* implies a dialogue, of exchanging thoughts with others. Let us consider this interesting text of Bion's on what *talking* implies.

> ... The problem is simplified if "thoughts" are regarded as epistemologically prior to thinking and that thinking has to be developed as a method or apparatus for dealing with "thoughts". If this is the case, then much will depend on whether the "thoughts" are to be evaded or modified or used as part of an attempt to evade or modify something else. If they are felt to be accretions of stimuli then they may be similar to or identical with beta-elements and as such would lend themselves to treatment by motor discharge and the operation of the musculature to effect the discharge. Talking, therefore, must be considered as potentially two different activities, one as a mode of communicating thoughts and the other as an employment of the musculature to disencumber the personality of thoughts ... (Bion, 1962a, p. 83)

The film shows that the task of the jury will require "thinking in an uncommon way". It will require conjectures based on suppositions that lead to a different perspective, one that might place the "facts" in a dimension in which a reasonable doubt is possible, which is the opposite of the certainty of those who avoid thinking. The Thinker is

76   ON MENTAL GROWTH

able to think of some very difficult situations by himself, or could imagine and think them; for other situations, he needs the exchange with other members of the jury.

He could think by himself of the impossibility of the elderly male witness hearing the words allegedly said by the boy. He could think that, if he were the boy, he would have wanted a lawyer who cross-examined the key witnesses to bring certain anomalies in their evidence to light. He could think that it would be useful to go to the neighbourhood and see the world as it is seen from there. This is what he did, and how he found a knife shop from which he bought a knife identical to the one owned by the accused, refuting the assumption, presented as a certainty, that the knife with which the crime was committed was special and rare.

Some lines from the script and points to note

1. "Oh God, there's always one" 2. "If you don't believe in the boy's testimony, why do you believe in the woman's testimony? She's also 'one of them'" 3. "It is possible for a lawyer to be stupid." 4. "Witnesses are just people. They could be wrong." Also notable is the moment in which they decide that each one will state their reasons for considering the boy guilty. It is worth observing how they sometimes treat the thinker with fury and irritation, because he has a different opinion, and sometimes with a disdainful arrogance, and how they consider him a sentimental fool. This demonstrates the arrogance of the psychotic part of the personality or, if we express it as links, it is a link of active disavowal, a minus K link.

Two of the members of the jury represent opposite character traits: Fonda, the one we call the Thinker, seems able to tolerate being alone and the slow process of thinking and investigating, and the other, whom we will call the Manic Salesman, does not tolerate the need for thinking or the time that this would take. The evacuative action is immediate, where the mind works like the musculature. The Manic Salesman does not think but acts, and does not tolerate being in contact with himself either; in fact, he does not tolerate any emotional contact.

It is worth noticing that the members of the jury are never identified by their names in the film, only by the place and number that

ILLUSTRATION OF THE IDEAS ABOUT THE ORIGIN AND NATURE OF THOUGHT 77

identifies them, if at all. I propose to name them according to selected facts about the characteristics of their personalities. My list follows the order in which they changed their vote from guilty to innocent:

A short biographical sketch of the characters in Twelve Angry Men

1. *The Thinker* says that although the young man's guilt is almost certain and the evidence seems very obvious, he cannot vote guilty without examining and speaking about it (he only wants to talk, to discuss the problem). The other members of the jury, in an obvious group action of the basic assumption dynamic, are hostile to thinking and press for the quick action they want; they show disdain for the task proposed by the Thinker (a task at the work group level), which is to discuss, to talk. As the opportunities for discussion arise, this stimulates conflict and the automatic agreement of the basic assumptions group's opinion seems to show cracks. When they reach a new deadlock, they feel trapped and out of options to escape. The Thinker then makes a proposition that is worth examining in detail. He proposes discussing the problem for a limited time (an hour) and then, after examining the situation, for everyone to vote in secret—he will not vote: if the result of the vote is guilty, he will accept it and vote guilty. Then they will conclude the matter and go to the judge with the verdict.

    Let us examine this proposition: as the vote is secret, it stimulates individual thought and being able to contain the basic assumption functioning of fight/flight. There is a transition towards the predominance of the work group dynamic. Each one is left to face his conscience. The scene has strong emotional impact. They vote, and the first crisis takes place: there is a vote for innocence.

2. *Old Man.* He is the first to change his vote. This change is based on his access to a selected fact (SF) that opened up for him the possibility of being able to think and come into contact with situations from his own life. This man's selected fact is derived from his experiences of social loneliness, experiences of being alone

78   ON MENTAL GROWTH

and of anonymity. He states that he knows the painful effect of anonymity in old age. He also shows a capacity for observation which becomes evident when he remarks on the impressions made by spectacles on the nose of another character (see *Obsessive Characteropath*, below).

(Throughout the book, we mention the hypothesis that Bion takes from Poincaré: that of the selected fact. This means that there are moments where problems are perceived as dispersed and it is impossible to establish a relationship with them. When the SF is uncovered, we can see the connection that we could not find before, because the SF harmonises and gives coherence to what was previously seen as disparate. Darío Sor, an Argentine psychoanalyst, conceived another selected fact, which he named SF1 to differentiate it from SF2, which is the one that harmonises. SF1 is the one that disarticulates what has already been articulated, so that thoughts can evolve and do not become crystallised.)

3. *Young Man from the Slums*. His vote for a guilty verdict was based on the need to cover up his past of having been himself a boy from the slums. He is stimulated to change his vote by the opening up of another perspective on his past: he can think then that his past can be *useful* as an experience. He is the second person to change his vote after the Thinker's proposition. Although he can become doubtful and he changes his vote, he cannot yet mobilise his past experience. He only does this when he overcomes his shame and remembers how a knife is handled. He says, "Why didn't I think of that before; how could I not have thought of it, if I so often used a kind of knife like the one used in the crime." He is amazed at his own resistance to thinking; at that moment, he feels more comfortable and takes off his coat. The coat is, for him, a sign of participation in the group's emotions and also a symbol of having attained a different social status, wanting to erase his lower-class experiences.

4. *Democratic Watchmaker*. He changes his vote because of his love of democracy and because he has a feeling that a guilty verdict might be an injustice. He is a scientist above all. A European immigrant, he knows the pain of social oppression. He changes his vote because of a reasonable doubt that occurs to him when

ILLUSTRATION OF THE IDEAS ABOUT THE ORIGIN AND NATURE OF THOUGHT 79

he is able to think about the absurdity of returning to the scene of the crime. He refutes the panic argument.

5. *Shy and Scared* can think and make observations when he is not scared, when he can get rid of the inhibition of a primitive super-ego represented by the *Violent Authoritarian*. He then faces the Violent Authoritarian and draws attention to the issue of the two knives.

6. *House Painter* (characterised by a deep respect for his elders). He possesses well-developed common sense. He makes the Thinker doubt. He uses the same "let's suppose" argument. He tells him, "Let's imagine you are guilty and you are declared innocent."

7. *Chairman of the Group*. This character makes an emotional outburst when *Bigot* hurts his self-esteem. He then tells him to be the one to chair their discussion.

8. *Amusing Case*, so named because he seems amused by the fact that the case involves death. He works in advertising. His vote oscillates. He is superficial and banal. His lack of contact (like a rigid mode of mental functioning) makes him propose explaining to the "emotional fool" (the Thinker) the points on which he is confused. At no moment of the film is he committed or willing to think. This is shown in several moments in the film, one of them being when he is playing tic-tac-toe after they agreed on an hour to talk.

9. *Manic Salesman* (he sells jam). His tendency to evade the problem is evident from the first moment. He is in continuous (evacuative) action, and he feels fenced in and seems not to understand the responsibility of his task within the work group. What he wants to do from the first moment is to escape, apparently to go to his basketball game, but it is actually a much deeper evasion he seeks. If he has to change his vote to be able to leave, he will. He is confronted by Watchmaker for his lack of values and disrespect for them, for not doing anything with conviction. Thinker calms Old Man when Salesman does not want to hear the reasons for the change in his vote. He tells him "He doesn't listen to any-body"; in other words, his actions tend to be evacuative, expulsive, and he is armoured against any possibility of introjection or thought.

10. *Bigot*, who declares himself an anti-liar when he says, "You know what this type of people are like, they lie." From the beginning of

80   ON MENTAL GROWTH

the film, he is shown to have a somatic, psychosomatic, or somato–psychotic problem, as Bion would say, manifested as a nasally based allergy, and displays disdain towards ethical values as well. He is absolutely bigoted, fanatical, and racist, and he gives the impression of being unable to change. He actually breaks down, but he does not change his verbal vote, although he eventually accepts changing his vote due to group pressure. He never goes through a crisis of thought, but accepts the others' vote because of the pressure of the group's dynamics, shown by their disdain for him and their isolation of him because of his racist statements. His final breakdown and the absence of a crisis are facts that show the absolute impossibility for him to change and to think. He shows no anxiety regarding the oscillation of the PS↔D function (oscillation between states of dispersion and integration. Bion described this oscillation as a matrix function of thinking, along with the container–contained relationship (see Chapter Six of the current volume).

When they register his irreversible mental damage for the first time, they stop talking to him, simply turning their backs or ignoring him. He is the film's biggest achievement. This person who does not talk, who breaks down, is psychically dead and this is how everyone treats him.

11. *Obsessive Characteropath*, a non-participating, unemotional observer. This is a person who changes his monolithic reasoning only when something touches his personal experience and in relation to the body; he has a revelation regarding the use of glasses, and above all when the marks on his own face impose themselves as evidence. This happens when he is asked if he sleeps with his glasses on, and, at that moment, he understands that the elderly woman witness—who says she saw the boy murder the father through the windows of a passing train—could not be telling the truth, because if she was lying down to sleep, she was not wearing her glasses.

12. *The Violent Authoritarian*. He is the last one to change his vote. He has to change his tendency towards violent and explosive projective identification. He has to dismantle his defensive violent character when he faces the circumstances of the loss of his son, a loss in which he played an important part. He feels a persecutory guilt, which alternates with violent reproaches with obvious

projective identifications that are related to his difficult relationship with his son.

I shall now illustrate Bion's concept of catastrophic change with some aspects of the film. (Note that catastrophic change is not a concept synonymous with catastrophe; it is something equivalent to a mutation or a discontinuity in evolution. As we will see in Chapter Nine, catastrophic change is a concept of change which does not imply a catastrophe. It has three characteristics: (1) subversion of the previous system; (2) violence; (3) invariance—something from the previous system passes on to the new system, but in a transformed state.)

The first catastrophic change in Violent Authoritarian is when he accuses his son, whom he has projected on to the Young Man from the Slums, of being a coward and not man enough. The motivations of his vote were also questioned. He has an unconscious conflict with his son, but he is not as deteriorated as the fanatical Bigot, and stimulates feelings of compassion in the Thinker, who helps him put on his coat at the end of the film. Compassion, respect for the truth, and consideration for life are described by Bion, in *Cogitations*, as characteristics to take into account in a scientific, psychoanalytical investigation, when its object of study is an animate object. Psychoanalysis is a science of relationships, and not of related objects. These three characteristics identify relationships.

> The concern for truth must be distinguished from a capacity for establishing contact with reality. A man may have little capacity for that through lack of intelligence, training or even physical endowment – he might be defective in one or more of his senses, to take an obvious example. Yet this same man can have an active yearning for, and respect for, truth. Conversely, a highly gifted and well-equipped person may have little concern for truth about the realities with which his endowment permits an easy contact. Such unconcern will clearly be a matter for attention for the analyst for whom the psycho-analysis of the patient has truth as its criterion.

> Concern for life does not mean only a wish not to kill, though it does mean that. It means concern for an object precisely because that object has the quality of being alive. It means distinguishing between objects because one is alive and the other is not. It means that the difference is an important one. It means being curious about the qualities of what

82 ON MENTAL GROWTH

we know as life, and to have a desire to understand them. Conversely, a lack of concern for life means regarding a living object as indistinguishable from, or as being unworthy of being distinguished from, a machine, a thing or a place. (Bion, 1992, p. 248)

Evolution of the relationship between the individual and the group, and of thought and thinking, in the film

Several rounds of voting are carried out, and they show the evolution of the capability to think. This evolution seems to be related with what Bion calls a catastrophic change in those who dared to open their former closed constant conjunctions (let me remind the reader that Bion uses the term constant conjunction to describe how the mind organises facts. This conjunction can be saturated, closed, or open to new experiences), and accept thinking in a different way. These changes must not be viewed as a competition (that is the perspective of those who cannot think: this rivalry in the context of thinking is characteristic of the psychotic part of the personality and is evidence of an activity that comes from the super-superego.)

The votes change in those who could gain access to the selected facts and who opened their minds to a different perspective. In the atmosphere of the group, it seemed sometimes that some viewed these changes as a competition or rivalry between the different opinions of the jurymen, focused on who was winning. At the beginning of the film, there is an attempt to reduce the whole problem to an agreement of the complete group to vote without discussing the case, an attitude that seemed like an attempt to calm the anxieties implicit in a decision concerning the life of a human being. It is equivalent to the "idea as a saviour", which can quickly make sense of things and calm the anxiety of not knowing, of vacillating between one path of thought and a different one. It is like the diagnoses arrived at on a first interview: they can be used to calm the anxiety stemming from some still-evolving conjunction that has yet to be fully understood.

Thinking, instead of an automatic group agreement of basic assumption, means opening the mind to some new idea, a thought without a thinker, which is trying to find a containing mind. The Thinker is the one who seems to be able to tolerate the thought without a thinker, which needs to find a means of expressing itself. Six of

ILLUSTRATION OF THE IDEAS ABOUT THE ORIGIN AND NATURE OF THOUGHT 83

the members of the jury are going to mobilise their PS↔D function (the oscillation between mental states of dispersion and integration) in different moments and under specific circumstances. They seem to be able to tolerate the thought without a thinker; they can contain the thought of a "reasonable doubt". The other six are divided into two groups of three who are unwilling to think about the issues; the members of the first group do so only when they have to face a crisis that implies catastrophic change. In the final group of three (the advertising agent (Amusing Case), the Manic Salesman, and the Bigot) the change is not authentic, or, at least, the nature of the change can be disputed: we can see this in the Manic Salesman and in the Amusing Case (the advertising agent).

We can consider that each one has a different configuration in the PS↔D oscillation. Each one also has a different point of resistance from where the catastrophic change related to thinking starts. A classification in Column 2 (Ψ) of the Grid—that of using a thought as a resistance—could be the following: the Thinker could contain and think the disruptive idea during the trial but he was aware that he was completely alone, having to bear by himself the burden of thinking without giving in to evacuating it through his actions. (He obtains something of his revenge when he confronts Violent Authoritarian and tells him, "We now have all the time to hear your reasons.")

I am using the film to illustrate the concepts that we have developed in this chapter. The oscillation between states of dispersion and integration (PS↔D) is one of the matrix mental functions for thinking, along with the container–contained function. The first one implies tolerance of doubt, of uncertainty in PS and of the finite–infinite relationship in D, since the resolution of a problem is a point of arrival and also of departure towards new problems not previously revealed. Out of all the possible interpretations, one of them must be chosen. The container–contained relationship of mutual benefit transforms crude emotions into thinkable elements by containing them and giving them a meaning.

Let us continue with an analysis of the characters throughout the film.

1. *Thinker.* We see his capability to be alone with himself and to be the only one that does not agree, without thinking, with the group. We see him alone and withdrawn, looking out of the

84   ON MENTAL GROWTH

window, and displaying tolerance of being alone. He can be alone with his thoughts and with the feeling of being separated from the group when he differs from the group mentality because he is thinking. He seems to have training in being able to think in the midst of pressure for action from the group. He thinks even when he is receiving what seems to be a bombardment of projective identifications, which is not an easy thing to do. And this moves the Old Man to change his vote.

2. *Old Man.* He changes his vote moved by what seems to be empathy, because of his identification with the situation of being alone, which he knows very well, and because he admires the Thinker's capacity to tolerate it. But he also says, "It's hard not to be afraid of being ridiculed." That is his problem. In his observations and contributions to thinking, he refers to people who are afraid of old age, afraid of being ridiculed and hide it, not because they are liars, but because, in a way, they are hiding the facts. In the film, we see him developing an open attitude towards the observation of facts, making use of his own painful experiences. He doubts the testimonies of the witnesses and he points out that the old and paraplegic witness—who testifies that he saw the boy running away after the victim's body fell and the woman, a key witness who says that she saw the boy commit the murder, might have given these testimonies out of fear of old age and being ridiculed. He himself seems to have suffered the loneliness of old age and the shame of not being acknowledged. In this sense, his supposition about the motives of the handicapped witness is a reflection of his own depressive feelings, of his experiences of loss in his own life.

3. *Young Man from the Slums.* He changes his vote once he overcomes the fear that leads him to try to hide his origins and dares to become aware—once he can start to think—that the accused was like him when he was a teenager in the slums and of the lies and the shame involved because of his background. He feels almost no receptivity to projective identifications when he is accused of being the first one to change his vote to "innocent". He knows about intimidation and, because of this feeling, he was unable to think throughout the trial. Only when he connects with his past can he discover that the question of the handling of the knife was different from how it was described in the trial and how the

Violent Authoritarian dramatises it; this is when the Young Man changes his vote with conviction. He can connect with his experience of having lived in a slum, and is then amazed that he had not thought of that before. We can understand what might have been the obstacles to him thinking about it. There are two options: the repression of his past (which the trial brings up again) or that he projectively identifies this past with the boy. My conjecture is that probably it was the repression of his past, so when he realises the discrepancy in the issue of the handling of the knife, there is a moment of true insight. Also, he does not seem to harbour the violence that is generated by a hypertrophied projective identification, something which is clear in Violent Authoritarian, for example, when he confronts the Young Man, accusing him of disloyalty for having voted against them, as if it were a game and not a question of life and death for the accused. We will be aware, later, that Authoritarian has a difficult relationship with his son.

At that moment of the film, we can assume that many of the members of the jury might have experienced some kind of projective identification, a phenomenon that happens often in the functioning of a group, and that does not produce insight, but the opposite. Another element that freed him (the Young Man from the Slums) from his isolation or repression was the value judgements directed towards the accused's past. (However, a lot of violence was needed to mobilise him; it seems that his painful past left strong inhibitions and submissive feelings. He refuses to express his ideas in front of the group.)

4. *The Democratic Watchmaker* (a European immigrant). He changes his vote when his democratic values are at stake, and he can authentically convince himself that there is reasonable doubt. He is a thorough observer of the facts, but he also experiences emotion and has sensibility: he believes in justice and in democratic ideals. It can be conjectured that he works alone when repairing watches. He begins to doubt when he compares the witnesses' timings and contrasts facts which can uphold his opinion with logical arguments.

5. *Shy and Scared* starts to gain in confidence, acting with conviction during the voting; he remains interested, he is not prejudiced, but

86   ON MENTAL GROWTH

he does not dare to think. When he allows doubt to enter into his simple thinking mechanism, he is able to maintain his line of thinking. He is scared of making decisions; only when he can find himself and think does he stop being scared and is able to confront Authoritarian's pressure.

6.   *House Painter* has few interlocutions. He is convinced that the boy is guilty. However, as the atmosphere in the group becomes more open to thinking, he can start resorting to his own experience and to thinking as well, which enables him to help uphold the fact that trains make a dreadful noise and do not allow for listening or talking. They (the workers) bang and make a noise while working and do not talk. He has an exchange of dialogue in the bathroom with the Thinker, asking him again if he thinks the boy is innocent. Thinker answers that he "doesn't know", but that it is possible. Thinker then asks him to suppose that the boy is innocent. House Painter says that he is not used to supposing, and asks Thinker to suppose that the boy is guilty and is declared innocent. At that moment, he is beginning to think. "Supposing" means the possibility of making hypotheses, of having access to imaginative conjectures which are obviously not certainties. He makes the Thinker doubt.

Some other facts worth highlighting

The weather changes; it becomes stormy and starts raining and that point in the film marks the moment of a catastrophic change in the group. Bion says that when two personalities meet, an emotional turbulence is created. This means that, in every encounter, there is always a specific emotional atmosphere, even if it is just one of boredom, or of "nothing is happening". In the film, the emotional atmosphere is first one of confinement and isolation. The lack of thinking generates situations with no real possibility of finding a way out, because either they lack, or there is no possibility of using, adequate instruments to solve the problems. Evasion can be used as an antidote to anxiety.

After voting, six maintain their vote of guilty because their thinking process is still disturbed. What kind of disturbance? It is different in each one of them. The first one to change his vote from guilty to innocent, because he only wants to leave to go to his game, is Manic Salesman. He is confronted directly by Watchmaker, who demands of him a responsible attitude; he does not want to accept a vote without the acknowledgement of responsibility, an innocent vote simply because the other wants to leave. It is the point of crisis for each one of them that shows responsibility towards the other and speaks of the seriousness of the vote and of pronouncing the accused innocent.

There is a critical moment in the scene when Thinker asks for a new round of votes.

Those who vote innocent, besides those who had already done so, are:

Chairman;
Amusing Case.

That is how they reach nine votes for an innocent verdict.

Bigot, Obsessive Characteropath, and Violent Authoritarian still have not changed their vote. The Bigot cannot change; he is dragged into it by group pressure.

When only the Bigot's vote is pending, he does not vote; he breaks down, but he is still unable to change. He suffers the mental deterioration that is a consequence of his fanaticism. It is an interesting fact that there is a group movement of unspoken physical rejection, with the members leaving Bigot alone and turning their backs on Bigot's discourse, which is devoid of ideas and consists of isolated and fanatic statements. He breaks down when he realises his isolation.

This moment is an opportunity that is seized on by Thinker, who calls for a new round of votes. Obsessive Characteropath, defeated in his omnipotence of logical thought, has to admit that he did not perceive the mark of the witness's spectacles, and he knows the implications of using glasses. Thus, he comes to have reasonable doubt, and changes his vote authentically.

This leaves Violent Authoritarian, who says that he is offended by the turn in the voting. He is furious, and he finally goes through an emotional crisis, symbolically murdering his son by tearing up his photograph, and then declaring his son innocent. In the end, Thinker shows compassion, not triumph, by helping Authoritarian to put on his coat, and, once on the street, they introduce themselves to Old Man.

88   ON MENTAL GROWTH

Amusing Case (the advertising agent): this is an "as if" personality, lacking an endoskeleton. He cannot think because he claims that it is too complex for him, but this is because he uses thoughts only to evacuate them and not to establish relationships and think. He only has "witty" phrases, amusing *clichés* that are not useful in maintaining a line of thought. He is the only one who retracts his vote one way and then the other. Angry, Salesman says that he is like a tennis ball that goes from one side to the other. When he finally votes innocent, he is disconnected. The situation overwhelmed him.

Manic Salesman (with a hat). His intolerance of thought and thinking is shown by his considering that, for him, problems do not exist, everything has an easy solution. He takes refuge in admiring sports figures. He knows about metaphors but does not use them for thinking; he is witty as a way of evading thought. The P↔D oscillation with which he operates places everything within the realm of superficiality. As soon as he enters the discussion room, he quickly goes to the coat rack to leave his hat, something that seems to mark his identity and, at the same time, his condition of always being hyperkinetic, of going somewhere else. At one point, when the Old Man feels wronged and he demands to know what Salesman means by saying that he changed his vote so he could go, the Manic Salesman evades the question without listening to him, and goes to the bathroom. That is the moment when Thinker intervenes; trying to calm the Old Man's anger, he says, "Don't worry, he'll never listen to you." Salesman is one of the first who has to defend his "guilty" vote and he refers to the accused's history, exhibiting prejudices that condemn the accused for his supposedly violent past. But his arguments lack consistency.

A few more comments

In the first round of votes, the result is: eleven for "guilty" and one for "innocent". We see several defensive reactions to the frustration of the preconception (an expectation that is open to a new experience) which at this level is a pre-determination: that is to say, it is not an expectation, but an affirmation of certainty that is unable to couple with any fact in order to transform itself into a conception or thought. The Thinker, with his "innocent" vote, defeats that automatic group consensus and does so because he wants time to be able to discuss the problem and think.

We see the use of disqualification: "Oh God, there's always one", says the Manic Salesman. (Disqualification is typical of the primitive super-superego that usurps ego functions.)

The group asks the Thinker to say on what basis he cast his vote, and his answer is interesting, since he claims that he does not believe the accused to be innocent but he wants to talk, to discuss, because what is being discussed is a young man who had suffered much and deserves discussion of the matter. Thus, he demonstrates consideration for life and truth, and respect for mental pain. When there is another proposal for each one to give their arguments on their "guilty" vote, it is a movement that opens the possibility of thinking, since they need to put their thoughts or beliefs into words, making them evident.

Moments of insight and obstacles for thinking

Those who allow doubt to penetrate their constant conjunctions (the way the mind organises the experiences) can have access to thinking. In the film, those who can disarticulate the conjunctions that they had organised during the trial are able to think. They are the first six who accept changing their vote, and do it with authenticity because they have seen that there is "reasonable doubt". This can be observed in the film because they say, "There was something that was bothering me and I didn't know what it was", or "How strange, I didn't think of this during the trial." For example, the one who knew how to handle switchblades in street fights did not think of it during the trial because of the pain that his past on the streets caused him. He might have stabbed someone in the past. Neither did he think that the accused could be the victim of an injustice on the part of the court-appointed defence lawyer, as is likely to have happened to him at some time.

Those members of the jury that are without prejudices have different motivations for maintaining their previous ideas.

1. The Salesman claims that he has experience of being a juror in previous trials and of life. But he uses his prior experience to avoid contact with the facts through a maniacal activity that never stops.

90   ON MENTAL GROWTH

2. The Obsessive Characteropath, who is wearing glasses, is holding on to sensory facts and putting forward what seem to be thoughts without conjectures, he argues with a logical, intellectual reasoning without contact with emotional experience. He is only attracted to "facts that are almost irrefutably proven", "facts without feelings". He is stubborn and obsessive. He is only moved if something is close to his direct sensorial experience and he leaves out feelings, feelings that cannot be avoided when the kind of learning is learning from experience. He never sweats or takes off his coat. He is armoured (even his body seems to be under the sway of the obsessive system). He upholds a monolithic vision, based on what, according to him, is irrefutable evidence: a witness saw the boy kill his father. He only starts to doubt when he realises the fact that you cannot sleep while wearing glasses.

3. The Bigot is angry with foreigners; he makes prejudiced judgements all the time about people who are born in certain places. A prejudice is a statement based on a generalisation that does not accept differences. He says, "They're all the same."

4. The Amusing Case (an advertising agent) has a shallow personality, similar to the type seen in television advertisements. He is superficial; he discovers the *impasse* but, in order to get out of it, he just makes a statement that is a kind of jingle. He cannot bear the depressive feelings or the pain of facing a problem that has no solution or that demands thinking. He uses symbols as they are used in advertising as the means to manipulate.

5. The Shy and Scared. Once he matures and can emerge from the position of "respecting authority", he defends the Old Man. He thinks that a crime always has a motive, which seems reasonable, but its opposite is not so reasonable: if we find a motive for a person, that does not mean that we have found the criminal, that the person with a motive actually committed the crime. But these ideas are not so rigid and isolated that they cannot undergo a crisis. His feelings of protection towards the Old Man are the motivations for his change of vote.

6. The House Painter's change comes through recovering his experiences as a worker, and this also leads him to collaborate and use his capacity to measure spaces. He helps the engineer in his calculations of the distance that the disabled witness, who "saw

the boy running from the house after having heard the fall of the deceased's body", would have had to cover.

Another classification

We can ask what the selected facts are for each one of the members of the jury, those that stimulate a crisis and so enable gaining access to thought. For example, in some of the jury members this is quite easy to see:

1. In the Thinker, this is his capability for having doubts and his consideration that a life is at stake.
2. In the Old Man, it happens when he comes into contact with his own experience of being alone and so understanding the Thinker's solitude. He can put his sense of sight at the service of observation (a highly preserved sense) associated to his thinking about his own experience and what people's lives are like.
3. In the Watchmaker, it is the fact of valuing the meaning of democracy. He is helped in his discoveries by his precision (taken from his profession) in the sequence of facts and the possibilities that they combine.
4. For the Young Man from the Slums, not thinking about his origins prevents him from developing thought; when he gets in touch with his background, which he had wanted to erase, he can use his experience to make discoveries, including knowing how a switchblade is used in the neighbourhood he comes from.
5. The Obsessive Characteropath, not being emotional, takes apparent "facts" as proven with the senses as selected facts, but he changes his vote and gains access to thinking when he realises the issue of the spectacles that is connected with his own body, and is able to work out that the female witness was not wearing her glasses at the moment that she claimed to have seen the crime, because, at the time at which the train passed, she had just got up, and you do not go to sleep with glasses on.
6. The Manic Salesman's selected fact stems from an evacuative action; achieving something no matter how (be it selling, going to the baseball game, or solving any situation quickly), so it is not a true selected fact and he does not gain authentic access to thinking.

92   ON MENTAL GROWTH

7. The Bigot does not gain access to thinking either; his statements are prejudiced generalisations that reaffirm his disdain for the object of his prejudices.

8. House Painter (worker) also appeals to his own experience when he gains access to thinking. Contact with this experience allows him to gain access to authentic thinking and the development of a separate mind.

9. Shy and Scared: his main feature is the need to be appreciated and to find something or somebody to lean on. When he can dismantle this relationship with what he feels as authority, something in him evolves and enables him to confront the Authoritarian. He then gains access to authentic thinking.

10. Amusing Case, although he changes his vote, is unable to make an authentic deep change. His personality is orientated towards the avoidance of contact with facts; he does so through the advertising vertex: advertising aims at selling something, so the statements of advertising imply something that causes amusement and amazement along with surprise, but it does not care about truth. He does not gain access to thinking either.

11. For Chairman of the Group, his function is to organise, and he tries to carry it out efficiently; he only gains access to thinking, and his method of organising begins to encourage thinking, when there are challenges to, and questioning of, his function (he is made the butt of jokes). It is also interesting to note that when he breaks away from the basic assumptions dynamic, he stops being the leader of the basic assumption, the primitive group activity, and that is when his function of organising the task in hand is questioned by the group.

12. The Violent Authoritarian tries to impose his prejudices. The massive projective identification of his conflict with his son becomes evident the moment he wants to demonstrate the use of the blade. He suffers a crisis and is able to change his vote when he understands that he wanted to kill his son in the person of the young man accused of killing his father.

An observation about the final take

The camera is focused on the wardrobe. It represents leaving something of one's appearance behind: when Thinker is leaving, he helps

Violent Authoritarian to put on his coat, which is a sign of compassion, an L (love) link. Bion says that in psychoanalysis—and, I suppose, at every time we are dealing with living objects—there is a need to combine the search for truth with compassion. We can see in the film that there are two characters who do not take off their coats: the Thinker, for whom clothing is not a symptom, and the Obsessive Characteropath, for whom not taking off his coat is a symptom of control and the absence of emotions.

CHAPTER SEVEN

Learning from Experience: alpha function and reverie

Introduction

1962 sees the publication of *Learning from Experience*, the first book that Bion publishes as such and not as a compilation of revised articles, as had been the case with the first two, *Experiences in Groups* and *Second Thoughts*. This publication introduces the third phase of Bion's developments if we consider the first one to be *Experiences in Groups* and the second one the understanding of the psychotic part of the personality. This third phase was named by Bléandonu (1994) "the epistemological period", and he frames it within the context of Bion trying to find a scientific language for psychoanalysis. Through this book and the two following ones (*Elements of Psycho-analysis*, 1963; *Transformations*, 1965), he develops the ideas of a "thought-thinking apparatus" and its negative, that is, the model where thinking fails, where thoughts cannot be thought and are fragmented, evacuated, or substituted by the construction of lies.

The discoveries Bion made throughout this period when he investigated the psychotic part of the personality led to the formulation of a psychoanalytical theory of knowing, meaning not a possession of knowledge, but a disposition to know as a link. Philosophy had been

96   ON MENTAL GROWTH

studying rational thought for a long time, but the philosopher lacks the psychoanalyst's experience of the personality problems that manifest as disturbances of thought.

In this book, Bion has already found a language and hypothesis of his own. We see him develop a psychoanalytical theory of knowing and thinking, and he is trying to find an approach to mathematical language. By adding to his experience as a psychoanalyst the philosophical and epistemological training acquired through his studies in Oxford, he can use them to develop a theory that can account for the phenomena of thought disturbances that he discovered in his clinical practice. At the same time, he aims to find a more precise language which is, moreover, "empty", or unsaturated, to avoid the risk of jargon and of the ossification which can obstruct the evolution of ideas. His experience with psychotic patients allowed him to observe their symbolisation disturbances and the very concrete language they used. A more abstract language for expressing psychoanalytic ideas is needed because, as Bion says in the book we are discussing,

> It appears that our rudimentary equipment for "thinking" thoughts is adequate when the problems are associated with the inanimate, but not when the object for the investigation is the phenomenon of life itself. Confronted with the complexities of the human mind, the analyst must be careful in following even accepted scientific method; its weakness may be closer to the weakness of psychotic thinking than superficial scrutiny would admit. (Bion, 1962a, p. 14)

This kind of language is expressed in the concepts of function and factor, of alpha function, and alpha and beta elements. By using these terms, Bion aims to provide precision and avoid the saturation of language or, paradoxically, as he puts it, to be as imprecise as possible to remain unsaturated.

> The term alpha-function is, intentionally, devoid of meaning. . . . Since the object of this meaningless term is to provide psychoanalytic investigation with a counterpart of the mathematician's variable, an unknown that can be invested with a value when its use has helped to determine what that value is, it is important that it should not be prematurely used to convey meanings, for the premature meanings may be precisely those that it is essential to exclude. (Bion, 1962a, p. 3)

LEARNING FROM EXPERIENCE: ALPHA FUNCTION AND REVERIE   97

In *Learning from Experience*, the Kleinian concept of projective identification is extended and modified, losing its aspect of an intrusive operation of one personality towards the inside of another one (the space of the mother's inside)—in it is an omnipotent phantasy. The concept of a realistic projective identification, a communicative one (a primitive means of communication), is related in this work to the new container–contained model, which Bion represents with the following signs: ♀♂, meaning container and contained, respectively, and going beyond the feminine and masculine meaning of the signs. Conceived like this, projective identification contributes to the idea that the personality does not end in the anatomy, because projective identification is not only an omnipotent phantasy but is also a primitive means of communication between infant and mother, and so the container–contained (♀♂) relationship takes on the value of a relational function. Later on, we shall see it as one of the matrix functions of thinking.

In the following section, I discuss the new concepts Bion developed in *Learning from Experience*, and then I take up the subject of links once more. I begin with some definitions and with the alpha function and reverie. Then I consider the function of dreams and dreaming, and the function of metabolising emotional experiences. I also describe the significance of models and their use in clinical practice.

I run ahead of myself slightly here to say that the alpha function refers to the development of a function which metabolises raw emotional experiences, thereby enabling them to be reintrojected. As we shall see later, instead of a hypertrophied projective identification and a beta screen due to the lack of, or to a breakdown in, a transforming container, which is one of the characteristics of the alpha function, we will have a contact-barrier and a "dreaming" screen, where raw emotions can be transformed into "dreams" and, therefore, acquire a meaning. My hypothesis is that the contact barrier and the "dream" screen are transformations of the maternal reverie once it has been introjected and assimilated by the infant's personality or, in an analytical process, by the patient's mental equipment.

The theory of functions and factors:
alpha (α) function and beta (β) elements

Function is the term used in mathematics to indicate the relationship or correspondence between two or more amounts. It can also be said

98   ON MENTAL GROWTH

to establish a relationship between two or more variables, or parameters. A function has factors that determine it. A clinical fact that can be observed is a function of a series of factors that can be correlated. The value of a function will depend on the way in which the factors are related.

Bion uses this term with two meanings:

1. As the equivalent of a mathematical variable—that is to say, an unknown quantity which can be assigned a specific value through its use—available for psychoanalytical research. Function and factor define personality traits. A clinical fact that can be observed is a function of a number of factors that can be correlated. Therefore, the value of a function, as an unknown variable, depends on the relationship between the factors.
2. He also uses function in a second sense, as direction. When used in this way, we can say that it has an aim or a purpose. Walking has the function of going from one place to another, or we can consider a symptom as "coming from" and "leading to". When the double sense of a function is clarified in psychoanalytical research, its unknown character is reduced and can become a factor.

The theory of functions and "alpha function" is an instrument for observation in psychoanalytical practice; it is useful for working without having to prematurely present new theories. Alpha function has no meaning, intentionally, in order to provide psychoanalytical research with an equivalent of the mathematician's variable, an unknown that can be assigned a value when its use determines what that value is. It must not be used prematurely to provide meaning. The α function is an unknown variable whose value must be discovered through psychoanalysis. We can conjecture that when we are with a patient in a psychoanalytical session, the meaning of what the patient says needs to be discovered. It is also an unknown.

Dreamwork alpha is an expression used in *Cogitations* (1991), posthumously published by Francesca Bion and containing Bion's ideas "in progress". Dreamwork alpha was transformed into alpha function in *Learning from Experience*. The investigation of alpha function implies the development of thoughts, of thinking and learning through emotional experience.

This function is meant to digest emotional experiences, transforming sense impressions of actual objects from the outside world and of objects associated with emotional experiences into "dream thoughts" which may then be used to "think". The alpha function operates on sense and the emotional impressions of which the patient becomes aware. If the operation is achieved, then "alpha elements" are produced which are able to be stored and to meet the requests of dream thoughts. The evolved consciousness, that which can perceive and understand what it perceives, depends on this function.

Bion extended the meaning of the word "dream" to include some circumstances in the analysis of severely disturbed patients. The emotional experiences must be "dreamed" (whether one is awake or asleep) in order to be assimilated by the personality. All dream thoughts are transformations of "undigested" facts. This function also differentiates between the conscious and unconscious through the creation of a contact barrier. "Dreaming" is part of the process of digesting the truth. Bion extends Freud's view that dreams are the hallucinatory satisfaction of an infantile desire: hallucination aims at ridding the psyche of what it cannot tolerate; dreamwork alpha operates in an opposite direction, towards containment and storage of emotional experiences. The alpha function does not operate only at night; it is a function that involves a continuous activity of digesting emotional experiences night and day. Only through their transformation into alpha elements can emotional experiences be metabolised and used in the different ways that Bion presents in *Elements of Psychoanalysis.*

The alpha function can act in reverse, and this leads to the dispersion of the contact-barrier. The alpha elements are stripped of that which differentiates them from beta elements, and this produces bizarre objects with fragments of ego and superego adhering to these beta elements.

Alpha elements are those elements that include visual images, emotional, auditory, and olfactory patterns, and are the particles of thought which are the "furniture of dreams" that can be developed into dream-thoughts while sleeping and unconscious thoughts while awake. These elements are produced through the differentiation between sense impressions and emotional experiences, not as facts, not as the "thing in itself" and its transformation into dream thoughts. An example would be the infant when he can differentiate the feelings of hunger, such as the need of a breast to feed him, from those feelings of satisfaction that result from his actual experience of feeding from the breast.

The α elements, produced by the operation of the alpha function, can be articulated and disarticulated and they form a reticulum that is a contact-barrier. Alpha elements are the precursors of memory, of unconscious waking thoughts and of dream thoughts. They are the elements of which models and dreams are made.

Beta elements are sense impressions and emotional experiences that are not differentiated from facts, from the "thing-in-itself". These elements cannot be used to develop thoughts; they can only be evacuated. As an example of beta elements, let us take the infant who does not differentiate between feelings of hunger and the need for a breast, so, instead of understanding that he is hungry, he experiences the sensations of hunger as a bad breast that is attacking him.

These β elements cannot be articulated; they can only agglomerate. However, if they are evacuated through realistic, communicative projective identification and find a transforming container, such as maternal reverie or the analyst's alpha function, they can be the beginning of a thinking process. In *Cogitations* (1991, p. 191), Bion says that they also have a function of communicating the emotions within the group.

At the beginning of the development of these ideas, Bion had not yet made these differentiations. It is only when he extends the notion of projective identification, through the formulation of the container–contained relationship in *Learning from Experience* that the bizarre object and the beta element could be differentiated. The bizarre object, described in "Differentiation of the psychotic from the non-psychotic personalities" (1967), can be visualised as a beta element with traces of ego and superego, which have been evacuated through a hypertrophied projective identification in inadequate and inanimate objects. Bion gives as an example a person who, through projective identification, projects his capability to see on to a gramophone, which is then perceived by the patient as looking at him. The infant's beta elements at the beginning of life, when he lacks alpha function, are named "beta virginal elements" by Meltzer (1973), who, furthermore, proposes differentiating them from bizarre objects, for which he suggests the name "betes".

Reverie can be defined as a detoxifying and digesting function, which the mother performs for the infant through her alpha function.

Bion uses this term to name the mother's capacity to receive the infant's projective identification of intolerable emotions, "dream" them, and return them to the infant already detoxified. Because they have been transformed by the mother's alpha function into something tolerable, the infant can now reintroject them and assimilate the emotional experience as a part of his personality.

The infant, being in himself unable to make use of the sense data, for example, feelings of hunger, has to evacuate his emotions into the mother, relying on her to transform them into something suitable to use as alpha elements.

If the projection is not accepted, the infant feels that the feeling— for example, the fear of dying—is stripped of meaning, so that what the infant receives is not an emotion made tolerable but a "nameless dread". Naming is a container; it is part of the containing function. These considerations about naming have significant implications for psychoanalysis and psychoanalytic technique.

Bion also defines reverie as

> the psychological source of supply of the infant's needs for love and understanding . . . if the feeding mother cannot allow reverie or if the reverie is allowed but is not associated with love for the child or its father, this fact will be communicated to the infant even though incomprehensible to the infant. (Bion, 1962a, p. 36)

This perspective views reverie also as a channel of communication.

The tasks left unfinished by the breakdown in the mother's reverie are imposed on the rudimentary consciousness of the infant. This can lead to the establishment of an internal object, hostile to projective identification, which means that, instead of an understanding object, the infant has a wilfully misunderstanding object with which it has identified.

Contact-barrier is a term used by Freud (1950[1895], p. 299) to describe neurophysiologic synapses. Bion borrowed it to name a structure that has both functions: of contact and of barrier (Bion, 1962a). It develops through the articulation of alpha elements that, in one moment, cohere and, in another, are disarticulated as they proliferate and form a reticulum. It is in a continuous process of formation, and marks the point of contact and separation between conscious and unconscious elements, creating the distinction between them.

The term emphasises the establishment of contact between the conscious and the unconscious and the selective passage of elements from one to the other. Alpha elements form a semi-permeable barrier which, at the same time, allows exchange in such a way that emotional experiences can be "dreamed" and stored, but it impedes the intrusion of phantasies and emotions into the conscious, which might disturb an appropriate assessment of the facts of external reality; it simultaneously preserves dreams, the psychic reality, from being overwhelmed by a hyper-realistic vision.

The change of elements from conscious to unconscious and *vice versa* depends on the nature of the contact-barrier. The nature, in turn, will depend on the supply of alpha elements and of the kind of relationship these elements have with one another. They may cohere or agglomerate, be ordered sequentially as a narrative—as in a dream— or be ordered logically or geometrically. Its function as a semi-permeable membrane allows for it to be awake or asleep, conscious or unconscious, and to differentiate past from present and from future. It acts as a barrier that prevents the mutual invasion between "dreams" and realistic facts, acting also as an articulating caesura that makes thinking and communication possible.

Container–contained (♀♂) is a term that describes a relationship that has as a model a container with receptive qualities and a contained with a penetrating quality. Bion uses the female and male symbols (♀♂) for this model, symbols that have an abstract quality but also contain the common matrix of the emotional experience from which they emerge. Both the container and the contained are models born from the emotional experience with the first objects. Thus, the breast can be conceived as the container (♀) of the mouth (♂). This model also develops as a conceptualisation of the relationship between the infant's projective identification, a contained (♂) with penetrating capability and the receptive quality of the container (♀) that is maternal reverie. It is also a model of the origin of thought, as the infant's realistic and communicative projective identification is received and transformed into alpha elements by maternal reverie. Bion does not conceive of the isolated development of each of these terms, so the object of investigation is the relationship between them. The observation of autistic mechanisms made me consider that the autistic functioning obstructs relationships between the container and the contained, so that what prevails there is isolation.

LEARNING FROM EXPERIENCE: ALPHA FUNCTION AND REVERIE 103

Depending on the quality of the emotion, the container–contained relationship can favour development or hinder it. If what prevails is envy, container and contained are stripped of their essential qualities, of meaning and vitality. This relationship is the antithesis of growth. Bion represents a despoiling emotion and a container–contained relationship joined by this parasitic emotional link with the minus sign: $-(\male\female)$. This is in contrast to the growth-stimulating relationship represented by: $\female.\male$ with the point being the representation of a link of love (L), hate (H), and the disposition to know (K). The fundamental difference between both types of relationships is that the latter has the possibility of development, based on tolerance of doubt, of ignorance, and of a sense of infinite. The $-(\female\male)$ relationship leads to deterioration. Bion proposes three forms of relationships.

1. Symbiotic: it is a container–contained relationship in which two come together for their mutual benefit and/or the benefit of a third party. Projective identification ($\male$) is used in a communicative manner and is detoxified by the container ($\female$) and transformed into meaning, thereby becoming a preconception open to new meanings. These characteristics of the relationship are factors of growth. The mother grows in her capacity to be a mother through her contact with her infant, and the baby, in turn, develops through his relationship with the mother.

2. Commensal: it is a container–contained relationship in which both co-exist side by side without making contact. The caesura is broad, so there is no conflict. We could think of it as not having achieved the conditions for the meeting between container and contained, such as in the example Bion provides with Aristarchus of Samos's heliocentric theory in 500 BC, which went unrecognised in its time, when the geocentric theory was predominant, until the evolution of the culture and instruments such as the telescope resulted in a clash between religious beliefs and scientific observation when Galileo put forward Copernicus's theory.

3. Parasitic: the relationship between container–contained is mutually destructive. Projective identification is explosive, and destructive for the container. It is, in turn, destructive for the contained. The container strips the contained of its penetrating qualities, and the contained strips the container of its receptive quality. This parasitic relationship is one of mutual despoiling,

not only of the pre-existing relationship, but also of its possibilities for future development. In this kind of despoiling relationship, container and contained can be considered to be related by a destructive combination of envy and voracity. Bion named this type of link minus (–)K. It is the kind of link that is characteristic of the murdering superego, which usurps the ego functions.

Enforced splitting is one of the different kinds of splitting described by Bion in *Learning from Experience*. These kinds of splitting are different from the classical ones described by Klein and the fragmentation introduced by Bion himself when he investigated the psychotic and non-psychotic part of the personality. With this term, Bion described a splitting between what is material and what is psychological–emotional. This mechanism arises as a "solution" for a conflict between the infant's need to survive and the fear of violent and conflicting emotions stimulated by the contact with the nurturing breast-object.

A strong fear of emotions can inhibit the infant's impulse to obtain sustenance. If fear of death through starvation compels the infant to resume feeding it does so, but at the price of developing an enforced splitting which is characterised by a relationship with the material product, the milk, but not with the breast as an emotional link. This state is stimulated by the need to get rid of the emotional complications of the awareness of life and of a relationship with objects that are alive. Steps are taken to destroy or hinder awareness of all emotions or feelings. Its purpose and effect is to enable the infant to obtain material comforts without acknowledging the existence of a living object on which these benefits depend. The need for love, understanding, and mental development is split off and transformed into the search for material comforts. Our postmodern culture can provide us with many examples of this kind of splitting.

Link. Bion defined psychoanalysis as a science of relationships, and he said we have to investigate the relationship between the objects and not the objects themselves, which are the anchors of the relationship.

A link is an emotion that relates container to contained. He described three links, which he named L (love), H (hate), and K (knowledge), as well as describing three negative despoiling emotions, to which he added a minus sign: –L, –H, and –K. Meltzer names them as anti-emotions, and describes them as hypocrisy, cynicism, and

LEARNING FROM EXPERIENCE: ALPHA FUNCTION AND REVERIE   105

philistinism. They are different variations of lies. Bion differentiated between lies and thoughts and described the difference between the liar and the thinker.

Bion's developments in *Learning from Experience* were, most of all, dedicated to the ideas about the K link, such as the disposition to know and not as the possession of knowledge, and the minus –K link is described as a link of active disavowal. The links of love and hate had already been considered, from a psychoanalytical perspective, by Freud and Klein. The K link, the disposition to know, is significant in psychoanalysis, because, when a –K link prevails—a tendency to misunderstand—the analyst lacks the fundamental collaboration of the patient, and, in psychoanalysis, as in dance, "it takes two to tango".

Some thoughts about these new terms

As we can see, in *Learning from Experience*, Bion develops one of his key notions: that the specific significant characteristic of the alpha function has to do with the capability to tolerate the difference between the "thing" and the "no-thing", between the object and the emotional impression or experience, or the difference between the idea and the fact. Described in terms of maternal function (reverie) or of the psychoanalytical function of the personality, alpha function is related not only to the modulation of anxieties, but also implies the mother's offering of a "gift" of meaning which enables the infant to tolerate its emotions. This enables the transformation of the emotions into elements that are dream thoughts. "Dreaming", in a broad sense, enables the formulation of emotional problems and dealing with mental pain through the meaning, and even the tolerance, of its absence and not equating it with the destruction of the object, the breast, that is the source of meaning. For Freud, thinking was a method of restricting discharge as a means of achieving a reduction in tension. For Bion, thinking is meant to modify mental pain instead of evading it, digesting emotional experiences so they can be assimilated.

Bion is giving a central role to the attitude with which the personality faces mental pain: alpha function and maternal reverie help to tolerate and modify the pain instead of evading it. This function allows the development of the contact-barrier, which is a semi-permeable membrane that both separates and relates the conscious and unconscious processes. This barrier is a fundamental element in adult life: it enables the development of "dream thoughts". In other words, this barrier determines our capacity to "dream reality" and keep dream life from being invaded by a hyper-realist vision, and also to keep waking reality from being invaded by "dreams". The infant incorporates not only the contents already processed by the alpha function, but also the function. We can say the same thing, differences notwithstanding, of the analytical relationship: the patient not only incorporates the content of the interpretation, but also introjects the function that metabolises emotional experiences.

The breakdown of alpha function can bring about what Bion called the beta screen, which has the characteristic of being formed by beta elements and being either evocative or provocative. The beta screen cancels the capacity to assign meaning to emotions and relationships, and can be accompanied by pathological mechanisms such as hallucinations and bizarre objects.

As I pointed out earlier, another possibility is that the alpha function is reversed with the dispersion of the contact-barrier. The significance of the beta screen is that, thanks to it, the psychotic patient can evoke or provoke emotions in the analyst, an emotional state that is an obstacle for the analyst's intuition and thinking. This provoking or evocation of emotions in the analyst has the aim of involving the analyst emotionally and, thus, not to receive psychoanalytical interpretations and understanding.

Let us now come back to links. We have already mentioned the three links described by Bion: L, H, and K. In analysis, the K link, or disposition to know, should predominate, at least for the analyst, with L and H always as necessary factors. Remember that we have already discussed how, in an analysis, the search for knowledge must be combined with compassion, unlike arrogant investigation carried out at any price. The search for truth at any price, without compassion, disavows the psychoanalytical object as a living, evolving object. Due to the animate characteristics of its object, psychoanalysis must combine the search for truth inherent in any scientific investigation with consideration for life.

Bion always stresses the significance of respect for the truth. I want to present this idea developed by Bion in *Second Thoughts*: that there are healthy and unhealthy psychotic patients, and, as we have seen in the light of these new ideas, the difference lies in the predominance of respect for truth, or the prevalence of an active link of disavowal, of misunderstanding, something Bion takes up in the final chapter of *Learning from Experience,* and which he names the –K link.

In *Cogitations,* Bion says,

> The concern for truth must be distinguished from a capacity for establishing contact with reality. A man may have little capacity for that through lack of intelligence, training or even physical endowment— he might be defective in one or more of his senses, to take an obvious example. Yet the same man can have an active yearning for, and respect for truth. Conversely, a highly gifted and well-equipped person may have little concern for truth about the realities with which his endowment permits an easy contact. Such unconcern will clearly be a matter for attention by the analyst for whom the psycho-analysis of the patient has truth as its criterion. Concern for life does not mean only a wish not to kill, though it does mean that. It means concern for an object precisely because that object has the quality of being alive. It means distinguishing between objects because one is alive and the other not. It means considering the difference is an important one. It means being curious about the qualities that go to make up what we know as life, and to have a desire to understand them. Conversely, a lack of concern for life means regarding a living object as indistinguishable from, or as being unworthy of being distinguished from a machine, a thing or a place. (Bion, 1992, p. 248)

Let us now return to the –K link, which can be defined as an attempt to preserve the power to create guilt, as if it were an essential ability. The emergence of a tendency to seek the truth is opposed by destructive attacks and the affirmation of moral superiority. This is related to the moral conscience without morality that we saw in previous chapters and which is in opposition to a scientific search for truth, however rudimentary. Bion seems to relate it to envy as well, which is a potential factor of negative or despoiling links. –K produces something akin to the emotional state corresponding to the breakdown or break-up of the container. In –K, if we are using the model of the mother–infant pair, the feeling would be as if the mother enviously took away the good and valid element of the fear of dying and gave back to the infant a worthless residue. Thus, the infant, who started out with a fear of dying, now harbours a nameless dread.

108   ON MENTAL GROWTH

Learning from Experience appears in Bion's work as a great effort to produce—with concepts that are abstract enough to be "published"—a reflection on the emotional experiences, in both awake and asleep states, mental states that, for him, are the counterpart of being aware or unaware of the experience. It also seems to be the first attempt to formulate a theory of emotions within the psychoanalytical framework, placing emotions at the core of mental life and growth. It is true that love and hate had already been considered by Freud and Klein, but Bion, besides considering these emotions, also includes the disposition to know as an emotional link.

Seventeen years later, in one of his last seminars, entitled "Making the best of a bad job", Bion says that when two personalities meet, an emotional storm is produced.

> If they make sufficient contact to be aware of each other or even to be unaware of each other, an emotional state is produced by the conjunction of these individuals . . . The result of remaining silent, or the result of making a remark, or even saying "Good morning" or "Good evening", again sets up what appears to be an emotional storm. (Bion, 1979, p. 321)

It is through apparently anodyne situations such as remaining silent, making a comment, or what appears to be a simple greeting, that this turbulence is produced. This storm might be unnoticed at first sight; however, these situations can be the preamble to, and the signs of, a session from which analyst and patient will leave transformed, and which will not be innocuous for either of them. Both members of the analytical couple will continue their psychic work, their transformations from this encounter, not only through psychic changes, the variations in mental states, the new associations and developments, but also through the alpha dreamwork which generates the waking and night-time dreams. As we are about to see, in Bionian clinical practice, the analyst has a new way of entering the scene, with the weight and density of his mental life, with his alpha function, and traversing the turbulences that keep his awareness alive, because, even for the analyst, the apparatus for thinking is still embryonic. This new inclusion in this part of his work is manifested at this point in the idea of "waking dream thoughts", which is one of Bion's strongest intuitions and one of his most transcendental contributions to clinical practice, although, at this early stage of his work, this might not be so evident.

However, Chapter XII of *Learning from Experience* already outlines reverie not only as a function, but also as a channel of communication between the mother and the infant which, if all goes well, will be the channel through which the baby's raw emotions will circulate towards the mother, who will, in turn, transform them and return them over the same channel, having transformed them into alpha elements. We can conceive of the analyst's alpha function and his "wakeful dreaming" of the patient, and the session as a communication channel as well, as a relational dreaming, the construction of a dream between analyst and patient. It is what will enable the patient to develop the reverie function, an internal alpha container that will, in turn, enable him or her to have waking dream thoughts without falling prey to hallucinations, or what Bion will later call "transformation in hallucinosis".

The hypothesis of alpha function has contributed to the giving of a new meaning to the analyst's function and to the understanding of psychic life and the coming into contact with oneself. Dreams generate dream thoughts through alpha function, and this idea not only provides new psychoanalytic tools, but is a revolution and an invaluable contribution to psychoanalytical technique, as we shall see in the following chapters.

CHAPTER EIGHT

The matrix functions of thinking: myths, dreams, and models

We are such stuff as dreams are made on
And our little life is rounded with a sleep.
(Shakespeare, 1951a, *The Tempest*, act 4, scene 1)

In this chapter, I want to introduce the reader to some of Bion's concepts, developed in the book *Elements of Psycho-analysis*, which explore in greater depth certain notions that are key to understanding his investigations of the function of thinking and of abstraction from a psychoanalytical perspective. This means considering the emotional factors involved in cognitive processes.

In this book, Bion proposes the Grid as an instrument for "playing" "psychoanalytical games", somewhat akin to the rehearsals or exercises that a musician carries out before a concert, meant as a preparation and training for the analyst before or after the session. In this book, I am not going to describe the Grid, but I want to mention it, so that the reader will at least be aware of its existence and maybe become interested in reading more about it. Anyway, as an introduction to the subject of this chapter, I want to sketch some guidelines regarding the Grid. One of Bion's scientific concerns was to develop instruments that would make it possible to record the emotional

112   ON MENTAL GROWTH

experience contained in the sessions, even if it is ineffable. The difficulties are obvious because, if one records a session, the words provide a literal record, while the emotional atmosphere cannot be registered by a machine. What happens between analyst and patient in the field of the session can only be conveyed as a transformation of the emotional experience.

Bion's aim with the Grid was to design an instrument that could help working in psychoanalytical research in the absence of the object and, therefore, outside the emotional turbulence of the session. He also wanted the instrument to help communication between psychoanalysts, with a notation system analogous to the pentagram for musicians.

The Grid is an instrument designed by Bion to record and classify the statements from both analyst and patient during the sessions. It is not an instrument like the microscope or the telescope, which provide an extension of the senses. The Grid is designed to record transformations. The record consists of both the linguistic expressions and the emotional experience that takes place in the session. It is a tool to help the analyst think, after the session, about the problems that come up in his daily clinical practice, so that he can elaborate on different observations made during the sessions. The Grid is not a theory; it belongs to the field of clinical observation.

The formulations design an evolution from apparently simple elements (such as a gesture, an exclamation) to complex formulations (such as dream thoughts, concepts, a scientific deductive system, etc.). It can be used to classify the analyst's thoughts and interpretations. It is applicable to any element of the communication between patient and analyst.

Formally, the Grid consists of Cartesian co-ordinates with two axes: the vertical one (the genetic) marks the development of thoughts in increasing degrees of abstraction, and the horizontal one defines the use of these thoughts. According to Bion's innovative epistemological vertex, thoughts precede thinking and stimulate the development of an apparatus to think them. This apparatus can be considered to be made up of functions, such as memory, attention, etc., which are categorised in the horizontal axis of "uses" of the columns.

What I am interested in conveying in this chapter is that, for Bion in psychoanalysis, it is crucial to be able to combine abstraction (for example, a theory) with a particularity (for example, a dream, a dream thought, a myth, a model). Bion calls the use of these particularities "A capacity for negative growth"; it means, for example, to make models, to use myths, etc., which he calls negative growth, with negative meant not as a negative value, but as a way to avoid arid abstraction and be able to grow in naïvety to achieve an unsaturated perspective of the statements or problems that are presented.

I now focus on the two matrix functions of thinking and some related ideas, and then on dream thoughts, myths, and dreams. In this book (*Elements of Psycho-analysis*), Bion not only develops some of the concepts of *Learning from Experience*, but he also makes some changes, such as the relationship between the concept of alpha elements, dream thoughts and preconceptions: the latter are no longer conceived as only a mental state of expectation adapted to a limited number of phenomena, but, in this new perspective, any statement can be transformed into a preconception as long as it is not saturated. So, a theory can be used as a preconception, if it is not transformed and used as a dogma. In the film *Twelve Angry Men*, which we used as if it were a kind of clinical illustration for the ideas we are presenting, the reader can see how, in the beginning, all the members of the jury—except the one I have named the "Thinker"—have saturated preconceptions, and, therefore, decided to condemn the accused to death, unwilling to open their minds to assess the evidence they had to discuss. The Thinker is the only one who harbours doubts and has decided to think without preconceptions. In the chapter I dedicate to the film, the reader sees our considerations about the different moments of crisis of each of the members of the jury, from which they gain access to having doubts and to thinking.

Among the transformations introduced by Bion in psychoanalytical theory and clinical practice are his conceptions about dreaming that he extended with the notion of alpha function, which goes on day and night, about the thinking function and the conscious–unconscious relationship.

Freud's conception of thinking is linked to the idea of sublimation, and it is at the service of reducing tensions. In the context of the Kleinian theory, thinking is associated to working through the depressive position and the process of symbolisation. We have already seen how Bion places thinking and the K link in a privileged position along with the love (L), and the hate (H) links. For Freud, thinking implied a reduction of tensions in the service of the reality principle, changing

114   ON MENTAL GROWTH

the aim and the object of the drive. Bion conceives a model in which we must differentiate between unavoidable pains and unnecessary ones. Those who cannot tolerate pain and avoid it cannot feel pleasure, either. The function of thinking consists in developing a capacity not only to differentiate between these two kinds of pain and modify the inadequate methods of facing it (the false solutions), but also to develop the capability to tolerate the pain. In the last part of his work, Bion also visualises the development of thinking as a function that was, at first, necessary for survival, and, therefore, one has to transform an inadequate apparatus, through the model of digestion and the pleasure–pain principle, and develop the function of thinking thoughts and containing primitive emotions in order to search for truth and to understand oneself.

As we described in the previous chapter, the alpha function, the capacity to dream in a broader sense, is at the centre of this development and the search for the truth. The conscious–unconscious relationship changes compared to Freud's formulations, and Klein's concept of total object is transformed with the introduction of the notion of vertices.

Freud changed many of his conceptions through the years, such as the first topographic model, which he later changed when he developed his structural theory of the id, the ego, and the superego. In this latter conception, the unconscious is no longer a place, but a quality, differentiating, of course, the repressed, dynamic unconscious from the non-repressed unconscious and the unconscious quality of the preconscious. For Bion, as we have seen, it is through the alpha function that the contact-barrier is generated, along with the conscious–unconscious relationship. It is the capability for "dreaming" that generates the unconscious through alpha function, because the contact-barrier is composed of alpha elements. This barrier enables us to remember and also to forget. The perception of psychic qualities requires a binocular vision of the conscious and unconscious.

As for the total object, I believe it is important to focus for a moment on the notion of vertices, which the model of the Gestalt school's experience helps us to understand. The experience of the perception of a drawing in which one can see a vase or two silhouettes, depending on one's focus, provides a model for reversible perspective which, in my opinion, complements binocular vision. We cannot see both the vase and the two silhouettes simultaneously, but reversible perspective provides different vertices of observation that must be taken into account.

In *Elements of Psycho-analysis*, Bion—who had already described enforced splitting in *Learning from Experience*—introduces a new kind of splitting, static splitting, in which, instead of a perspective that is reversible, in an analytical situation we come across a reversion of perspective. Analyst and patient see the process of analysis from two different vertices; while the analyst assumes that they are in an analytical situation, the patient silently views it differently. In his book on theory of psychoanalytic technique, Etchegoyen (1986) provides an interesting clinical illustration: the patient is a homoeopathic doctor, who does not seek analysis because he wants to understand himself and wants to know the truth; instead, he is silently and secretly using the analysis to gather data for his professional activity. In everyday metaphoric language, we would say that he is secretly upsetting the apple cart. The aim of the reversion of perspective is to avoid mental pain. In my opinion, although Bion does not make it explicit, this reversion of perspective is present in his later formulation of transformation into hallucinosis, which raises very serious clinical problems that we cannot tackle here, but I do want to mention this defence mechanism as one of Bion's conceptions that transform psychoanalytical theory and clinical practice.

In *Elements of Psycho-analysis*, Bion extends the notion of the selected fact, relating it to the new concepts he is developing: "constant conjunction" and the PS$\leftrightarrow$D oscillation, the latter of which he defines as a mental function of oscillation between mental states of dispersion and integration.

Constant conjunction

This notion is related to Bion's disturbing idea of thoughts without a thinker. It is not the thinker that creates thoughts; thoughts stimulate the development of an apparatus for thinking. When these thoughts intersect with the thinker, we are no longer facing an infinite, formless void, and when these "thoughts without a thinker" are housed in the thinker's mind, they become a constant conjunction, a pattern, the connecting pattern, waiting for us to discover it in analysis.

116 ON MENTAL GROWTH

Constant conjunction is a term that Bion borrowed from the philosopher David Hume; he gave it a meaning of his own, in the context of his developments of the thinking function. In this framework, the term implies a pattern, how each individual organises his or her emotional experiences, an act of organisation that is specific to each person. Bion describes some of the characteristics of making constant conjunctions, associated to the investigation of the thinking function and the process of abstraction. Considering psychoanalysis as a science that investigates relationships, and not the related objects, is also linked to the investigation of this notion of constant conjunction.

- For a conjunction to achieve certain durability it has to be linked with a name; it does not have to be a verbal one, but can be linked by an image, etc.
- The development of conjunctions is stimulated by persecutory and depressive anxieties. The "constant conjunction" avoids dispersion, with its primitive connotations of fragmentation anxieties, and it attenuates the feeling of uncertainty and the intolerance of frustration.
- Depressive anxieties related to a loss, to mourning, also stimulate the development of constant conjunctions, because these conjunctions help to preserve the experience in spite of the pain of the loss.

The term "constant conjunction" is related to the fact that it names a pattern, a situation that has a certain stability and permanence. These constant conjunctions are, however, exposed to modifications because of catastrophic change: this is one of Bion's later concepts, related to a notion of psychic change and to the idea of a discontinuity. It does not refer to a catastrophe, but to a kind of psychic change, following the model of a mutation.

- When these constant conjunctions are associated with a process of mental growth, they can be considered temporary or in transit. When they become fixed, they can be associated with symptoms, character traits, beliefs, and they become stereotypes, inhibiting mental growth.

Selected fact

This term was used by the mathematician Henri Poincaré, who thought that the facts that science selects are valuable, are those that harmonise and give coherence to known facts that were previously seen as scattered and not related to each other. Bion thinks that this formulation resembles Klein's description of the paranoid–schizoid and depressive positions. He uses this term to describe the "fact" that the psychoanalyst realises or discovers in the process of synthesis. A selected fact is an emotion or an idea that gives coherence to what is dispersed and introduces order into was previously seen as disorder. The selected fact is the name of an emotional experience of a sense of discovery, of coherence. The name of the element that links those that have not been seen until then to have a connection is used to specify the selected fact.

The matrix functions of thinking

Bion described them as the matrix functions for the generation of thoughts and the development of the possibilities of using them for thinking: the $♀♂$ (container–contained) relationship and the PS↔D oscillation (between states of mind of dispersion and of integration).

The container–contained relationship $\{f\}$ $\{m\}$

The container–contained relationship is based on two models: (a) the model of the army: one army keeping another at bay, containing its progress. This model can be applied, for example, to the relationship between the psychotic and non-psychotic part of the personality; (b) the model of the relationship of communication between the infant's emotions (the contained) and the mother's (the container) mind/breast. As we have seen, Bion (1962a) defined projective identification not only as an omnipotent phantasy, but as a kind of primitive communication and exploration. Projective identification enables the infant to deal with primitive emotions through maternal reverie.

Projective identification is a content searching to be received by a container. Bion conceives the $♀♂$ function as a relationship related

ON MENTAL GROWTH

with the development of thoughts, a relationship that can have different characteristics to be investigated, from those leading to mental growth, such as a mutually beneficial relationship (symbiosis), to a parasitic one of despoilment and mutual destruction. Bion thinks of this matrix as a kind of primitive communication, projective identification, through which the infant evacuates his unbearable emotions, which are the content in search of a container, and this searching is a kind of exploratory probe. If everything goes well, he finds a container in the mother's breast/mind and she, with her reverie (alpha function), detoxifies these unbearable emotions so that the infant receives them already detoxified and can incorporate and assimilate them as a tolerable aspect of his personality.

The need of a breast, which, if not there, is a "no-breast" or an absent breast and, in the primitive mind of the infant, is experienced as a bad breast, is transformed through the mother's reverie, so that, together with the actual experiences of breastfeeding, the infant's anxieties are attenuated through the love and meaning provided by the mother's alpha function. In this case, it is a mutually beneficial container–contained relationship: both members experience growth. The relationship can also be one of despoilment, parasitic. In this case, the result is mutual destruction. As we already saw in the previous chapter, the relationship can be commensal.

PS↔D oscillation

Bion took the concept of the positions from Klein, and transformed it into a mental function: the PS↔D oscillation. Bion names this function PS (referring to the paranoid–schizoid position) and D (referring to the depressive position) and includes between them a two-way arrow marking the oscillation. This function is an oscillation between mental states of dispersion, the PS point (paranoid–schizoid dispersion) and of integration or synthesis of the depressive position, the D point. Bion transformed Klein's positions into a mental function, one of the matrixes of the thinking process. This function becomes relevant when, once primitive emotions have been detoxified, it enables tolerance of persecutory anxieties related to the experience of dispersion and depressive anxieties implicit in the fact that the integration that is achieved is not a definitive one; it is, in turn, a new starting point. This

THE MATRIX FUNCTIONS OF THINKING: MYTHS, DREAMS, AND MODELS 119

function allows for the toleration of the dispersal of the facts that need to be understood. These facts are still without meaning, until the moment when they can be integrated, related, and understood through the finding of the selected fact, which harmonises them.

The D point is unstable (the point of integration), and, when a new oscillation takes place, it will be transformed into a new PS, which will, in turn, begin a new cycle. Once the PS↔D oscillation enables the finding of a constant conjunction, the meaning can be investigated through the container–contained relationship. The PS↔D function outlines the observation of the whole object (with its good and bad aspects), and the exploration through the container–contained inter-action ($\female\male$)—that is, the one that enables the discovering of mean-ing—enables a meaning to be found. The PS↔D function helps the toleration of the depressive anxieties stimulated by keeping different aspects of the same object in the D point. The experience of discover-ing the selected fact and the finding of meaning also imply tolerance of the pain of confronting the conjectures—the preconceptions—with the facts that are observed.

This function outlines the object of investigation and its psychoan-alytic field, enabling tolerance of uncertainty, of dispersion in moments of "not understanding", and of transitory moments of inte-gration, with emotions associated to the discovering of the selected fact, which harmonises what was previously seen as dispersed (Bion, 1963). (Bion took the notion of selected fact from the mathematician Poincaré as the fact that gives coherence to facts that were previously seen as dispersed and not related.)

Discovering the selected fact is a powerful stimulus for mental growth when the individual develops emotions that facilitate the capability to become aware. These emotions are tolerance of doubt, tolerance of a sense of infinity, and of ignorance. A consciousness that has evolved towards awareness implies the ability to find an opera-tional selected fact, not a projective one (through projective identifica-tion). Dreams and playing are privileged activities for the discovery of the selected fact.

Mental growth is stimulated when the individual develops emotions that facilitate becoming aware. As I have already said, these emotions are doubt that is tolerated, tolerance of a sense of the infi-nite, and towards not knowing. The evolved consciousness, evolved towards becoming aware, implies the ability to find an operational, a

120   ON MENTAL GROWTH

non-projective, selected fact (one that is not related to projective identification). As said before, dreams and playing are privileged activities for this selective fact. These functions are complemented by a symbiotic ♀♂ relationship of mutual benefit, a function that allows the discovering of meaning.

PS↔D is the equivalent of a physiological function of the mind that contributes to the development of constant conjunctions, the discovery of meaning, and the development of the capacity for thinking. This function is responsible for the connection between thoughts already created by the ♀♂ function. In the PS↔D oscillation, a deep emotional change takes place, which implies the great capability of the mind for flexibility. I end this chapter with part of a poem that speaks of the poet's gift to "dream" in this extended sense, one which he says is to give "shapes to airy nothing":

> The poet's eye, in a fine frenzy rolling,
> Doth glance from heaven to earth, from earth to heaven;
> And, as imagination bodies forth
> The forms of things unknown, the poet's pen
> Turns them to shapes, and gives to airy nothing
> A local habitation and a name.
> Such tricks hath strong imagination,
> That, if it would but apprehend some joy,
> It comprehends some bringer of that joy;
> Or in the night, imagining some fear,
> How easy is a bush supposed a bear!

(Shakespeare, 1951b, *A Midsummer Night's Dream*, act 5, scene 1).

CHAPTER NINE

The function of dreams and myths as instruments with which to investigate mental life

B efore developing Bion's extension of the concept of dreaming, I want to mention some points as an introduction to this issue, which is salient in the transformation of clinical practice introduced by Bion's ideas. I want to remind the reader what we have seen in previous chapters regarding Bion's differentiation between *rudimentary* consciousness as equivalent to a sense organ that perceives psychic qualities but does not understand what it perceives, and *evolved* consciousness that perceives and is aware of what it perceives. This means differentiating between being conscious and being aware: infants and psychotics are conscious but they are not aware of what they perceive. To achieve awareness, which is essential for psychoanalysis and to be able to think thoughts, an alpha function is required—Bion calls it a function, taking the notion from mathematics where a function establishes a fixed relationship between two or more variables. A relationship is established between different parameters. For there to be a solution to a function, it must have one less unknown variable than the data. The patient can be conscious, but not be aware of what he/she perceives. We are referring to problems that we meet in our clinical practice where no neurotic conflicts are discernible at first sight; this does not mean that these conflicts do not

122   ON MENTAL GROWTH

exist, but the main problems of the severe disturbed patient are not related with repression. In this kind of mental pathology, the problem is that mental functions are missing or have flaws, and these are the functions we need to formulate and think through emotional problems.

As we have seen in previous chapters, the hypothesis of a contact-barrier implies a semi-permeable membrane separating the conscious from the unconscious, which is built and articulated with alpha elements. It is "dreaming", in the extended sense defined by Bion, which generates the alpha elements and, therefore, also generates the elements that are part of the contact-barrier that separates and connects the unconscious and the conscious. When some mental functions are missing or fail, we, as analysts, are not faced with neurotic problems of repression or of making conscious what is unconscious, which are repression-related problems.

Freud, as we know, thought that only neurotic patients could be analysed and Bion's concepts also differ from Klein's, for whom unconscious phantasies are correlated with instincts, and for whom there are always unconscious phantasies. Bion's investigations with patients in whom the psychotic part of the personality predominates, discovered that there might be an absence of phantasies and dreams because the thinking process was disturbed and, thus, the emotional problems could not be formulated; hence, they could not be solved. Taking mathematics as a model, we can say that if a problem cannot be formulated, neither can it be solved. This is why the development of the capacity to "dream" is essential to be able to represent an emotional problem and, therefore, have the ability to solve it.

> Let us suppose that the patient is capable of the process of the formation of a presentation or idea. Is that to say that the patient is capable of α-function and can transform the sense impressions, be they what they may, into α elements? No, he can have visual images on which, as Freud says, ideation depends . . . I shall include the capacity to have visual images amongst the factors in α function, but it is only one factor—although an important one. It makes storage possible because visual images are a kind of notation. One patient talked of lines and dots making up the film cartoon; it sounds like the elements of geometry (Euclidean). But before dream-thoughts are possible, it is necessary to find the selected fact and to use it for initiating the paranoid–schizoid and depressive position interplay. This means that α

THE FUNCTION OF DREAMS AND MYTHS AS INSTRUMENTS . . .   123

elements cohere, separate, cohere again, separate again, converge, and diverge, and so on.

In distinction to this method of employing α elements are two others: they can be strung together temporarily, in time, in a narrative sequence (as is the case in dream), and they can be connected logically, which is linear as in Euclid. (Bion, 1992, pp. 223–224)

This extract is one of many in which we can follow Bion's attempts to elucidate the similarities and differences between psychoanalysis and other disciplines, such as geometry, hence the reference to Euclid. Bion is trying to find out which is the ideal method for registering and storing emotional experiences; therefore, he says that there is a need to postulate an alpha function, which he defines as the one responsible for the development of dream thoughts. He also realises the significance for psychoanalysis of the function of myths and dreams as tools to investigate emotional problems of the group and/or the individual's mental life.

Weaving dreams and myths into a narrative is a way of keeping a constant conjunction together and storing it; it acts as a web that "traps" the selected fact. In order to be able to think, the chaotic experiences, or the "void and formless infinite", require a transformation so that a constant conjunction can be conjugated.

When Bion sets out in *Cogitations* to interpret what he names a racial myth (the myth of Babel), by which he means something that is a characteristic of mankind, he says he intends to use this tale in a similar way to scientists using a pre-existing mathematical formula o solve a new problem. The mathematical formula might have been invented without any intention of its being used by a scientist; however, the scientist might decide that, in spite of the mathematician's claim that the formula has no meaning, he has found a realisation, an equivalent to the mathematical formulation. This is what Bion intends to do with the myth. Therefore, he says that he is not going to interpret this story; he wants to use it as a tool to interpret a problem. Bion conceives that a myth or a model is a tool that the analyst has to help his patient with thought disturbances to formulate his emotional problem. This is a first step: we could say that it is a kind of construction, although different from that which Freud considered a construction. It does not refer to the past; it is a tool to formulate an emotional problem or experience, so as to help the patient repair his

124   ON MENTAL GROWTH

mental functions. Freud did something similar when he named a psychological conflict the Oedipus complex.

However, this consideration of dreams is different from that which Freud proposes for the psychoanalytic elucidation of a dream or myth. Bion does not disagree with Freud, but he adds his understanding of the function of dreams and myths as tools for formulating an emotional experience or problem. For Freud, dreams can reveal an unconscious conflict disguised by censorship because of repression), which can become conscious through the interpretation of the dream (Freud, 1900a). Freud thought that only neurotic patients could be analysed. Bion analysed patients who had symbolisation disturbances that needed to be repaired. For Bion, dreams and myths are also interpreters of psychic reality. Patients with thought disturbances cannot "dream". This method of using myths implies recognising that the story is a social version of the phenomenon known to the individual as a dream, and even has some similarities with the selected fact that has been consciously looked for: it is an emotional experience that has been transformed by the alpha function.

In *Cogitations* (pp. 227–229), Bion again equates myths with algebra, in terms of their function as an unknown and of having the potential to mate with a realisation. He also mentions the function of dreams to investigate problems or future emotional experiences, as their elements can be transformed into preconceptions; in other words, with an unsaturated part such as an unknown algebraic variable, there is a kind of "Memoir of the Future" that is open to mate with new experiences. In psychoanalysis, Oedipus is the name of a conflict: what the characteristics are of the Oedipus conflict in a particular patient in analysis is what the psychoanalytic therapy has to find out.

Dreams, unlike myths, have a very low level of generalisation, but, although this might be a disadvantage if the issue is the mental life of the group, it is, in fact, an advantage when the issue is something as idiosyncratic as the mental life of a specific individual, such as a patient in analysis. Bion thinks that the individual's dream has to be understood as having the function of stating that certain alpha elements are constantly conjugated. The alpha function has then served the purpose of making it possible to store, communicate, and publish a constantly conjugated emotional experience. This constant conjunction is like a dream, and this dream has made it possible to register this conjunction (to note a pattern). Thinking about severe pathologies, Bion wonders whether it could be that as there are people who are inadequately equipped to understand or do mathematics, there also might be people who are ill-equipped to use myths and dreams to think their emotional experiences, or who cannot even dream. His experience with psychotic patients showed him that these patients could not dream, could not have phantasies, because of their thought disturbances. In my opinion, Bion takes dream and dreaming as an instrument equivalent to algebra: it can be used to formulate and represent a problem, which is the precondition for finding a solution. When the psychotic part of the personality prevails, the patient cannot formulate—dream—his emotional problems, and, in consequence, he cannot think about them or solve them. In order to use dreams and myths as equivalent to the use of algebra, as in other sciences, we need to know how they have been constructed and what rules should be observed if we are going to make a preconceptual use of the "myth–dream–formula". Bion differentiates preconception as a level in the increasing complexity of thought, Row D in the Grid, from preconceptual use, in columns 4 (attention + reverie) and 5 (enquiry) of the Grid.

In *Elements of Psycho-analysis*, Bion says that Freud discovered psychoanalysis in the Oedipus myth and that psychoanalysis then enabled him to understand the Oedipus complex. What he calls oedipal preconception, which is not the same as Klein's oedipal precursor, is an important part of the ego function of investigating the relationship between the real parents. I think that when Bion refers to oedipal preconception, he means the capability to have unconscious phantasies, a capability which is disturbed in psychotic patients when the psychotic part of the personality prevails.

The capability to develop and use a symbolisation process is a precondition for being able to have unconscious phantasies. Patients with a disturbed thought process cannot dream or have unconscious phantasies. Freud thought that only neurotic personalities could be analysed; Bion is speculating that the capability to think and the symbolisation process can be repaired. If it is missing, or lacking in vitality, as is my experience with autism, psychoanalytical research and working through the oedipal conflict is not possible because there are disturbances of the symbolisation process that require the previous development of this preconception through repairing

126 ON MENTAL GROWTH

the symbolisation process. Bion aims to demonstrate that certain emotional problems in psychoanalysis could be solved if we recognise that the elements of the problem can be adequately represented by this "algebraic formula"; in other words, myths, dreams, and models (Bion, 1992, p. 229). This means that, as Freud did with the Oedipus myth, we need to recognise certain constant conjunctions and then we can give them the form and/or the name of a myth. Dreams and myths are a way of formulating emotional experiences. Therefore, we need to establish the rules for this use of dreams and myths.

> There is no doubt that mathematicians have formed a method of recording and communicating their formulations which makes teaching of the formulations and their use assume an enviably uniform and stable discipline – at least to me who proposes that myth and dream should be regarded as corresponding to algebraic calculi and therefore as capable of yielding, after scrutiny, the tools that can interpret, through their suitability to represent a problem, the problem itself, and so open the way to its solution. (Bion, 1992, p. 230)

We can understand this idea about the function of "dreaming" if we have in mind the incapability to dream displayed by Bion's patient, as we can see in the clinical material about the sunglasses he presents in "Differentiation of the psychotic from the non-psychotic personalities". Bion describes how this patient tried to use the sunglasses that Bion had worn some months previously as a sign that agglomerated his emotional experiences and not as a symbol. He needed to use the concrete fact of the sunglasses that Bion wore some months earlier not as a memory of a fact, but as a sign. In my book, *The Aesthetic Dimension of the Mind* (2007), I compare Bion's clinical material of the "sunglasses" and his dream, described in *Cogitations*, in which he analyses having dreamt of a negro. About his dream, Bion says that the negro is a real fact, but it is also an image; it is an ideogram used by his dream to digest emotional experiences. So, the ideogram "negro" is a dreamlike thought that generates meaning. The sunglasses, mentioned in the clinical material of Bion's patient, are also used as a proto-ideogram, in which the glasses that his analyst was wearing some months previously are not used by the patient as the memory of a real fact, but as an ideogram in which he agglomerates some undigested experiences. The patient uses the concrete fact of Bion wearing the "black glasses" as a "thought"; he needs the

THE FUNCTION OF DREAMS AND MYTHS AS INSTRUMENTS . . .   127

analyst to transform it into a "dream thought" through his alpha function. This "dream thought" of the analyst is a transformational container and a process of mental digestion of the emotional experience that makes re-introjection possible for the patient. These are steps which put an end to the evacuative haemorrhage of hypertrophied projective identification, because the "dream thought" of the analyst acts as a container for the emotional experiences of the patient. These ideas open up an opportunity of analysis for very disturbed patients.

Before considering the fundamental rules for the use of myths and dreams, I want to differentiate two functions.

1.   For the dreamer or the group or culture that constructs the myth.
2.   For the psychoanalyst in psychoanalytical practice.

In my opinion, for the dreamer and for the culture, dreams and myths have:

1.   The function of registering emotional experiences as constant conjunctions and of digesting or metabolising the emotional experience, since the dreamwork transforms beta elements (conscious but not available for awareness because they are experienced as "things in themselves") into alpha elements, which are no-things, conscious or unconscious, but available for awareness. The process of symbolisation implies a triangular relationship between the symbol, the symbolised object, and the observer, the one who observes this relationship. This observation of the relationship is part of the process of becoming aware. The function of the dream and of dreaming—in this extended sense—is a factor in the development of the capability of becoming aware.
2.   A function of registering, first through visual images, and then in the dream narrative. In a dream that is told, the constant conjunction remains conjugated, through combining alpha elements in a narrative sequence, including the temporality that conjugates emotional experience in a temporal sequence. This function is a psychoanalytical tool— if the psychoanalyst can use it as an interpreter of the experience—taking different elements of a myth or dream to make models for undigested emotional experiences.
3.   A function of private communication, which can become public when the dream is told in analysis. (Bion calls public

128   ON MENTAL GROWTH

communication the kind of communication that can draw attention and is useful for becoming aware. He calls private communication the intrasubjective communication.)

The psychoanalyst can use the myth or dream as an algebraic formula, and he has to find its realisation as a preconception. In other words, the dream or its different images can be used to make a model for an emotional experience and be used to interpret it. Which are the rules that Bion defines for scientific–psychoanalytic use of dreams and myths as a representation and an interpreter of an emotional problem?

The first point is that all dreams have one, and only one, interpretation, which means that its elements are constantly conjugated. What Bion means is that a dream and a myth formulate the emotional experience in a pattern. The second is that every dream has a corresponding realisation, which it therefore represents. (The term realisation simultaneously means materialisation, experience, and becoming aware of the experience.) So, we can speak of Oedipus, but, of course, with each patient we have to find out what the Oedipus conflict of that patient is, and identify its effects. The third point is that certain factual experiences will never be understood by the patient, and, therefore, will never be experiences from which he can learn, unless he can interpret them in the light of a dream or of the myth created by the group. To conclude this chapter, I propose definitions of the concepts of model and myth within Bion's ideas, and a very interesting, though brief, reference to the function of myths according to Plato.

Model

Model making is part of the psychoanalyst's equipment. Its flexibility contrasts with the rigidity of the theories as a conceptual system. If the analyst can build appropriate models he will avoid the temptation to create *ad hoc* theories. A model helps to find a correspondence between clinical problems and psychoanalytical theories. It can be easily discarded because it does not have the status of a theory, although, should it prove useful on different occasions, it could eventually be transformed into a theory. The model is built with elements related to sense experiences, and helps to bridge the gap between clinically observed facts and those psychoanalytic theories with higher levels of abstraction. When the analyst builds the model, he must also be aware of the model used by the patient. The model is useful for restoring contact with the concrete experience of psychoanalytic investigation, when this contact has been lost due to the use of abstractions far removed from experience and associated with the theoretical system. When Bion developed the Grid—and before that in *Elements of Psychoanalysis*—he put forward the idea of a negative growth, meaning the need to gain in naïvety by resorting to Row C of the Grid, which is the one for dreamlike thoughts. Any experience can be used as a model for future experiences.

This aspect of learning from experience is related to, and, in a certain way, is identical to, the function that Freud attributes to attention, a function which, from time to time, periodically goes out to seek "samples" in the outside world, so that its data may already be familiar in case an urgent need arises.

The value of a model, as a factor of the function of attention to emotional experiences and the psychic reality, is that its data can become familiar and is, therefore, available for future emotional experiences.

Before an emotional experience can be used as a model, its sensuous data needs to have been transformed into alpha elements, in order to be stored and be available for abstraction. If a model is needed for an emotional experience, then the individual can select the elements he needs from the storage of alpha elements which, as in the case of visual images, carries resonance of the emotional experience in which the alpha element was formed.

Myth

Myths are the kind of thoughts that Bion classified in Row C of the Grid, together with dreams and models. He suggest that the analyst can use myths to form "a picture gallery" of verbal elements, to be used as models for different aspects related to emotional experiences at the intersection between clinical experience and psychoanalytic theory. This implies using them as a preconception open to unknown facts, or to those facts that have yet to happen, which the myth, acting as a receptive net, could help to display and highlight. "The Oedipus

130 ON MENTAL GROWTH

myth may be regarded as an instrument that served Freud in his discovery of psychoanalysis and psychoanalysis as an instrument that enabled Freud to discover the Oedipus complex" (Bion, 1963, p. 92). Myths and dreams are psychoanalytic tools to formulate emotional experiences.

Bion added other myths to the well-known Oedipus myth: the Garden of Eden, the Tower of Babel, the Death of Palinurus, and the burial at the cemetery pit in Ur. He suggested freeing myths from their narrative structure, which is the only way of relating the elements of a constant conjunction, and using each element in a way analogous to that of the algebraic unknown in other sciences. He also suggested including the myth as one of the dimensions of the psychoanalytical object, together with common sense and passion. Any interpretation has to take into account these three dimensions.

The function of myths according to Plato

Mythology consists in keeping the idea of eternity within the categories of space and time. Plato ranks enthusiasm very high, whether manifested in the form of a sentimental rapture, or a religious or poetic one. He recognises in these three aspects the unsatisfied impulse that takes the individual over and exalts him, taking him towards something that overwhelms him. To illustrate that this goes beyond the individual, the philosopher resorts to myths; they are imaginary narrations that explain the world through plausible hypotheses. They transfer timeless truths to the changing times; they try to respect the proportions that make up the structure of the intelligible model and extend the reasoning through an invocation of dreamlike states. These myths are also works of art. They are, in short, allegories whose insufficiency and inadequacy is felt by Plato first and foremost, because he knows better than anyone that there are truths that images cannot express. This is the source of a very peculiar irony in which the thinker indicates that he is not the victim of the language in which he thinks, because he needs the language to think, so he can be able to deal with, or at least suggest, what is ineffable. The myth is the medium through which what is timeless becomes narration in the interlocutions of men, and the One can find its place in the borders of what can be formulated. With this resource, the invisible becomes

intelligible to mankind and, if not perfectly visible, at least perceptible. Thanks to the myth, the ineffable can be narrated and what cannot
be communicated is communicated.

In *Elements of Psycho-analysis*, while considering the relationship
between generalisation and particularisation, Bion puts forward the
idea of a negative growth, not in the sense of a negative value judgement, but as a way of going from the highest levels of abstraction to
dreamlike thoughts, myths, and Row C in the Grid. This negative
growth provides another vertex and, again referring to Plato, allows
the ineffable (of the emotional experience) to become able to be
narrated and communicated. Particularisation is not the same as materialisation. The myth is used as a model, as a selected fact. It is quite
evident that, in order to find the selected fact, one needs tolerance of
frustration and a capacity for synthesis, as well as intuition. Borges'
masterful story "Funes el memorioso" (Funes the memorious, 1944)
provides an illustration of how, for the mind of Funes (who wants to
make an infinite dictionary in which a dog has a different name
depending on if it is viewed sideways or head on), it is impossible to
find the selected fact. Borges' story can be used as a model, Funes' infinite dictionary cannot. (Funes is a character in Borges' story who
cannot forget and is bogged down in every small detail.) When particularisation also uses poetic language, it keeps alive the spark of the
emotional experience.

CHAPTER TEN

A theory of knowing–dreaming–thinking: emotional links and the container–contained relationship

I n this chapter, I try to develop some concepts and expand on others mentioned in previous chapters. First of all—and anticipating *Transformations* (1965), where we will come across a kind of mathematics that is similar to that of Lewis Carroll—I focus on the increasing use that Bion makes of Greek letters and mathematical symbols, or the *quasi* mathematical way in which he presents his ideas, from *Learning from Experience* (1962a) up to and including *Transformations*.

Bion was concerned with giving a scientific status to psychoanalysis. In *Cogitations* (1992), he thinks over and over again about the problems of psychoanalysis as a scientific discipline.

One of the conditions for a scientific status is finding a language that enables the formulation and communication of ideas with the least possible amount of ambiguity, so that the hypotheses that express these ideas may be contrasted with experience; in the case of psychoanalysis, that means the experience in psychoanalytical practice, in the session with the patient. This language of abstract signs that Bion began to use is related to the need to make psychoanalytical statements more precise, because, since they are made in conventional, non-mathematical language, unlike "hard" sciences, they can lend themselves to ambiguity.

134 ON MENTAL GROWTH

Psychoanalytical formulations in both theory and clinical practice need to preserve an unsaturated quality, analogous to an unresolved mathematical variable that can, in turn, be "saturated" by experience. It is what he begins to call preconception in "A theory of thinking" in *Second Thoughts* (1967). Then, in *Elements of Psycho-analysis* (1963), he also gives the name of preconception to one of the uses of thoughts, also as an unknown variable in the service of attention and enquiry functions. This means that preconception is a stage in the generic development of thoughts (row D in the Grid), and it is a use (columns 4 and 5 in the Grid). In this sense, even a psychoanalytical theory can be used in a preconceptual manner. Bion uses mathematicians as a model: for example, when they discover a mathematical formula for which they have no practical application, but later on an application is found for it in practical mathematics. This is what happened with the discovery of projective geometry.

When the reader finds these abstractions, which often have a negative emotional impact and sometimes produce rejection and irritation, he must keep in mind that Bion's purpose is not to be obscure, but to highlight the problem of communication and, above all, to show that when the psychotic part of the personality predominates, there is always the danger of confusing signs with things. The word "dog" does not "bark", the word "cat" does not "meow" nor does it have fur. By using letters, or dots, lines, and arrows, Bion is using signs and mathematical terms as models.

The question of difficulty in communication comes up not only among scientists or psychoanalysts, but also between patients and analysts. The "hard" sciences found a significant instrument for progress in the development of mathematics and the invention of algebra. Psychoanalysts' scientific language does not differ from conventional language, and, in communication with their patients, they also have to use the same conventional language that they would use in a social conversation; however, the use of this language in psychoanalysis requires precision, at least on the part of the analyst. Conventional language has the disadvantage of having been born in relation to the sensory objects of the external world, and now, in psychoanalysis, it has to be used for making contact and for the understanding of the personality, whether one's own or someone else's. So, on the one hand, we find abstraction in Bion's work: the α function, the α and β elements, the links he names with their initials: K (for knowledge),

A THEORY OF KNOWING–DREAMING–THINKING 135

L (for love), H (for hate). On the other hand, we also find in Bion a reappraisal within psychoanalysis of dreams and myths, as we have seen before. We shall come back to this later when we speak of dreams and myths.

In *Learning from Experience*, Bion says that the hypothesis of an apparatus for thinking is built on a digestive model. In order to expand our understanding of this, let us keep in mind that, when investigating thought disorders and α dreamwork, Bion considered that the emotional experience studied by psychoanalysis can be a digested or an undigested one. For this experience to be digested, it has to undergo a process of metabolisation. This process is achieved, as we have seen, through α function, which transforms sensory and emotional impressions into α elements, which are able to be stored and thought.

In *Cogitations*, which included his most private reflections, he called the alpha function dreamwork alpha. For a sensory impression or an emotional experience to become lasting and have the ability to be stored, it has to be transformed into ideograms: for example, if there is a pain, the psyche has to have an image of a tearful face, or rubbing an elbow, etc. This image functions as a model, a container that not only lodges that particular painful experience, but also determines the way in which that experience is registered. The incarnation in that sensory form, which then has the function of a model, fulfils the same function that Freud attributed to attention, since the model provides the possibility of approaching new experiences, and dealing with mental pain, equipping the patient to metabolise these new experiences. These models, which can be constructed from dreams, myths, stories, etc., work for psychic reality meeting the stimuli half-way, as Freud established for the function of attention, which takes occasional samples of the external world, so that the personality can then be familiar with certain stimuli.

Bion says that undigested facts can be assimilated by the mind when they become "dreams". Just as sensory impressions register actual objects from the external world, "dreams", or models transformed in ideograms that are associated with an emotional experience, are one of the ways that this experience can be to registered and can be used as unsaturated "psychological data" to face new experiences with adequate mental equipment.

As I pointed out in the previous chapter, "dreams" (in the extended sense, while sleeping or awake—alpha function is continuous throughout day and night) at an individual level and myths at a group level articulate the alpha elements into a narrative, and are in themselves instruments; that is, they are tools to be used for approaching emotional experiences. From this point of view, we can say that they are preconceptions, unsaturated, unknown variables that we can use to approach new emotional experiences and find a meaning to enable their digestion.

Let us now raise the following question: which are the implications of the relationship between the notion of a function and the three emotional links (L, H, K) that Bion develops in *Learning from Experience*, which are the fundamental core of emotional experiences? We will also then have to examine the meaning of these three links.

We already know that, in *Second Thoughts*, Bion draws attention to the significance of the linking function. We must keep in mind that he has suggested that the emotional digestion of experiences provides nutrients for the mind through truth, which keeps the mind alive and enables it to grow through learning from experience. As we have already said, "dreams" generate alpha elements and the meanings we can give to our emotional experiences are the nourishment of the mind. So, we human beings obtain our nourishment from meanings, and dreams, in an extended sense as postulated by Bion, generate meaning.

I also want, once more, to draw the reader's attention to the fact that the alpha function operates on those emotional experiences of which the personality is aware. Failure to use the emotional experience, evacuating it, has disastrous consequences for the development of the personality, and this disaster can range from psychotic deterioration to the psychological death of the personality.

In *Learning from Experience*, Bion develops his ideas about the K link, the disposition to know. It is very likely that he has taken into account that love and hate had, until then, been the centre of psychoanalytical research, especially after Klein. In Bion's investigation of the process and the disorders of thought, he focuses on the K (knowledge) and –K links (minus K, meaning active disavowal).

As much as in the L (love) and H (hate) links, the K link (disposition to know) as an emotional link also implies mental pain. The personality's attitude when facing the mental pain of modification or evasion is fundamental for the development of the personality. Truth is the nutrient of the mind and lies are its poison. Evading mental pain

A THEORY OF KNOWING–DREAMING–THINKING   137

requires the use of some form of lies or cheating and, because of this, it is toxic for the development of the personality.

We could say that what was previously conceived within psychoanalysis as defence mechanisms is transformed by Bion into mechanisms that modulate and deal with mental pain, making the truth more digestible through α elements, dreams, myths, etc., which are a way of approaching truth through providing a representation, or a veil for truth. Some other mechanisms are used for evading truth by creating lies and hallucinations with β elements and bizarre objects. Another way of evading truth is through what seems to be a thought but is actually a concretisation, where words or representations are not used at a symbolic level, but as "things in themselves" and are treated as such and not as thoughts. The alpha function provides the personality with a kind of experience from which stems a "feeling of confidence" in discerning the truth, similar to the confirmation of sensory data through common sense. Common to more than one sense of one person, or shared by the senses of two or more people, this feeling of confidence is related to the creation of the contact-barrier between conscious and unconscious representations of emotional experience, which has been processed by the alpha function. The alpha elements, as we have seen, are not experienced as the thing-in-itself, but as an abstraction and representation of the experience. In being represented in this conscious and unconscious way, it provides a binocular vision of the experience, from which emerges this feeling of confidence in its psychic and/or external reality.

Emotions conceived as links change our psychoanalytical perspective. Meltzer said that Freud conceived emotions as a kind of "noise in the machine", or as somatic manifestations or mental states perceived as emotions. For Bion, on the other hand, emotions are links between the container and the contained. Thus, he tells us that container and contained are liable to undergo conjunction and be permeable to each other. So, container and contained within a permeable conjunction stimulate a change in the personality towards mental growth. We can once again take the mother–infant relationship to illustrate this: if it is mutually beneficial (symbiotic), both mother and infant grow.

Coming back to dreams and their function in mental life, I want to mention Bion's ideas where he says that learning depends on the capability of the container to remain integrated and, simultaneously, to lose rigidity. I believe that dreams, myths, and models are ideal tools for functioning as a container that stimulates a process of mental growth: dreams, models, and myths can remain integrated and, unlike theories, can also have plasticity and are easily disposed of.

Bion continues by saying that this combination of integration and plasticity are the qualities of the mental state of an individual who can keep his knowledge and experiences and, nevertheless, be prepared to re-elaborate past experiences so that he can be receptive to the new idea. Container and contained must be kept within a constant relationship through emotions as a link, which, in turn, must be capable of transformation.

A film used as a clinical illustration

To provide the reader with a more vivid understanding of the notions we have been examining, I propose once again to use a film as an illustration, this time one directed by Ingmar Bergman: *Smultronstället* (*Wild Strawberries*, 1957). First, I need to introduce two terms that date from a later period in Bion's work: catastrophic change and caesura, and revisit the term selected fact.

Selected fact (SF)

This is an expression that Bion took from the mathematician Poincaré: it refers to the discovering of the fact that gives coherence and harmonises elements that were previously perceived as disparate. The selected fact highlights one fact above the rest for its capability to provide coherence. The selected fact conjugates previously scattered experiences into a specific configuration, named constant conjunction. The notion of SF is significant in psychoanalytical work because it is a very powerful tool for investigating psychic reality. The SF facilitates discovery by starting a transformational system with an indeterminate direction. It is an opportunity that provides a great variability to the analytical experience.

In the film, we can see how the first dream sets off a transformational system which produces a disarticulation of the former constant conjunction implied in how Isak, the protagonist, relates to his

A THEORY OF KNOWING–DREAMING–THINKING 139

emotional experiences, which is by disconnecting from his emotions. In the first scene, we see Isak sitting at his desk; he is shown as a solitary person who has devoted his life to science and has cut himself off, disconnected from human bonds. His surroundings are filled with photographs: his long-dead wife, his son who lives in another city, his mother, etc. The only living being that we see is the dog. In Swedish, the full name of the protagonist means: Is = ice, Borg = castle. Bergman commented on the character,

> I modelled a figure who, from the outside, resembled my father, but who was entirely me. I at thirty-seven years, isolated from human relationships, relationships which I had cut off, self-affirmative, introverted, not only quite a failure but a true failure; although successful and capable, and organized, and disciplined. (1990, p. 21)

I quote some of Bergman's comments about the emotional context in which he made this film because I think it shows that making it might have been for him a process of digestion of emotional experiences similar to those that Isak elaborates in the film with his dreams and his journey. Bergman says,

> The divorce from my third wife was still violently painful to me. It was a strange experience; loving someone you could not live with . . . I was in a bitter struggle with my parents. I did not want to and could not speak to my father. My mother and I would look over and over again for a temporary reconciliation, but there were too many skeletons in the closet, too many infected misunderstandings. We tried, because we really wanted to make up, but we failed continuously . . . I was looking for my father and mother, but I could not find them . . . (1990, p. 21)

In the film, the selected fact (or connecting pattern) that links a constant conjunction, such as the way in which Isak had articulated his emotional experiences, is the theme of the film: a lack of affection, an emotional poverty, emptiness, an unforgiving attitude, expressed in Isak's first comment, in which he says he has become distant, that he has drifted apart from people. It is interesting that Bergman comments that, through *Wild Strawberries*, he was asking his parents to: "Look at me, understand me, and—if possible—forgive me" (1990, p. 21).

The final scene of the film—after a trip with his daughter-in-law where he could elaborate some formerly undigested emotional

140   ON MENTAL GROWTH

experiences (alpha dreamwork)—shows a change in this constant conjunction: Sara takes Isak's hand and leads him to a sunlit clearing in the woods. From there he can see his parents, together, who look at him and wave to him. This image of the parental couple has its complement in the film's previous scene, in which his son and daughter-in-law say farewell to him, having come together and made peace, and in the change in Isak's son, who accepts not only his wife, but also her pregnancy and the fact of having a son. The warmth of, and reconciliation with, human links in these scenes are a selected fact that contrasts with the selected facts of coldness and isolation that are expressed in different scenes, before the change, such as the relationship between Isak and his housekeeper, with his daughter-in-law at the beginning of the trip, and in the scene with his elderly mother.

Bergman comments,

> I was portraying myself in the figure of my father and searching for explanations to the bitter fights with my mother. I thought I understood that I was an unloved child, raised in a cold matrix and born during a physical and psychic crisis. Later on, my mother's diary confirmed my idea: my mother had violently ambivalent feelings towards her miserable moribund son. (1990, p. 22)

However, we must notice that, in the film, Isak achieves a realisation, a digestion of these experiences, as well as of his oedipal conflict. The first dream is a model that includes elements of his isolation: in the first image, he is walking alone through deserted streets, flanked by derelict buildings which appear to close in on him. There is no sound until the handless watch appears (identical to the one he pulls out of his pocket in the dream, and to his father's, which he finds in his mother's home). The meeting with the watch, in the first dream, is the first time that the living body is perceptible; Isak sweats, his heartbeat can be heard.

Catastrophic change

This is a concept created by Bion, taking as a model René Thom's catastrophe theory. It refers to the fact that transformations happen through ruptures and qualitative leaps, as mutations in the evolution.

"Catastrophic", as has been explained before, is not synonymous with catastrophe in the usual sense, it is more like a mutation.

Catastrophic change has three characteristics:

1. It opens up the pre-established system: in the film, the system of dissociation of the emotions.
2. It is violent, not in a destructive sense, but in the sense of being abrupt, and because of the strength of the problem that appears now without its container. This can be illustrated within the film by the decision Isak makes after the first dream: to travel by car instead of by plane. This decision will give him the time and opportunity to go through emotional experiences that had remained dissociated, which contributed to his emotional freezing. When he connects again, he goes through the wild strawberry patch of the original title in Swedish, where he connects with his memories and his dreamlike waking thoughts.
3. Invariance: something of the former system transfers into the new system, but transformed. An example of invariance is the relationship with Isak's daughter-in-law at the beginning of the trip: it is a relationship of mutual coldness and rejection. Isak makes scornful comments about women; his daughter-in-law retaliates by not wanting to listen to his dream. It is a relationship of rejection and mutual incomprehension, which is reflected in the film in the relationship of the couple whom they meet on the road as a result of an accident. We can also think of this violent encounter as the meeting between two aspects of Isak's personality and his unresolved oedipal problems. The meeting that appears in the film as a violent crash takes place after Isak picks up Sara and the two youngsters, who seem to be current replicas of his teenage situation with his sweetheart, also named Sara, and his brother. Could this unresolved emotional situation have been transformed into the image of the couple in the other car who mistreat each other so badly?

Other examples of invariance are represented by Isak's mother, both as a young woman and as an elderly one, and by himself through his lack of emotional contact. We could consider the watch with the missing hands, which he finds again in his elderly mother's home, as invariance: the watch belongs to Isak's father. We can conjecture that

ON MENTAL GROWTH

the father–son relationship lacked emotional contact, a lack which reappears in the relationship with the superego and analytical aspects of the second dream, and in Isak's relationship with his son, who has to learn to return loans, and also in the relationship between his son and his wife: the son does not want them to have the child she is expecting.

Catastrophic change can also be illustrated by the final scene, in which the system of coldness, isolation, lack of forgiveness, and resentment turns into a warm scene of reconnection and reconciliation. The parents are together, distant but looking at Isak, whom, in turn, Sara takes by the hand.

Bergman commented,

> . . . the impulse behind *Wild Strawberries* was a desperate attempt of justification directed towards indifferent and mythically exaggerated parents. . . . My parents became people of normal proportions many years later; my childish bitter hate melted and disappeared. Mutual affection and understanding brought us together. (1990, p. 21)

Caesura

This is a fertile concept of Bion's, which can be onsidered as an "in-between zone" with different characteristics. It can be thought of as a gap, as a contact-barrier, as a river that might grow rough and choppy or feature calm waters, but which hide a swamp underneath; it can be a marsh; it can be a wasteland, etc. It is in these zones where the meeting between different parts of the personality or mental states can occur, and they are, therefore, areas of conflict and of potential catastrophic change. The growth of the personality is conceived after the model of a palimpsest: it is not linear or like a rubber band, but is more like the layers of an onion. Between the layers are caesuras, and to go through them can stimulate a turbulence that was latent, and now becomes evident. In the film, stimulated by the diploma he is about to receive for his fifty years as a scientific investigator, Isak connects with the emotional problem of the passage of time, which, until then, was immobilised by his emotional disconnection. This immobility is represented in the film's first scene by photographs of his dead wife, his son, etc.: a static, motionless world. The dream

A THEORY OF KNOWING–DREAMING–THINKING   143

stimulates the kind of change that is related to going through a caesura which has the characteristics of a frozen desert.

Some thoughts on Wild Strawberries

Up to now, the manifest content of a dream has been studied as a transformation that is meant to hide something, and that through an interpretative method would reveal what is hidden. An incoherent, conscious, manifest content was hiding a coherent, unconscious content that had to be revealed. This line of thinking has been fruitful and continues to be so. We often perceive the narrated content of a dream as an inexhaustible source of knowledge to allow us to understand the unconscious mental life of the person who dreamt it.

A new vertex of observation is that the dream is a means of developing constant conjunctions and producing critical changes in the dreamer. When Bion says that dreams have a low level of generalisation, unlike myths, he is using generalisation in the sense of the applicability of the dream to other people, or the possibility of its expressing universal problems for the group. A person cannot be nourished through other people's dreams, unless it is the "dream" of an artist, expressed in an artistic work; artists express this kind of dream in their ideas, pictures, music, etc., achieving a transformation which offers sensitive people the possibility of connecting and changing after being exposed to the artist's work.

We are using the film *Wild Strawberries* to try to illustrate some of Bion's ideas and as a preconception (an unsaturated expectation) that can be used as a technical tool in the analyst's consulting room in the search for new realisations (experiences which combine the materialisation of the preconception and the awareness of the experience). We can use films as models to incarnate for the patient some of his emotional experiences as a means of constructing models that help the representation and elaboration of undigested emotional experiences.

So, the images and ideas of a film, a dream, a story, or a myth can be used as models to formulate the emotional experience of the patient in the consulting room.

Oscar Wilde said that a peasant who has not seen a storm painted by Turner does not know what a storm is like. This refers to a kind of very successfully achieved transformation, using a powerful type of

144 ON MENTAL GROWTH

reverie, which is a central factor in the development of the mind's aesthetic dimension, or "dreaming condition".

An emotional experience does not have univocal sensory correlatives, unlike the relationship with sensory objects, which have impressions provided by the senses, liable to be transformed into sensory data. Emotions have no colour, flavour, or smell, etc.; they can acquire sensory correlatives, such as Freud describes in the relationship between anxiety and the accompanying physiological and sensory perceptions from the trauma of birth. Which is the equivalent of a sensory impression for emotional experiences, and how can it be given durability so that it can be thought?

It would seem that the nearest equivalent is ideograms: as I mentioned before, an emotional experience has to be transformed into an ideogram in order to acquire durability and be available for storage. Dreams seem to be a very fertile source for the generation of ideograms. Myths are more universal; they are like "dreams" at a cultural level. Then there are also the artists' "dreams", which perform a reverie function for the human being.

New openings into unexplored fields or problems require new forms for their depiction and approach. Artists open new doors towards previously unknown aspects and new vertices for observation. As an example, we can think of the discovery and development of perspective in the Renaissance, or the Impressionists, who discovered a new "way of seeing", decomposing light, focusing more on it than on the object it has an impact upon, or Cubism and its decomposition of the human figure, seen simultaneously from different vertices and in different moments.

Bion partially developed the idea of a training for psychotherapists or psychoanalysts based on using and playing with myths (the collective dream).

Every psychoanalyst can choose his myths and select its different elements. If he spontaneously makes an association with a patient while doing that, he will have discovered a new vertex from which to approach the clinical problem. This task lies outside the psychoanalytical session, and it could be equated to a musician's warm-up exercises before a concert. Bion said that a psychoanalyst or psychotherapist should have a wealth of myths available as preconceptions in the search for realisations. As we have seen before, we can take other elements of the oedipal myth to investigate the question of

A comment on Wild Strawberries

The film begins by introducing its protagonist, Isak, a seventy-eight-year-old man who lives alone apart from his housekeeper and seems to be cold, selfish, and devoid of emotion. He has devoted his life to his scientific work, apparently, according to the first scene, without having allowed himself to be touched to any great degree by emotion. We see photographs of his long-dead wife, and of his son and daughter-in-law. It is the eve of a trip to the city where he will receive a diploma and medal in recognition of his fifty years as an eminent doctor and scientist. In this first scene, he comments that people's relationships are practically reduced to criticism, which is why he has isolated himself. This first scene already anticipates the problem of emotional isolation: his relationships are with "things", photographs, and, although Isak describes who is in the photographs, they are not containers of memories, of emotional bonds.

The reference to criticism expresses a second problem which emerges throughout the film in different images: Isak's criticism and intolerance of his daughter-in-law, the criticism of the young mother (in the family lunch with the deaf uncle), of the boy with the dirty hands (a superego reference to masturbation), and his old mother's criticism of those who do not visit her, etc.

This super-superego is incarnated in the figure of the man who mistreats the woman in the episode of Isak and his daughter-in-law's meeting with the couple in the car that almost crashes into theirs. These images also express other problems: the couple's relationship, which is portrayed throughout the film through memories, this time with affection, of Sara, his childhood sweetheart, in the wild strawberry patch. It follows the problem of the triangle when the female member of the trio of hitchhikers (who is also named Sara) is accompanied by two suitors, a replica of Isak's situation with "his" Sara and his brother, etc.

What I want to exemplify with this use of the film is how we can take the images of a dream, as I am taking those of the film, to formulate models and express an emotional problem: it might be

146   ON MENTAL GROWTH

emotional isolation, it might be Isak's superego's characteristics, it might be the emotional relationship, the oedipal triangle, the father–son relationship, etc. When approaching a dream in this way, the problem being tackled depends on the selected fact, which becomes the point or vertex from which the observation is made. The problem is formulated in images that narrate the different emotional elements; once formulated, then it can be thought and a meaning can be found.

The other point I wish to make is how the first dream produces a critical change in Isak, one that unfolds throughout the film. I want to draw attention to the fact that I am not concerned with the plot; the narrative is just a way of linking the events. There are elements in the film highlighting turning points of significant emotional change: the decision to travel by car, taken after the dream, leads to an emotional contact with his daughter-in-law and the problem of Isak's son, as emotionally frozen as the father, if not more so.

The stop-off at the strawberry patch connects Isak with memories and dream-like waking thoughts with emotional significance. These dream-like waking thoughts can be seen as a true dreamwork alpha. The meeting with a grateful ex-patient at the petrol station, whose wife he treated during childbirth, connects him with the aspect of his profession that deals with people and their gratitude.

The meeting with his very old mother, who is cold and resentful, refers once again to a world of inanimate objects. These are some aspects that exemplify the different paths that can be taken, depending on the chosen vertex.

I shall now take the elements in Isak's first dream to exemplify how we can deconstruct a dream into its elements and take each one, independently, from the narrative.

1. Deserted street.
2. Derelict buildings to one side.
3. Winding streets, thereby limiting visibility.
4. A perplexed man walking.
5. A sign that stands out on the pavement: it seems like an advertisement for spectacles; in one eye there is a watch with no hands.
6. He goes back, retraces his steps, he looks at the watch again. He takes out a pocket watch that has no hands either. It is the one that is found at Isak's mother's house and is his father's watch.

A THEORY OF KNOWING–DREAMING–THINKING   147

7. The sound of heartbeats is heard.
8. A creaking sound, like that made by a cradle, coming from the hearse.
9. The sound of horses' hooves.
10. The image of a man's back.
11. The image of a man with no face or with a flattened one.
12. The image of a man falling and his head spilling liquid on the pavement.
13. The image of horses dragging a hearse that is missing a wheel.
14. The image of a wheel hanging from a streetlamp.
15. The image of a wheel rolling by, almost running over Isak.
16. The image of Isak behind the now stationary hearse.
17. A coffin that falls off the hearse.
18. An image of the open coffin from where a hand comes out and wrestles with him.
19. Isak looks at the corpse in the coffin and sees that it is himself.

Isak's first dream

We hear the dream being narrated and see the images: he is on a deserted street, derelict buildings can be seen on one side, and because street is winding, its end cannot be seen. We see Isak from the back, walking along the pavement. He suddenly sees a sign that stands out; it seems to be the advertisement for an optician, depicting two eyes. In one of them there is something like a bird, and in the other, a watch without hands. When he sees it, Isak takes out his pocket watch, which has no hands either. We will find out in the film that it is his father's watch. But, as presented in the dream, we see that the protagonist feels disturbed: we hear heartbeats, he sweats and needs to lean against a wall.

The heartbeats and sweating are the first signs of emotion. Isak looks towards the end of the street and sees a figure going away; he approaches to touch it, and when it turns around he sees a deformed, crushed face; the man falls and liquid spills from his head, pooling into a black shadow on the ground. At that moment, we hear the sound of horses' hooves and, coming from the bend in the street, we see a horse-drawn hearse heading straight for the protagonist. No one is driving, and the horses seem to be out of control. One of the axles

148   ON MENTAL GROWTH

gets caught on a streetlamp, the horses continue pulling, and we hear sounds that seem reminiscent of the rocking of a cradle. The horses continue to pull, and the axle joining the wheel to the hearse breaks. The wheel comes off and almost runs over Isak. A coffin falls from the hearse, making a lot of noise. Isak approaches it and looks inside; the coffin is half open and a hand is hanging out. When Isak comes nearer, the hand grabs his hand and pulls at him with great strength; he resists, the coffin opens, and inside the coffin he sees himself. At that moment, he awakes in anguish. He gets up, goes towards the window, and looks outside. It is already day because it is 1 June, summer in Sweden, and the days are as long as the nights are short.

The dream brings about a significant change: he looks for his housekeeper and tells her that he has changed his mind about the trip he is about to take; he will travel by car instead of by plane, as originally planned. The housekeeper represents opposition to change: she reproaches him for his decision, and adds that he is a selfish old man who does not consider her, who has served him for forty years and that she will not pack his suitcase. Isak replies that they are not married and he will pack it himself. The housekeeper grudgingly packs it and makes his breakfast. While he is having breakfast, his daughter-in-law (played by Ingrid Thulin) appears and asks if she can go with him. In the following scene, they are in the car; Isak, who has shown no interest in his daughter-in-law and makes an attack on women by expressing his opinions on smoking, wants to tell her the dream. She does not want to listen.

In the next scene, they reach the "wild strawberry patch" (the translation of the original title in Swedish). There, Isak experiences several images that imply emotional contact and digestion of emotional situations that, until then, had been frozen. They meet a group of hitchhikers, consisting of two young men and a woman named Sara, who is adored by both of her companions. For Isak, this invokes his teenage sweetheart, also called Sara, with whom he used to pick strawberries, but who he now "sees" flirting with his brother Sigfrid, whom she eventually marries. He also observes the scene of a family meal, arranged to celebrate a deaf uncle's birthday, at which the father is absent. This dreamlike meeting is duplicated in the meeting with the young Sara at the strawberry patch, again demonstrating a triangular situation. This illustrates how the connection with his emotional experiences also enables him to encounter them in waking life, thus making a new elaboration possible. This can be seen in his changing relationship with his daughter-in-law.

However, the encounter with emotional experiences also brings other encounters that could be conceived as a container–contained relationship.

- There is a car crash (the car, a container, crashes because it has wandered off the road, almost colliding with Isak's vehicle; what it contains is an embittered middle-aged couple who constantly bicker, hurling venomous insults at each other).
- After having invited Sara and her companions to travel with him, Isak ends up inviting the bickering couple (who represent his image of his own unhappy marriage) to travel with him. It is interesting to see how the inclusion of this couple makes the space claustrophobic until Marianne, Isak's daughter-in-law, stops the car and demands that they get out, out of consideration for their younger passengers.
- The man of the couple later appears as part of Isak's dream about a test, which focuses on the problem of the primitive, arbitrary, and cruel superego.
- As the film develops, it includes poetry, a visit to Isak's ancient and cold-natured mother, and the dream with his wife and the conversation with his daughter-in-law.
- Can the dream that begins with Sara (lovingly taking care of a baby), the daughter-in-law's pregnancy, and the rejection of Isak's son (whose nature is so like Isak's) be related to pregnancy and having a child?

The end of the film shows the reconciliation of Marianne and Isak's son through the dream meeting with a united couple: Isak's parents greeting him, his father next to his mother, fishing. In the first memories at the beginning of the film, it was only the father who was with Isak. There is also a development in the relationship with the father. The watch with no hands that he finds in the first dream and then in his mother's house is an element that represents the relationship with his father, as well as with the notion of time. The passing of generations and acceptance of this provides an emotional notion of time, such as the time when the breast used to be and is now gone, and is also related to a couple who generate babies, a new generation.

150   ON MENTAL GROWTH

We can, therefore, ask why the relationship with his father is represented by the watch. What happens with the passing of time and how is it presented in the film? The watch is an instrument that places one within a timeline, a temporality; if the internal relationship with the parents breaks down and they become cold and critical, and mistreat each other, then the mental and emotional instrument for situating oneself in life and relationships, both in terms of generational succession and in the mature processing of situations of childhood ambivalence, appears to be failing.

Could Bergman's making of this film, the process of creating and filming images, have provided him with the opportunity of formulating, registering, and digesting emotional situations that, while undigested, were toxic and stimulated inhibitions?

CHAPTER ELEVEN

Transformations

"The psycho-analytic problem is the problem of growth and its harmonious resolution in the relationship between the container and the contained, repeated in individual, pair, and finally group (intra and extra psychically)"

(Bion, 1970, pp. 15–16)

"Of all the hated possibilities, mental growth and maturing are the most feared and hated"

(Bion, 1979, p. 53)

"Time has often been regarded as being of the essence of psychoanalysis; in the growth process it has no part. Mental evolution or growth is catastrophic and timeless"

(Bion, 1970, p. 108)

"I would make a distinction between existence – the capacity to exist and the ambition or aspiration to have an existence which is worth having – the quality of existence, not the quantity; not the length of one's life, but the quality of that life"

(Bion, 1979, p. 249)

152   ON MENTAL GROWTH

The book *Transformations* is subtitled *Change from Learning to Growth*. In this book, Bion approaches the intuitions that will be presented as "catastrophic change" and "transformations", "evolution" towards O, becoming oneself, and at-one-ment. In this new turn of his ideas, O designates an epistemological vertex: ultimate reality is unknowable. Bion also refers to this O as the starting point from which something evolves in each session and also, quoting Milton, O marks the infinite, formless void. Getting ahead of myself a bit, I will say that, since *Learning from Experience*, what he now designates as K transformations refer to the disposition to know the personality, the psychic reality. In this new approach of psychoanalysis, in this book, Bion says that it is not enough to know about, it is necessary to become "it"; it is what he describes in his abstract formulation as the transformations of K↔O. Within this change, he differentiates between doing psychoanalysis and talking about psychoanalysis, something that again has deep connotations for psychoanalytical practice, and expands on the notion of emotional commitment of the analytical couple and the emotional turbulence that is inherent in psychoanalysis. These K↔O transformations are the way in which Bion indicates "becoming", becoming "oneself", being in at-one-ment. The resistances, from either patient or analyst, are described by Bion as resistances to this becoming, and are linked to the anxiety stimulated by the search for "truth".

I digress a little before going on with examining *Transformations* to add a factor to these resistances: in the seminars that Bion gave at the Tavistock when he was already nearing the end of his life, he said something surprising but, at the same time, coherent with the ideas of catastrophic change and emotional turbulence: ". . . It took me very a long time to realize that the actual experience of being psychoanalyzed was a traumatic one and that it takes quite a long while before one recovers from it" (Bion, 2005, p. 1).

To modulate the implications of these statements, and before expanding on *Transformations*, I want to paraphrase something that Meltzer (1978) says about *Transformations*: he says, with a sense of humour, that in order to develop tolerance for the reading of this book, we should imagine a contemporary Leonardo designing his flying machines, producing wonderful drawings, fireworks, and mechanical toys. To be able to understand this book, our task is to take Bion's intentions seriously and fight against the feelings it might provoke, such as resentment, the suspicion that he is mad, the humiliation of reading quotations from authors that we might barely have heard of if we are lucky, and, above all, the exasperation with his attempts at "mathematisation". Bion explicitly says that he does not agree with the dictum that a system cannot be considered scientific unless it is expressed in mathematical terms. However, how can we tolerate the proliferation of maths *à la* Lewis Carroll, with his maths-style notations, featuring not only Greek letters but also words, plus arrows, dots, lines, etc.? Sometimes, when faced with this assault on our capability to think, we might have the impression that the book seems as though it was written by Bion's patient B, and we could quote many sentences that sound like those of the patient who talked about "the girl who left her knickers lying about". Before deciding to abandon this book, let us consider another viewpoint from which to tackle it.

We might wonder where this modern Leonardo is heading. Taking the Leonardo metaphor further, we could say that, in *Learning from Experience*, Bion tried to build a flying machine called alpha function, and that, in *Elements of Psychoanalysis*, he broached the development of the Grid as a navigational instrument to enable us to get our bearings as analysts within the cosmos of thought and thinking. *Transformations* looks for other navigational instruments: it calls for the sextant as a model, an instrument that enabled navigation without a coastline in sight. It is an instrument that is not an extension of our senses, such as the microscope or the telescope, but an indirect medium used by the navigator to orientate him in relation to very distant objects, analogous to the fragments of the personality that we come across in a psychoanalytic treatment.

This navigator of the cosmos of thought and thinking that Bion proposes seems to be a mixture of a serious psychoanalytical game and some elements used by mathematicians. This serious game proposed by Bion seems to be related to our need to make psychoanalytical observations. This is essential for our work as psychoanalysts and a significant part of Chapter Three of *Transformations* seems to deal with it. Afterwards, we need to apply the instruments we already have to apply them to the data we have observed, and then assess how inadequate these instruments are, in order to make changes and apply them once more to observation.

This book seems to show not only Bion's ideas, but also how he thinks, his method of thinking. The theory of transformations is not a

154   ON MENTAL GROWTH

psychoanalytical theory of the personality, but a theory of the psycho-analytical observation of personality. Bion developed and used the terms transformation and invariance for the observation of specific clinical facts and for the theory of the psychoanalytic technique. So, the concept of *transformation*—already used in other disciplines, such as projective geometry—is introduced by Bion into observation and psychoanalytical clinical practice as an instrument for the investigation of psychic reality.

As mentioned at the beginning of this chapter, the book's subtitle is *Change from Learning to Growth*. Bion made a Copernican turn in postulating that, epistemologically, thoughts precede the apparatus for thinking them and stimulate the development of this apparatus, and in proposing alpha function as indispensable for the development of an evolved conscience associated to an unconscious, capable of being aware, different from a rudimentary consciousness. When following the evolution of his ideas, we see that, in *Transformations*, he surprises us again by introducing the concepts of mental growth, catastrophic change, and at-one-ment, which is becoming one with oneself.

Mental growth refers, on the one hand, to "catastrophic change" and becoming one with oneself as an ongoing but simultaneously discontinuous process with the quality of a mutation. On the other hand, this growth also refers to the formulation of different levels of abstractions of thinking, with varying degrees of complexity, and to the plasticity of the use of thoughts. (The rows and columns of the Grid.) These two axes of the Grid imply that we have to observe not only the level of abstraction of thoughts but also how the patients are using them. Thus, a patient can tell many dreams in a session, but use them as a defence mechanism in order to evade thinking.

Bion has two interesting models to illustrate the idea of transformations:

1.   The model of the painter transforming a poppy field into a picture through the media of paint and the canvas.
2.   The model of a lake reflecting the trees and being disturbed by the wind, and the observer seeing only the reflection of the trees in the water. It is the same image as Plato's cave, but with the images altered by emotions L, H, and K.

He also uses a third model, of water which appears to be very still until a stick is introduced and then we see the movement.

Meltzer says that in this book (and, I would add, starting with the notion of alpha function) there is an implicit idea of a process of working through implied in the notion of growth. It seems to imply a change from Freud's conception, which mostly saw the dreamwork as being in the service of censorship, hiding the truth; in Bion, on the other hand, every "dream" (in a broader sense: for Bion, "dreaming" is associated with alpha function, which operates day and night and transforms crude β (beta) elements into α (alpha) elements, apt for thought and thinking) is an elaboration to give shape to the nascent thought. Where he seems to agree with Freud is in placing thoughts and dreams between impulse and action, something fundamental to dealing with emotional problems in the absence of objects.

The key point of this book, besides mental growth, is truth. Both points are related. It does not mean an absolute, unattainable truth, but truth more in the sense of sincerity, as respect for facts the way they are and not the way one would want them to be. Bion tells us that "If truth is not essential to all values of the Ta β (the final outcome of the analyst's transformation), Ta β must be regarded as expressing a manipulation of the emotions of the patient or the public and not an interpretation" (Bion, 1965, p. 37). In Chapter Four of *Transformations*, Bion draws an analogy between the painter and the analyst:

> That the analyst works on his patient's emotions as a painter might work on his canvas would be repugnant to psycho-analytic theory and practice. The painter who works on his public's emotions with an end in view is a propagandist with the outlook of the poster artist. . . . The analyst's position is akin to that of the painter who by his art adds to his public's experience. Since psycho-analysts do not aim to run the patient's life but to enable him to run it according to his lights and therefore to know what his lights are . . . (Bion, 1965, p. 37)

The theory of transformations is not a psychoanalytical theory but one intended to improve psychoanalytical observation. In this book, Bion comes closer to the intuition that he will later name catastrophic change: it is what he begins to conceptualise in this book as "transformation in O". This kind of transformation is different from transformations in K (the knowledge link) that refers to the disposition to know about psychic reality, while transformations in O are related to "becoming".

156   ON MENTAL GROWTH

The idea of transformations is linked to Bion's epistemological vertex: the ultimate reality is unknowable; we can only know it through its transformations. Bion gives ultimate reality the same characteristics that Freud gave to the nature of the unconscious: it is unknowable, and we can only know it through its derivatives (by-products). The aim of this theory is (a) to develop the analyst's capability for observation and (b) facilitate contact and communication between patient and analyst. Bion claims that every kind of communication in an analysis, such as dreams and symptoms, among others, can be investigated with this concept. The process of transformation has different characteristics in each of the transformational processes described by Bion, and is specific and characteristic of "that patient", "that moment" and "that transformational medium". The transformational process is produced within what Bion terms a "medium", consisting of the patient's emotional experience. The analyst also conducts his transformation in a "medium", and we can consider that both media together configure what we call the analytical situation. As we shall see below, we differentiate different kinds of transformation: thus, the patient who makes a transformation in a projective medium needs to receive from the analyst a transformation (interpretation, construction) in a transformational medium of thought.

Bion's investigation describes three types of transformations, to which he later adds the transformation in K (from $O \rightarrow K$), the transformation in O ($K \rightarrow O$) and the transformation of $O \rightarrow O$.

From an unknowable ultimate reality, a starting point, an unknown origin, O, something evolves in each session. Bion describes a transformational process that he names T p. α (when it is the patient's) and a product of this transformation that he describes as T p. β. The same goes for the analyst: the transformational process there is T a. α and the product of the transformation is T a. β. Bion also describes transformational cycles: the patient carries out a transformation of whatever evolves from his O, the analyst receives the product of this transformation, and, in turn, he carries out a transformation of the patient's transformation. This is an initial transformational cycle, and there could be a second, a third, etc. (This denomination of α and β is not related to α function or α and β elements described in the chapters dealing with thinking.)

I shall now expand on the complex notions we are dealing with. Bion uses two concepts as keys: (i) invariance: the element that passes from one transformational system to another, although transformed; (ii) the medium: in which the transformation is carried out.

There is "something" in each of these three kinds of transformations (projective transformations, rigid transformations or transformations in thought, and transformations in hallucinosis) that will allow recognition of the invariant, that is to say, the original traits, which it is both possible and necessary to recognise in their transformations, even if they pass through transformed.

Investigating transformations, Bion took the example of the poppy field as a stimulus for the painter at one extreme, and, at the other, the painted picture. He did this to provide a model that could clarify an aspect or a part of the whole: the part that takes place in the artist's mind.

He claims here that the domain of the psychoanalyst falls between the point where a man receives a sensory impression, and the point at which he provides an expression for the transformation which took place. The principles of investigation need to be constant no matter what the medium is; it can be a musical medium, a visual one, a verbal expression between two people, etc. There has to be some constant element, whether the investigation deals with a healthy or unhealthy mind. Here, he uses the model of the trees reflected in the lake. The trees (the O) cannot be seen, and the visible reflection depends on the turbulence of the setting.

Bion classifies transformations, according to their transformational medium, into the following.

1. Transformations in rigid movement, taking Euclidean geometry as a model. I prefer to call them "transformations in thoughts". In this kind of transformation, the emotional elements already contain the potential for thought and thinking, however embryonic. Invariances are easier to recognise, such as in the case of the painter and the poppy field, when he refers to the model of Monet's painting. The picture itself is a transformation of the painter's emotional experience in contemplating the poppy field. The transformational medium is the painting as a creative artistic thought. What makes us recognise the poppy field on the canvas is the invariance. Besides, each painter, and, I would add, each dreamer, has a personal "style" that imparts a strong element of invariance to his transformations. This enables us

158   ON MENTAL GROWTH

to differentiate a painting by Goya from one by Velázquez, or by Picasso, etc. In this kind of transformational medium, transformation in thoughts and thinking, we can say that analyst and patient meet in the same invariance field when both can think.

2.   Projective transformations (taking projective geometry as a model). In this kind of transformation, a process of deformation takes place that makes it difficult to recognise the invariance. In this passage from Euclidean to projective geometry, topology, properties such as distance, proportions, or angles, lose their meaning. The Möebius strip could give the reader an idea of this model. In psychoanalytical communication, we find these transformations in the different modalities of projective identification. This enables us to also consider the invariance, the O, the unknowable, the O of the emotional experience, from the point where a projective transformation evolves, a kind of transformation that is generating a huge deformation. The emotional experience then is difficult to recognise because projective identification is operating. In clinical practice, we have to consider the difference between realistic projective identification, which has a communicational quality, and hypertrophied projective identification. When the container–contained relationship fails, projective identification becomes hypertrophied, and this implies more difficulties in clinical practice. When referring to this kind of transformation, Bion describes the position in which the analyst finds himself as analogous to that of someone who hears the description of a work of art that is made from an unknown material and to an unspecified scale. The analyst's task—when this kind of transformation arises in the analytical field—is more difficult, because the members of the analytical couple do not share the same points of reference, although they seem to share the same language. Hence, the need for the analyst to find the medium for setting up a common relational field, which will help in the evolution of O↔K so that the subsequent evolution of K↔O can take place. Meltzer (1967) refers to the analyst's need to modulate his interventions to the transformational registration range of the patient. In my opinion, the analyst needs to help his patient develop a communicative projective identification. Here is where the ideas of reverie and the analyst's alpha function are again significant. However, if we include the ideas of catastrophic

change, emotional turbulence, and becoming in at-one-ment, which are crucial points related to mental growth, the analytical task becomes more complex and compromised for both members of the analytical couple. The negative capability to remain in an atmosphere of doubt and mysteries without resorting to reason and certainties—used as defence mechanisms—is a discipline that the analyst must develop. In psychoanalytical clinical practice, this discipline is demonstrated through the attitude of "no memory, no desire and no understanding".

3. Transformations in hallucinosis, which is not synonymous with hallucination. It is a transformational system that the patient carries out in a medium of rivalry with the analytic method, in a relationship of inferiority and superiority as the only one available. In this transformational medium, misunderstandings, perspective reversals, and transformations into $-K$, as well as lies, are in the foreground. This type of transformation seems to generate (T β patient) relationships tinged with hallucinosis as a final product and to provoke "contact" with a world devoid of life and meaning. If we, like Bion, consider that transformations in thought need a dynamic PS$\leftrightarrow$D to create constant conjunctions, and that these, in turn, need a name to link them in order to be given meaning, we are approaching one of the more important issues implicit in the concept of transformations in hallucinosis: the issue of lies (Pistiner de Cortiñas, 2007). In this kind of transformation, language is used as an action and has no relation with the "experience" to express it; on the contrary, it is used to inhibit thought. Bion claims that what lies behind transformations in hallucinosis is mental pain. In my opinion and clinical experience, it is a very difficult issue to tackle, and even more so to change. The fundamental clinical problem is that if the question of rivalry between the methods of analysis and hallucinosis is not cleared away from the analytical situation, there is no chance of change or evolution, except towards the deterioration of either the patient or both members of the analytical couple.

As we have already mentioned, Bion adds two transformations which take into account the direction in which the transformations are made: the transformations from O$\leftrightarrow$K, the transformations from K$\leftrightarrow$O and the transformations from O$\leftrightarrow$O. The latter ones have to do with at-one-ment. Mental growth is related to transformations towards O; transformations towards K are more or less useful in clinical practice, depending on the amplitude of the diameter. While transformations towards O can be represented by a model using a spiral, transformations towards K refer to a circle; this is why the larger the diameter of the circle, the more opportunities there are for enquiry.

Another kind of transformation is that in −K of active disavowal: this is part of the transformations in hallucinosis in which there is a rivalry with O. In this kind of transformation, there is neither recognition nor acceptance of an ultimate reality, of an unknowable truth, and −K is considered to be the superior truth. We can easily recognise this kind of transformation, presented as absolute truth, in fanaticism.

In *Attention and Interpretation*, Bion outlines a relationship between (a) the mystic, whom I believe could be conceived as the O, or the creative and/or destructive idea, which evolves; (b) the Establishment, that is to say, the institutionalisation of the idea, which can contain it or can destroy or deform it by crushing its potential, "putting it to sleep", weighing it down with bureaucracy, etc.; (c) the group that needs the institutionalisation of the Establishment in order to embrace the new idea.

The psychoanalytic idea and each transformation towards O in an analysis can be exposed to one of these fates or evolutions. In Chapter Thirteen, we are going to speak about tropisms, a hypothesis that is inspired in by changing the medical model in psychoanalysis for one of mental growth. The hypothesis of transformations from O and towards O contain the idea of prenatal potential, which can evolve and be developed, so it implies a model of metal growth more than a model of mental healing or cure.

Before going on I want to mention that one of the consequences of the notion of *Transformations* is the change in the concept of resistance in clinical practice: resistance is conceived as related to "truth"; it is activated and becomes manifest only when the threat seems to be in contact with what is believed to be real, to be true. There is no resistance to what is perceived as false. Transformtions towards K are feared when they threaten the evolution of transformations towards O. From a clinical point of view, transformations of K towards O are special cases of transformation and of particular interest to the analyst, since they have the purpose of favouring mental growth and the patient's process of maturing.

CHAPTER TWELVE

The difference between reparation and transformation

The Kleinian concept of reparation, associated with the depressive position, implies a previous attack or the unconscious phantasy of an attack. In this notion of unconscious phantasy, defined as the psychic correlation of the instincts or drives, there is no distinction between a phantasied attack and one that has been acted out. The depressive position implies a configuration of total object relationships, defences, and depressive anxieties that lead to guilt and reparation. Reparation is associated with the integration of the object, the acknowledgement of the object's and the ego's good and bad aspects, feelings of depressive guilt as a consequence of recognising the total object as the one that has been attacked, and the reparation of damage to the object and the ego.

Transformation does not imply a previous attack: in an evolution of O, the ultimate unknowable reality, the infinite and formless void of the origin or of tropisms, as Bion describes them in *Cogitations*: "The tropisms are the matrix from which all mental life springs. For maturation to be possible they need to be won from the void and communicated" (Bion, 1992, p. 34). I deal with tropisms in the next chapter; I mention them here because my attention was caught by their similarity with the formulation of O as a formless, infinite void, although, as a formulation, it is clearly more complex. Bion describes them as the matrix of all mental life, and that they need to be won from the infinite void. As we shall see in the following chapter, Bion says that he conjectures that the patient who comes to analysis has a predominance of the tropism of creativity. He also refers to becoming mature, which we can conceive as mental growth and the need for tropisms, as primitive aspects of the personality, to be communicated to an object that can receive and transform them.

In my opinion, a creative transformation towards mental growth implies a reverie function—which has intuition, receptivity, understanding, compassion, and consideration for life as characteristics—as a receptive container that modulates the primitive anxieties of the infant with love and understanding in a combination of the K and L links. It is a transformational container that possesses the necessary conditions for the catastrophic primitive anxieties—the threat of an imminent catastrophe—to be transformed into a mental function: the dynamic oscillation PS↔D.

As we have already seen, this is the function that enables the observation of the constant conjugated conjunctions, the observation of the relationship, the connecting pattern. It might not have a meaning yet, but once the conjunction is observed, it demands a meaning, which is provided by its nomination, related to the discovery of the selected fact that harmonises previously scattered facts and links them with its name. A meaning is achieved through experience (realisation) in a mutually beneficial container–contained relationship: the relationship transforms the container, as much as the contained, towards mental growth. It limits it within the context of the finite–infinite relationship, includes the notions of space and time, and enables a new transformational cycle towards mental growth through the K↔O transformations, which imply becoming one with oneself.

In transformations towards K, the problem is related, on the one hand, to the presence and absence of the object, and, on the other, to the state or condition of the object, whether fragmented or whole. It is in this sense that we must consider (in a metaphoric sense) geometric and arithmetic transformations. As for geometric transformations, they include the process of generation of meaning through dreamlike images, the visual–geometrical representation, such as Leonardo's drawings of hair, which can be used to express turbulence through an image. The O of the tropism is the primitive emotion which, when

THE DIFFERENCE BETWEEN REPARATION AND TRANSFORMATION   163

detoxified, can be creatively transformed. If we use the model of the lake and the trees that reflect in the water, these models are an evolution of this O, a transformation in an environment of a calm emotional atmosphere, as is the one of the reflective surface of a calm lake. In a psychoanalytic treatment, the analyst can use this kind of model to communicate with the patient and represent emotional experiences. This kind of approach, in my clinical experience, is very useful with patients with symbolisation.

Klein differentiates manic reparation from an authentic reparation but, besides what we have already said, that reparation implies a previous attack, in her hypothesis of reparation, the differentiation from the concept of transformation is that the latter is related to the tolerance or intolerance of the finite–infinite relationship that Bion puts forward for each process of transformation in thought or thinking. As an example, we can think of the interpretation that the analyst must choose to give to his patient out of the infinite possibilities of interpretation. When we choose, we need to have tolerance for the infinite–finite relationship, and this choice seems to be one of the difficulties of the psychotic part of the personality.

The transformation in thought requires the detoxification and metabolisation of the primitive emotions, whether we consider the work of art of a genius, such as Leonardo, or the process of becoming mature of every human being. Through this detoxification process, we can gain access to the levels of symbolic transformation in both geometry and arithmetic (taking both disciplines as a model). The number is then transformed from its emotional roots, from three into the name of a feeling and into an element of the capability for thinking: for example, the Oedipus conflict. The same can be said of the transformation of the oedipal triangle—no longer loaded with the primitive emotional content, having been detoxified of the corresponding emotions—into a finite space; first, that of the real parents, and, in a geometrical transformation, into the triangle of the Pythagorean theorem, as a transformation of the triangular oedipal situation. Bion's formulation, the notion of space occupying the place where the breast used to be but is no longer, means that the notion of space occupies the place of the absence of the object, as the silence in music, as a caesura, as a notion of otherness. The breast is an Other, that can be present or absent.

The emotional turbulences, those that are disturbing for the personality (taking now the model of the reflection in a lake that is blurred by a wind), have a different kind of transformation in a work of art, as the hair in Leonardo's drawings shows. Leonardo's painting is a transformation in art, a special and very talented kind of thinking. In his paper "Caesura", Bion proposes the model of Picasso's drawing on a glass pane that can be seen from both sides as a creative model of the contact-barrier, a semi-permeable membrane, a caesura that separates the conscious from the unconscious. On the one hand, the alpha elements that are produced allow investigation of the relationship between the real parents and a transformational relationship, through this realisation of the relationship is preconceived by the oedipal preconception. As has already been mentioned, the new transformational cycle towards mental growth is that of $K \leftrightarrow O$. As we have already established, transformations in K mean "knowing about", and, as I see it, transformations in O in psychoanalysis mean, for example, some moments of insight that are different from just knowing. These transformations in O are transformations in *being*.

In "arithmetical transformations" which, according to the Bionian hypothesis, elaborate and transform the anxieties of fragmentation described by Klein due to phantasied attacks of the object; catastrophic anxieties related to the whole or fragmented state of the object and the ego are reflected through the modulation of this anxiety into calm water, having been detoxified through reverie–alpha function. This detoxification enables the transformation of what Klein described as the paranoid–schizoid and depressive positions in Bion's dynamic $PS \leftrightarrow D$ oscillation, a mental function that is an oscillation between states of mind when facing uncertainties, still unintegrated situations, and moments of integrated objects or situations. This transformation leads towards the discovery of the selected fact, and the nomination links the experiences with the infant's language skills. So, the infant says "da-da-da", and this utterance is transformed by the name provided by the mother—"yes, daddy!"—and links the experiences to a name in the infant's mind. In the evolution of $K \leftrightarrow O$ and of $O \leftrightarrow K$, the name becomes polysemic, metaphorical, and can continue acquiring new meaning with new experiences. In clinical practice, using Klein's theory, we could consider this in terms of reparation; with Bion's hypothesis, we can consider it as a transformation into thought through the metabolisation of primitive anxieties.

CHAPTER THIRTEEN

Tropisms and mental growth

In psychoanalysis we usually speak of instincts. Bion speaks also of tropisms, so I want first to introduce the reader to what is meant by tropism. The definition of tropism is that plants can detect changes in the environment and respond to them. The most frequent response for plants consists of growing slowly in a certain direction, as defined by the stimuli. These may be:

- positive, when the plant grows towards the stimulus;
- negative, when the direction is the opposite.

Viral tropism

From a cellular point of view, there is also the so-called viral tropism, when a type of virus has a highly specific attraction towards a particular cell, determined in part by the surface markers in that cell. The virus develops a specific ability to attack the cells selectively, as well as the host's organs, and often certain cell populations that are found in the organs of the host's body.

166   ON MENTAL GROWTH

The autistic frozen desert and the psychotic turbulence

> I would make a distinction between existence – the capacity to exist –
> and the ambition or aspiration to have an existence which is worth
> having – the quality of the existence, not the quantity; not the length
> of one's life, but the quality of that life. (Bion, 1979, p. 249)

In her autobiography, entitled *In Praise of Imperfection* (1987), author
Rita Levy Montalcini, an Italian physician who won a Nobel Prize for
her discoveries about neurotransmitters, has some interesting ideas to
which I will now refer. She praises the imperfection of man, who is
born premature and incomplete, but with great potential for development, unlike other species, such as insects. Montalcini speaks of the
evolution of our species and, above all, the evolution of the brain,
which has grown and mutated. However, the mutations mostly
affected the cortex, the grey matter associated with intellect, with
reason, the intellectual side which, besides mutating, can continue
evolving towards mental growth, not only biologically, but also
because it receives cultural influences. But there is another system, an
older one: the limbic system. Bion calls it thalamic, or subthalamic,
and speaks of subthalamic terrors. The limbic system cannot mutate
because it regulates emotions or their biological reactions—such as the
adrenalin discharge—as well as such vital mechanisms as breathing
and heartbeat. The relationship between the evolved cortex, which
receives the influences of culture, and the limbic system is not prede-
termined, and there might or might not be established connections,
which can also have varying characteristics.

Bion speaks about tropisms in his posthumously published book,
Cogitations. In those of his works published during his lifetime, his
only references to this hypothesis—in my opinion—are in the discussions of of narcissism and socialism in Chapter Six of *Transformations*.
We do not know the date at which this hypothesis was formulated,
but, in my opinion, they are related to the idea of an embryonic mind
that he puts forward in his paper "Caesura", with the hypothesis of
somatic anticipation of what will later be transformed into emotions.
This notion of tropisms is also strongly related to the conjectures
about prenatal and protomental functioning that we find in his work
from *Experiences in Groups* onward.

The tropism hypothesis is also related to the investigation of
the characteristics of the primitive mind and its possible evolution,

referring to a primitive kind of communication: realistic projective identification and the environmental circumstances that this kind of communication meets. As we will see, these circumstances allude to a human environment that we also find in his work relating to maternal reverie, alpha function, etc., and which contribute to psychoanalysis with an understanding of mental growth and its obstacles. I am going to anticipate some of these ideas and develop them later on. In *Cogitations*, Bion says that tropisms are seekers of objects that can receive them and, at the same time, transform this type of primitive communication. He says that, therefore, tropisms can be communicated.

In this chapter, I refer to mental growth in connection with the development of potential through the transformation of primitive, proto-emotional, prenatal aspects, and I approach this subject from the perspective of tropisms. The development of potential in the human being is an evolution that can either fail or be achieved in different ways.

These ideas have important implications in psychoanalytic clinical practice. Psychoanalysis has investigated the primitive mind from its beginning and, as for all the hypotheses presented in this book, these are disturbing and generate turbulence which we need to face; this implies that it also demands of the reader a change that, in a way, illustrates this turbulence.

To go deeper into the hypothesis I am proposing, I use elements of Bion's ideas, which I consider vital for understanding this author's journey from the first notions about primitive mechanisms (already present in *Experiences in Groups*) and disturbed functioning (the psychotic and non-psychotic part of the personality) to his formulations on learning from emotional experience and the elaboration of a notion of the personality's development towards mental growth. This will help us understand the options available for the transformation of tropisms and its consequences for personality.

In *Cogitations* (1992, p. 34), Bion refers to tropisms as follows:

> Tropisms may be communicated. In certain circumstances they are too powerful for the modes of communication available to the personality. This, presumably, may be because the personality is too weak or ill-developed if the traumatic situation arrives prematurely. But when this situation does arise, all the future development of the personality depends on whether an object—the breast—exists into which the

168   ON MENTAL GROWTH

> tropisms can be projected. If it does not, the result is a disaster which ultimately takes the form of loss of contact with reality, apathy, or mania. . . . If such an object exists, a breast capable of tolerating projective identification which is thrust into it (for it is to projective identification in relation to the breast that I have now returned), then the outcome may be supposed to be more favorable, although in suspense.

Why does Bion say "in suspense"? Because the result depends on the transformational quality of the breast–object–container: if it is an object with reverie that can accept projective identifications and transform them so they become tolerable for the infant's personality, the infant will then be able to reintroject that part of his personality. My hypothesis is that tropisms are linked, on the one hand, with O, since Bion says that they need to be rescued from the infinite formless void, and, on the other, with their development as emotional links. My conjecture is that tropisms become emotional links L (love), H (hate) and K (disposition to know) through the mediation of a breast that is capable of receiving and transforming them, giving them a meaning. This conjecture is a bridge to understanding certain technical considerations in clinical practice, in order to develop an adequate container–contained relationship.

As we have already considered in the first chapters of this book, after *Experiences in Groups* and *Second Thoughts*, Bion presents his theory of emotions as the central core of psychic life and, in this sense, the K link, the disposition to know, is as primary and fundamental a link as love (L) and hate (H).

With this conception of the K link, several psychoanalytical concepts are reassessed, and even changed, due to his theory of reverie, dreamwork alpha, and the alpha function. The reader should remember that the K link, as an emotional link (as the disposition to know and not as the possession of knowledge), differs substantially from the Freudian conception of knowledge as the product of the sublimation of childhood sexual curiosity, and neither is it conceived as an epistemophilic instinct, as in Klein. Could we conceive of a tropism as the disposition to know that is transformed into a K link through a containing object that provides meaning?

With these changes in the vertex of observation, the first object— the breast, the mother (and the analyst in the analytical process)— becomes an object that provides containing forms and meanings of what evolves from O, which—as we discussed in Chapter Nine—Bion borrows from Kant in naming it unknowable ultimate reality, and from Milton to define O as the formless, infinite void. In the evolution of the personality, the encounter with this meaning-providing object is fundamental, either through maternal reverie or the analyst's alpha function.

Meaning is the nutrient of the mind, of the personality. The infant's personality, as that of the patient's in analysis, might be too weak for these powerful means of communication. If they do not find an object equivalent to the nourishing breast that can receive the tropisms and transform them, or if it is hostile to this primitive form of communication, the situation becomes traumatic and could have disastrous consequences, as we shall see. The containing object that provides meaning fosters understanding, learning from experience and wisdom. It is an object that contributes to the development of the mental equipment that is needed to face changes, to grow, and contain the turbulence that this process generates.

This object provider of meanings is different from the breast provider of services, such as the toilet-breast (Meltzer, 1967) or the gratifying or frustrating breast (Klein, 1952). Neither does it equate to the total breast-object of the depressive position, although, in my understanding, if everything goes well, the evolution of the mother mind–baby mind relationship includes both the capability of integration and the tolerance of moments of depression and uncertainty.

The container–contained relationship has a fundamental role here. With the idea of maternal reverie as a container of the primitive projective identifications of the infant and as a psychosomatic channel of communication through which the mother transmits what she feels for the baby and the father, the environmental factor acquires a psychoanalytical meaning for the first time. The notion of tropism complements this psychoanalytical understanding of the environmental factor as the setting, or emotional atmosphere. With this conception, the equivalent of the nourishing breast is a breast whose function of being receptive to primitive kinds of communications and providing meaning is fundamental for the process of humanisation and mental growth. This is the context in which the description of a catastrophic anxiety emerges, possibly the most fundamental state of helplessness of humankind as thinking beings: the fear of an imminent catastrophe. When reverie fails to transform the

170 ON MENTAL GROWTH

primitive states of mind and emotions, this anxiety becomes a nameless dread.

As I have already mentioned, Bion defines tropisms as seekers of objects and says that they can be communicated. I refer to the extract from *Cogitations* (this volume, pp. 167–168) to draw the reader's attention to Bion's description of tropisms which can be too powerful in relation to the means of communication available to the personality.

Tropisms as seekers of objects that can be communicated

One way of describing this communication is that the infant launches a primitive emotion into outside space, through projective identification, which is also a primitive method of communication, as we saw in Chapter Three. Through his crying, screaming, kicking, and his gaze, the infant transmits the emotion as a probe seeking an object that can contain and transform it. Freud had already stated in the *Project* that the infant's crying, when in contact with a fellow human being, becomes communication.

Once again, why does Bion say *in suspense*? The patient needs us to be receptive to his modes of primitive communication and to be able to modulate his catastrophic anxieties. If this communication finds an object with reverie that can accept projective identifications and transform it so that it becomes tolerable for the patient's (or infant's) personality, he will be able to reintroject that part of his personality; otherwise, the situation becomes traumatic because it is too premature, an important factor in Bion's ideas. Another factor is the too weak or underdeveloped personality, which increases the possibility of the situation becoming traumatic. A relevant question is whether or not, in Bion's theories, the notion of traumatic situation is associated to the conception of an undigested fact. In my opinion, the model of undigested facts is a very good model that leads to the model of one of the aims of psychoanalytic treatment: the digestion or elaboration of undigested facts, a notion that has been fundamental since Freud's developments. In clinical practice, the patient depends on the analyst's alpha function to receive and transform the traumatic situation, with all its defensive deformations.

In terms of what interests us from a clinical standpoint, out of the three tropisms that Bion describes (parasitism, murder, and creation), he suggests that the one which predominates in the patient who comes to analysis is the one of creation, which implies the seeking of an object with which projective identification might be possible as a realistic method of communication. In *Cogitations*, he also states that the infant's tolerance of frustration is not of primary importance, because, I suppose, that it also depends on the mediation of reverie, but it is a factor which is interesting for the psychoanalytic clinical practice. A patient who comes with little tolerance of frustration will have more difficulties with a psychoanalytical treatment that inevitably implies frustration, and will need more of the analyst's alpha function and capability to modulate the catastrophic anxieties and traumatic states of helplessness.

In my opinion, by classifying them as tropisms, Bion includes them within the characteristics of life (even predators and parasites are part of life, and not of the inanimate world. We have already seen that there are viral tropisms that attack healthy cells).

In human beings, the tropisms described by Bion are greatly dependent on transformations. They can evolve towards transformations in thought, can become more virulent, or even wither or freeze. Obviously, to dream of a murder, write a detective novel, or paint a picture depicting a murder is not the same thing as commiting the act of murder itself. When tropisms freeze, as in my hypothesis regarding autism, the patient can sometimes express it from a non-autistic part of his or her personality, such as a patient of mine, Pablo, did by saying that he felt he was "withering". The consideration that creation is the tropism that predominates in the patient who seeks analysis is of great clinical importance.

Unlike instincts or drives, tropisms are not theoretical hypotheses, they are observable: taking phototropism as a model, it is obvious that plants seek light, or, in the case of roots, the earth. One of the essential traits of tropisms is their sensitivity to environmental changes. A flower has certain needs regarding light, temperature, etc.; if it does not find them, it withers. We shall return to this point in connection with maternal reverie.

I think that it is important now to resume my hypothesis of the relationship between transformation of tropisms and emotional links, which are channels of communication between the inner and outer reality (Pistiner de Cortiñas, 2007). My hypothesis, interpreting some of Bion's ideas and his subsequent developments, is that the encounter

172   ON MENTAL GROWTH

with this container object that provides meaning transforms tropisms into emotional links of love, hate, and the disposition to know. The infant not only communicates the tropisms through the primitive means available to him, but also attempts to control them. I resume the idea because I am now interested in describing the relationship between the tropisms and the *self* and what are in my opinion the *disastrous consequences* that Bion mentions in the quotation from *Cogitations*. As I have said above, if all goes well for the infant or the patient, tropisms, transformed into emotional links, return to the personality that has identified them through projective identification to an object that can receive and return them as something with a tolerable meaning, as a part of the personality that now can be assimilated. If all does not go well, they can undergo different transformations which I shall discuss later on.

Regarding the self, what I find very interesting and in line with some of Winnicott's notions (among other authors who take into account the infant's initial helplessness and the environment that surrounds his emotional development), is that Bion gives priority to the emotional links with the self: this first transformation of tropisms into links of love, hate, and self-knowledge is necessary for the development of emotional growth in the personality. These L, H, and K links with the self are top priority; Bion calls them narcis-sism (hyphenated) and, according to how they develop, this development is reflected in the object relationships (that Bion calls social-ism). This formulation is a revolution, considering the Kleinian hypothesis of envy, guilt, and reparation, where the priority is given to the link with the object and not with the self. The development of emotional links with the self is a precondition for discovering the other and how the nature of the object relationships will be.

With the tropism hypothesis, the development of the mental equipment and the matrix functions for thinking are very much related to these "environmental" circumstances. A primordial source of catastrophic anxiety for Bion, as we have described in other chapters, is that the infant has no notion of absence, so the absence of meaning is experienced not only as a nameless terror, but is also perceived as if the source of all meaning had been lost or destroyed. In Chapter Six of *Transformations*, Bion says that if the infant does not find this transformative object for which he has a meaning, it seeks a god for whom it does have meaning. This is the god that we have already mentioned several times: the super-superego, the moral conscience without morality. This primitive superego, hostile to primitive communication, is described by Bion as a murderer of the ego and is one of the central obstacles to a creative transformation that can generate a new evolution towards mental growth. Moreover, the object that rejects this primitive means of communication (projective identification) is internalised by the infant and becomes an internal object that is hostile to this kind of communication. This causes many difficulties and misunderstandings that are a challenge in psychoanalytical clinical practice. The infant's or patient's personality also rejects the tropisms and, as we shall see, they can then remain lodged in the means of communication, which, paradoxically, prevents them from being useful for that communication: if the eyes are used for projective identification, instead of seeing they project, while if speaking is used in an evacuative way, it cannot be used to communicate, etc. We can understand that this adds to the clinical difficulties, since psychoanalytical treatment depends on the existence of communication. In psychoanalysis, discovering these objects and getting the patient to develop genuine ego functions clears the way to dismantling the crystallisations, the exoskeletons, and to the process of becoming more authentic with himself.

So, a relevant question arises, representing a true challenge in psychoanalytical theory: is the tropism hypothesis a different way of defining the object relationship—at a very primitive level—as a search for a containing object? Is this what Bion later includes in the notion of innate preconceptions, clearly a much more complex hypothesis? Are tropisms what he will later describe as the links that form the matrix of contact with reality? If we think of the definition of tropism as the way in which plants can detect changes in the environment and respond to them, the idea of the relationship between the tropism brought by the infant and environmental conditions becomes very significant.

> The tropisms are the matrix from which all mental life springs. For maturation to be possible they need to be won from the void and communicated. Just as a breast, or its equivalent, is necessary for the infant life to be sustained, so it is necessary that a mental counterpart, the primitive breast, should exist for mental life to be sustained. (Bion, 1992, p. 34)

Meaning is the nutrient of mental life.

174   ON MENTAL GROWTH

My hypothesis, which I have already advanced, is that in these descriptions of unknown date included in *Cogitations*, we find a precedent for the idea of O, the infinite formless void from which something evolves, and, in the light of these ideas, in my opinion, what evolves is the tropism, the matrix of mental life, which can be transformed into a link, in the relationship with a breast with reverie, or, in the session, through the analyst's alpha function. It is the evolution of OA↔K, an evolution in which what is formless takes on the form of a link. In my opinion, the whole personality could be included in O, as what is not yet transformed. The personality *must* evolve; therefore, these transformations are always necessary to prevent crystallisation or ossification and deterioration. For an evolution towards growth, it is necessary to develop a *shape* out of the infinite formless void—in other words, a meaning, a narrative container skin, which I referred to when speaking of dreams, myths, and models. Yet, in order to dismantle what has been crystallised or the disastrous consequences that Bion refers to and which open the path to evolution and mental growth, there is another necessary step: the transformation of K→O in order to become that which was obtained through K.

Taking psychoanalytical clinical practice into account, I am going to insist, at the risk of repeating myself, on the ideas I have been developing throughout this book. The optimal transformation for the construction and discovery of emotional meanings is dreamlike thought and the playing that is the continuation of dreaming in waking life. In the light of these ideas, I think that what evolves from O, if we consider it as the primitive tropism, can be transformed into an emotional link of love, hate, and disposition to know through the mother's reverie and, in session, through the analyst's alpha function. This implies developing functions or mental equipment for the patient to enable him to develop a mental skin and, at the same time, become more authentic. Therefore, a new step is the transformation of K to O, becoming that which one has discovered one is becoming, and being in unity with it. Considering these ideas from the point of view of mental growth as well as from an analytical process, both the development of self-knowledge and becoming one with oneself are necessary.

I refe again to the extract from *Cogitations* this volume, pp. 167–168) about communication to expand on other possible circumstances and transformations that can lead to mental deterioration and to which Bion refers as disastrous consequences:

In *Cogitations* (p. 34), Bion continues by saying,

Just as a breast, or its equivalent, is necessary for the infant life to be sustained, so it is necessary that a mental counterpart, the primitive breast, should exist for mental life to be sustained. The vehicle of communication – the infant's cry, tactile and visual senses – is engaged in order not only to communicate but also to control the tropism. If all goes well the communication, by projective identification, leads (as Melanie has described) to the deposition in the breast of the tropisms that the infant can neither control, modify nor develop, but which can be so controlled and developed after they have been modified by the object.

If this breaks down, then the vehicle of communication, the contact with reality, the links of every kind of which I have spoken, suffer a significant fate. This applies particularly to the communicating particles that are felt to lie with their enclosed tropisms, rejected by psyche and object alike.

In order to develop these hypotheses, I add that in the infant the vehicles of communication, its crying, its way of looking at things, its way of listening, etc., are his contact with external reality, along with intuition, which we might consider here as a transformed tropism and as a contact with internal reality. So, contact with both external and internal reality requires the factor of tropism transformation.

Here, we find once again a precursor of O; tropisms must be won from the void and be communicated through reverie of the alpha function. As I have already described throughout the book and in this chapter, what happens if they are rejected is that they return as a catastrophic anxiety, which leads to helplessness and its possible reverse side: an arrogant, omnipotent, and omniscient super-super-ego, an object that is hostile to this kind of primitive communication. Furthermore, if they are also rejected by the infant's personality, they become more virulent, settle in, and become parasites of the means of communication; in other words, projective identification is hypertrophied, and contact with reality deteriorates. This happens in psychotic turbulence.

In the case of autism, my conjecture is that when faced with an apathetic response in an infant who is highly sensitive to the object's mental states, it is possible that projective identification as a means of communication is halted, and that tropisms freeze and are substituted

176   ON MENTAL GROWTH

by adhesive identification. The disastrous consequence is that the connection with reality withers; this maight be what we mean when we say that projective identifications stop.

We have mentioned that, among the disastrous consequences if this search fails, is the transformation of this anxiety into a nameless dread, an anxiety that reflects the lack of meaning, which is felt as a loss of the breast-object as the provider of meaning for the emotional experience. I insist on the idea that the infant at first does not have the notion of absence, so when the meaning is absent, the infant experiences it as if it had been destroyed, and if the outcome is a psychotic turbulence, the infant feels that the object has rejected the tropism and stripped it of meaning. In this case, the consequence for the personality is a deterioration that could result in psychic death.

I would like to mention three disastrous consequences which I have already touched on before and am now going to expand: psychotic turbulence, which I am going to separate according to two different transformational forms, and a third disastrous consequence of another type, which I have named the autistic frozen desert.

The psychotic world has a violent turbulence tinged with attacks on links and linking, and a hypertrophied primitive means of communication (projective identification), which was realistic in its origin but became excessive due to a lack of containment. When there is a rejection of the infant's projective identifications, and there is also an inversion of the reverie channel, the mother's projective identifications are received by the infant instead of she being the one who receives and contains this primitive kind of communication. We must bear in mind that reverie is also a psychosomatic communication channel (with David Liberman, we called this type of maternal rejection "the mother who rejects" or, worse, "the mother who throws bombs", meaning that she uses projective identification with her infant not as a means of communication, but as an evacuation of feelings she cannot tolerate and contain (Liberman et al., 1983)); in this case, when there is an inversion of the direction of this channel, we will probably see the consequences as psychotic turbulence or psychosomatic disorders. What predominates are projective transformations, hypertrophied projective identifications, and, instead of the infant reintrojecting an object with a capability for reverie and an alpha function, what returns to the infant is this super-superego, which Bion describes as a moral conscience without morality, that usurps the functions of the ego of discernment, attention, and proof of reality, among others. It is also possible for tropisms to remain at the level of the somatic mechanisms that anticipate emotions, such as, for example, the adrenalin discharge, and, thus, the body can become ill with one of the mysterious self-immune illnesses that still require investigation. The hypothesis of the tropism might contribute some elements to the research and understanding of the psychosomatic disturbances.

I want now to differentiate between what happens with patients in whom what predominates is projective transformations and those who function mostly with transformations in hallucinosis. With the hypothesis of a container–contained relationship that can be symbiotic, commensal, or parasitic, we can identify a situation where projective transformation prevails, when the violence of the projective identifications that have not been contained and given meaning by the reverie function tend to be evacuated and do not allow the development of ideograms, which are the sensory impressions formed by the images that are the furniture of dreams. Ideograms are evacuated through a hypertrophied projective identification, so the means of communication, of contact with internal and external reality, are invaded by the tropisms because they are rejected both by the infant's personality and the object, as we have seen. The eyes are not used for seeing, or the ears for hearing, etc., but for projective identification.

A vicious circle emerges in which there is no differentiation between the sense impression and the object of the external world. However, in this case, if what predominates is the tropism of creation, the analyst's alpha function can transform crude, primitive emotions into alpha elements, the analytic process generates an adequate container, and the patient can start reintrojecting what he evacuated, transformed into tolerable aspects of his personality; also, the patient could, through this process, develop his own alpha function. The patient also becomes capable of distinguishing between psychic and external reality. When that happens, we find that these patients start to dream, to value their dreams, and to generate a space in their inner world for alpha function and dreamlike thoughts, which are the providers of emotional meaning, which provides nourishment for the mind and is a very significant factor in mental growth.

In transformations in hallucinosis, what predominates are envious rivalry and the arrogant super-superego. The method of transformation into hallucinosis is considered superior to the psychoanalytical

178   ON MENTAL GROWTH

method. Contact with reality has been more damaged than in the projective transformations of the tropisms; it is also possible that what predominates are the tropisms of parasitism and murder which have not been transformed into dreams, and these generate intolerable terror and mental pain along with a toxic system of lies. However, when this kind of transformation predominates in analysis, as I pointed out in Chapter Ten, the first task is to consider and modify this rivalry of methods, as far as possible; if this is not achieved, instead of a space for the development of dreamlike thoughts, we are left with a hallucinotic space; it is not the transformation of a "poppy field into a painting" (Bion, 1965), or even a projective transformation that can generate a kind of void that provokes mental pain in the patient. In the hallucinotic world, dreamlike elements have been substituted by lies and hallucinosis; it is a toxic world, not only for the mind of the person who is generating lies, but also for the mind of those who come into contact with such toxicity.

Another possibility is that the response to the search for the tropism of an object with which projective identification is possible might be lack of answer, an apathy, such as in autism. In the case of apathy as a result of maternal depression, if combined with an infant who is very sensitive to the mental states of the object and an absent father, my conjecture, as I have already pointed out, is that the tropisms wither or freeze, resulting in what I have called the autistic frozen desert.

Psychoanalytical exploration in autistic children reveals conditions of "non-contact", of a halting of projective identifications, substituted by adhesive identifications linked to a particular fusion of their own bodies with the body of the object. The tactile sense predominates, resulting in the child using objects to produce autistic sensations, which is different from an object relationship because what matters is the sensation the object produces: for example, when the child holds it in his hand. For the autistic child, a toy is not an object to play with; it is something hard to hold on to, which generates tactile sensations that enable the child to feel connected. Autistic infants are intolerant of the awareness of separation between tongue and nipple; they experience this separation not as an absence of the object, but as a hole in their own bodies. Such a feeling of separation is terrifying, which leads the children to develop spurious soothing sensations that result in further disconnection from others.

A body which is felt as being full of holes protects itself from terrifying experiences by wrapping itself in a whirlwind of self-generated sensations, which strengthen the lack of attention to shared realities and hinder the awareness of normal sensations.

Disconnections leave holes in the place where relationships should be.

I illustrate these ideas with a clinical experience by referring to a patient whom I will name John. He was born at a time when his mother had just lost her own grandmother, the woman who had raised her because her own mother had suffered from depression all her life. When John was born (a Caesarean birth), his mother, confused, believed that he had died. Afterwards, she became very depressed and could not tolerate the baby's intense gaze. The father was absent most of the time and John started breastfeeding only when the father returned and they were able to go on a family vacation. However, the mother's depression and fragility continued, as well as the father's absences. The baby began showing signs of autism, avoiding all visual contact. The parents decided to seek consultation and John started an analysis when he was three years old.

In this analysis, he demonstrated a capability for making contact and communicating from a non-autistic part of his personality, while, at the same time, falling back again and again into clinging to autistic manoeuvres (the protective shell described by Frances Tustin) and autistic objects of sensation, inanimate objects that generated spurious sensations. These manoeuvres and objects belong to a lifeless world that is different from the psychotic world (Pistiner de Cortiñas, 2007). In an advanced stage of the analysis, John oscillated between moments of playing and moments of taking refuge in the sensations of his autistic world, such as turning his back and licking the window pane, disconnecting himself from all human contact.

Maternal depression and paternal absence combine with the infant's high sensitivity to the object's mental states; the response of the breast-object that nourishes mental life is not that of rejection, but apathy; it is a lack of an answer. We can hypothesise this absence of reverie as an emotional disconnection of reverie as a communication channel and that, in the case of autism, the tropisms are faced in a kind of void without vitality. It is not rejection, such as in psychotic turbulence, but more an absence of emotional connection. In the autistic zone of non-transformation, tropisms are stripped of vitality,

180 ON MENTAL GROWTH

frozen, and the development of embryonic thinking stops, which truncates the development of a consciousness capable of awareness. We find a diminished, truncated consciousness (Pistiner de Cortiñas, 2007). Among the functions that are most affected by disconnection, annulment, and isolation are memory, attention, judgement, and curiosity. These undeveloped, arrested functions, the isolation, and the emotional and cognitive disconnection allow for the conjecture of frozen tropisms and their lack of transformation into L, H and K links.

We can see this kind of devitalisation in clinical practice when the method the patient uses to face problems or unresolved issues is an oscillation between devitalisation and automation through rituals, where the animate world becomes inanimate. People are either non-existent or are treated as things that can be controlled or erased, and mimetic language is used to generate the illusion of non-separation. When this process can be reversed, we discover that the patient perceives all that is vital as dangerous and has sought refuge in an inanimate world, as a kind of protective shell, in the words of Tustin, surrounded by "things" and isolated from all emotional contact.

A fundamental question for clinical practice is how we can help these patients to escape from this frozen, inanimate world and access the possibility of a creative transformation of their tropisms.

In my book, *The Aesthetic Dimension of the Mind* (2007), I put forward the hypothesis that there is a need to create for the personality a "space for playing" and discuss this. I also propose other technical resources, such as the personification of emotions and the need for a more active intervention to stop the autistic manoeuvres (such as John's licking of the window pane) that keep the child or the adult in that arid world with untransformed terrors.

Escaping from that arid world, where tropisms remain frozen, and creating a space for playing provides the patient with the possibility of not only transforming the tropisms into play and playing, but also implies opening a space for the oedipal preconception to be vitalised and, thereby, enabling exploration of the relationship between the real parents. This exploration permits the bridging of the caesuras between the infant's part of the personality and a more mature understanding, from another perspective of the infantile part of the personality. Both dreaming, in Bion's extended definition, and playing are vital developments for the differentiation between psychic and external reality and contribute to the vitalisation and transformation of tropisms.

Dreaming and playing also develop and provide spaces for projection in which, as is the case with reverie, dreamlike imagery and play give back parts of the personality with a meaning which now, having become more tolerable, can be reintrojected. In my clinical experience, I could see that what these children or adults stimulate in the analyst is tenderness, unlike the violence of the psychotic turbulence, which requires other technical resources. Furthermore, I have observed that when these patients emerge from their autistic world, they very often lean towards aesthetic developments, such as painting, music, or theatre. These are means of expression of emotional states of mind with reverie that, as often happens with works of art, also have a reverie function for other people.

The same goes for the patients in whom excessive adaptation to external reality functions as an exoskeleton; when they can abandon their prosthetics and generate an endoskeleton, often through dreams and playing, their evolution towards mental growth is to find more poetry and more life in their lives.

As for psychotic turbulence, if we are dealing with problems arising from hypertrophied projective transformations, then, although we sometimes face a toxic atmosphere and misunderstandings generated by transformations into –K, of active disavowal, the analyst's alpha function—if all goes well—slowly enables tropisms to be transformed by creating a relational space in the session for dreaming and playing and prevents tropisms from becoming parasites of the means of communication with internal and external reality. This space for dreaming and playing, related to the development of mental functions, also opens up the field to substitute atonement, thanks to the alpha function, which enables us to differentiate between dreams, external and internal, and psychic reality. Atonement is related to the primitive super-superego, the at-one-ment, that way of being in unity with oneself described by Bion as becoming one with oneself. In my opinion, Bion is playing with words when he suggests that at-one-ment is like being in unity with oneself, in contrast with atonement, a word which means expiation and which I relate to the super-superego.

The development of the matrix functions of thinking, starting with embryonic thought, also opens up a space in which the patient can exist and feel that he can be himself. The development of this space and the notion of time as a fourth dimension—linear time—also opens up the possibility of growing up while accepting limits and responsibilities.

THE GRID EXTENDED

	1 Definitory Hypotheses	2 ψ	3 Notation	4 Attention	5 Inquiry	6 Action	7 Fanatic use	8 Autistic use	...n
A β-elements	A1	A2				A6	A7	A8	
B α-elements	B1	B2	B3	B4	B5	B6	B7	B8	....Bn
C Dream Thoughts, Dreams, Myths	C1	C2	C3	C4	C5	C6	C7	C8	....Cn
D Pre-conception	D1	D2	D3	D4	D5	D6	D7	D8	....Dn
E Conception	E1	E2	E3	E4	E5	E6	E7	E8	....En
F Concept	F1	F2	F3	F4	F5	F6	F7	F8	...Fn
G Scientific Deductive System		G2					G7	G8	...Gn
H Algebraic Calculus									

Figure 1. Bion's Grid.

NOTE

1. *Bhagavad-Gita* is an important sacred Hindu scripture. It is a book that contains very profound aspects of Hindu philosophy. It is considered to be one of the most important religious classics of the world, and is part of the epic text *Mahabharata*. It has 700 verses. *Bhagavad-Gita* means "the song of Bhagaván" (God, the one who is almighty). Its content is the conversation between Krishna and Aryuna on the battlefield just prior to the beginning of the battle of Kurukshetra. Answering the moral dilemma and confusion of Aryuna, Krishna explains to him his duties as a warrior and a prince.

REFERENCES

Aronofsky, D. (Dir.) (1998). *Pi*. Artisan Entertainment.

Baranger, W., & Baranger, M. (1968). *Problemans del Campo Psicoanalítico*. Buenos Aires: Kargieman.

Bergman, I. (Dir.) (1957). *Smultronstället*. AB Svensk Filmindustri.

Bergman, I. (1990). *Bilder*. Barcelona: Tusquets.

Bion, W. R. (1950). The imaginary twin. In: *Second Thoughts* (pp. 3–22). London: Karnac, 1984.

Bion, W. R. (1954). Notes on the theory of schizophrenia. *International Journal of Psychoanalysis*, 35(2): 113–118.

Bion, W. R. (1956). The development of schizophrenic thought. *International Journal of Psychoanalysis*, 37(4–5): 344–346.

Bion, W. R. (1957). Differentiation of the psychotic from the non-psychotic personalities. *International Journal of Psychoanalysis, 38*(3–4) [reprinted in: *Second Thoughts* (pp. 43–64). London: Heinemann, 1967].

Bion, W. R. (1958a). On hallucination. In: *Second Thoughts* (pp. 65–85). London: Karnac, 1984.

Bion, W. R. (1958b). On arrogance. *International Journal of Psychoanalysis*, 39: 144–146.

Bion, W. R. (1959). Attacks on linking. *International Journal of Psychoanalysis*, 40: 308–315. Also published in *Second Thoughts*, London: Heinemann, 1967 [reprinted London: Karnac, 1984].

186   REFERENCES

Bion, W. R. (1961). *Experiences in Groups*. London: Tavistock.

Bion, W. R. (1962a). *Learning from Experience*. London: Heinemann.

Bion, W. R. (1962b). A theory of thinking. *International Journal of Psychoanalysis*, 43: 306–310.

Bion, W. R. (1963). *Elements of Psycho-analysis*. London: Heinemann.

Bion, W. R. (1965). *Transformations: Change from Learning to Growth*. London: Heinemann.

Bion, W. R. (1967). *Second Thoughts*. London: Heinemann. [reprinted London: Karnac, 1984]

Bion, W. R. (1970). *Attention and Interpretation*. London: Tavistock. [reprinted London: Karnac, 1984].

Bion, W. R. (1976a). Emotional turbulence. In: *Clinical Seminars and Other Works* (pp. 295–305). Oxford: Fleetwood, 1987 [reprinted London: Karnac, 1994].

Bion, W. R. (1976b). On a quotation from Freud. In: *Clinical Seminars and Other Works* (pp. 306–311). Oxford: Fleetwood, 1987 [reprinted London: Karnac, 1994].

Bion, W. R. (1976c). Evidence. In: *Clinical Seminars and Other Works* (pp. 312–320). Oxford: Fleetwood, 1987 [reprinted London: Karnac, 1994].

Bion, W. R. (1977). *Two Papers: The Grid and Caesura*. Rio de Janeiro: Imago [reprinted London: Karnac, 1989].

Bion, W. R. (1979). Making the best of a bad job. In: *Clinical Seminars and Four Papers* (pp. 321–332). Oxford: Fleetwood, 1987 [reprinted London: Karnac, 1994].

Bion, W. R. (1980). *Bion in New York and Sao Paulo*. Strathtay, Perthshire: Clunie Press.

Bion, W. R. (1982). *A Long Week-end*. London: Fleetwood [reprinted London: Karnac, 1991].

Bion, W. R. (1985). *All My Sins Remembered: Another Part of a Life and the Other Side of Genius: Family Letteras*. London: Fleetwood [reprinted London: Karnac, 1991].

Bion, W. R. (1991). *A Memoir of the Future. Book I: The Dream; Book II: The Past Presented; Book III: The Dawn of Oblivion*. London: Karnac.

Bion, W. R. (1992). *Cogitations*. London: Karnac.

Bion, W. R. (2005). *The Tavistock Seminars*. F. Bion (Ed.). London: Karnac.

Bléandonu, G. (1994). *Wilfred Bion, his Life and his Work*. London: Free Association Books.

Borges, J. L. (1944). Funes el memorioso. In: *Ficciones* (pp. 485–490). Buenos Aires: Emecé.

Brecht, B. (1939). *Leben des Galilei*. Zurich: Surhkamp.

Einstein, A. (1931). *Living Philosophies*. New York: AMS Press.

REFERENCES   187

Etchegoyen, H. (1986). *Los fundamentos de la técnica psicoanalítica*. Buenos Aires: Amorrortu Editores.

Freud, S. (1897). Letter to W. Fliess, 21 September 1897. *S. E.*, *1*: 259. London: Hogarth.

Freud, S. (1900a). *The Interpretation of Dreams*. *S. E.*, *4–5*. London: Hogarth.

Freud, S. (1911b). Formulations on the two principles of mental functioning. *S. E.*, *12*: 218–226. London: Hogarth.

Freud, S. (1921c). *Group Psychology and the Analysis of the Ego*. *S. E.*, *18*: 67–143. London: Hogarth.

Freud, S. (1923b). *The Ego and the Id*. *S. E.*, *19*: 3–66. London: Hogarth.

Freud, S. (1927e). Fetishism. *S. E.*, *21*: 152–157. London: Hogarth.

Freud, S. (1950[1895]). *Project for a Scientific Psychology*. *S. E.*, *1*: 281–391. London: Hogarth.

Green, J. (1947). *Si j'etais vous . . . [If I Were You]*. London: Eyre, 1950.

Grotstein, J. (2009). *". . . But at the Same Time and at Another Level . . ."* (Volume 1). London: Karnac.

Heimann, P. (1950). On countertransference. *International Journal of Psychoanalysis*, *31*: 81–84.

Jonze, S. (Dir.) (1999). *Being John Malkovich*. USA Films.

Klein, M. (1946). Notes on some schizoid mechanisms. *International Journal of Psychoanalysis*, *27*: 99–110 [reprinted in *Envy and Gratitude and Other Works 1946–1963*. London: Karnac, 1997].

Klein, M. (1952). *Some Theoretical Conclusions Regarding the Emotional Life of the Infant*. London: Hogarth.

Klein, M. (1955). On identification. In: *Envy and Gratitude and Other Works 1946–1963* (pp. 141–175). London: Karnac, 1997.

Liberman, D., Grassano de Piccolo, E., Neborak de Dimant, S., Pistiner de Cortiñas, L., & Roitman de Woskoboinik, P. (1983). *Del Cuerpo al Símbolo, sobreadaptación y enfermedad psico-somática*. Buenos Aires: Kargieman.

Lumet, S. (Dir.) (1957). *Twelve Angry Men*. United Artists.

Mandelbrot, B. (1982). *Fractal Geometry of Nature*. New York: Henry Holt.

Meltzer, D. (1967). *The Psychoanalytical Process*. London: Karnac.

Meltzer, D. (1973). *Sexual States of Mind*. Strathtay, Perthshire: Clunie Press.

Meltzer, D. (1978). *The Kleinian Development, Part III*. Strathtay, Perthshire: Clunie Press.

Montalcini, R. L. (1987). *Elogio dell'imperfezione*. Rome: Garzanti.

Pistiner de Cortiñas, L. (2007). *The Aesthetic Dimension of the Mind: Variations on a Theme of Bion*. London: Karnac.

Racker, H. (1948). A contribution to the problem of countertransference. *International Journal of Psychoanalysis*, *34*: 313–324.

188 REFERENCES

Racker, H. (1953). Los significados y usos de la contratransferencia. In: *Estudios sobre la contratransferencia*. Buenos Aires: Paidós [also published in *Psychoanalytic Quarterly, 26*: 303–357, 1957].

Segal, H. (1957). Notes on symbol formation. *International Journal of Psycho-Analysis, 38*: 391–397.

Shakespeare, W. (1951a). *The Tempest*. Tudor Edition. London & Glasgow: Collins Clear-Type Press [reprinted June 1953].

Shakespeare, W. (1951b). *A Midsummer Night's Dream*. Tudor Edition. London & Glasgow: Collins Clear-Type Press [reprinted June 1953].

Spitz, R. (1968). *La Premiére annee de la vie de l'enfant*. Paris: Presses Universitaires de France.

Trotter, W. (1916). *Instincts of the Herd in Peace and in War*. London: Unwin.

INDEX

abstraction, xiii, 15, 40–41, 44, 49,
    64–65, 111–113, 116, 129, 131,
    134, 137, 154
anxiety, 6, 20, 24, 30, 40–41, 45, 51, 54,
    68, 72, 80, 82, 86, 144, 152, 170, 176
    catastrophic, 2–3, 23, 30, 44, 49,
        164, 169–172, 175
    claustrophobic, 21
    depressive, 116, 118–119, 161
    fragmentation, 116, 164
    infant's, xxii, 118
    intense, 40–41
    modulation of, 105, 164
    overwhelming, 39
    paranoid, 40, 43, 48, 53, 56
    persecutory, 118
    primitive, 162, 164
    psychotic, 23, 56
    unbearable, xxii
Argentine Psychoanalytic
    Association (APA), xi
Aronofsky, D., 34, 39

Baranger, M., xi
Baranger, W., xi
Bergman, I., 10, 138–140, 142, 150
Bion, W. R. (*passim*)
    alpha
        elements, 96, 99–102, 109,
            113–114, 122–124, 127, 129,
            134–137, 155, 164, 177
        function, xiii–xix, xxi–xxiii, 15,
            19, 22, 25, 31, 34, 65, 69,
            96–101, 105–106, 108–109,
            113–114, 118, 121–124, 127,
            134–137, 153–156, 158, 164,
            167–171, 174–177, 181
    basic assumption (BA), 5–6, 28, 77,
        82, 92
        dependence, 5
        dynamic, 77, 92
        fight or flight, 5
        group, 5, 73, 77
        pairing, 5
        principle, 69, 72

190   INDEX

beta elements, 21, 75, 96, 99–100,
106, 127, 134, 137, 155–156
caesura, 102–103, 138, 142–143,
163–164, 180
cited works
A Long Week-end, 1
A Memoir of the Future.
Book I: The Dream;
Book II: The Past Presented;
Book III: The Dawn of
Oblivion, xvii, 11
A theory of thinking, 10, 62, 134
All My Sins Remembered: Another
Part of a Life and the Other
Side of Genius: Family Letters,
1, 6
Attacks on linking, 10, 35–36, 47
Attention and Interpretation, xxiv,
7, 9, 68, 74, 151, 160
Bion in New York and São Paulo,
28
Cogitations, xiii, 11, 16, 29, 51, 59,
66, 81–82, 98, 100, 107,
123–124, 126, 133, 135, 161,
166–167, 170–175
Differentiation of the psychotic
from the non-psychotic
personalities, 10, 13, 15, 19,
23, 27, 36, 100, 126
Elements of Psycho-analysis, 9–10,
95, 99, 111, 113, 115, 119,
125, 129–131, 134, 153
Emotional turbulence, 10
Evidence, 10
Experiences in Groups, 3, 5–7, 9,
51, 95, 166–168
Learning from Experience, 9, 18,
28, 30, 36, 59–60, 62, 65, 67,
75, 90, 95–98, 101, 104–105,
107–109, 113, 115, 117, 133,
135–136, 152–153
Making the best of a bad job, xiii,
xxi, 10, 108, 151, 166
Notes on the theory of
schizophrenia, 9–10
On a quotation from Freud, 10
On arrogance, 10, 30
On hallucination, 10
Second Thoughts, 7–9, 13–15, 23,
26, 30, 60, 62, 95, 100, 106,
134, 136, 168
The development of
schizophrenic thought, 10,
15
The imaginary twin, 7, 9, 32
The Tavistock Seminars, 152
Transformations: Change from
Learning to Growth, xx, 9, 95,
133, 155, 178
Two Papers: The Grid and Caesura,
10
Grid, xviii, 64, 83, 111–112, 125,
129, 131, 134, 153–154, 182
H, 103–104, 106, 113, 135–136,
154, 168, 172, 180
–H, 104
K, 103–106, 113, 134, 136, 152,
154–156, 158–160, 162, 164,
168, 172, 174, 180
–K, 61, 76, 104–105, 107, 136,
159–160, 181
L, 93, 103–104, 106, 113, 135–136,
154, 162, 168, 172, 180
–L, 104
O, xiii, 152, 155–164, 168–169,
174–175
Bléandonu, G., 95
Borges, J. L., 131
Brecht, B., 67
British Psychoanalytical Society, 7–8

Carroll, L., 133, 153
catastrophic, xxii, 141, 151 *see also*:
anxiety
change, xiii, xix, xxiii–xxiv, 2,
81–83, 86, 116, 138, 140–142,
152, 154–155, 158–159
fears, 31
feelings, 23
communication, 14, 28–32, 35, 60, 62,
66, 68, 102, 112, 117, 133–134,
156, 167, 169–170, 173–177, 179

analytical, 62
channel of, 101, 109, 169, 171
difficulty in, 134
disorders, 68
existence of, 173
function of, 35
intrapsychic, 36
intrasubjective, 128
modes of, 167
organ, 51
primitive, xxi, 20, 29–31, 61, 65, 97,
117–118, 167, 169–170, 173,
175–176
private, 35, 127–128
problem of, 134
psychoanalytical, 158
psychosomatic, 176
public, 35, 127–128
quality, 158
realistic, 20
vehicle of, 31, 171, 175
verbal, 35
conflict, 13, 77, 92, 103–104, 121, 124,
142 *see also*: oedipal, Oedipus,
unconscious
emotional, 22, 41, 50–51, 104
of ideas, 23
neurotic, 22–23, 36, 121
psychological, 124
conscious(ness), 16–17, 19, 21, 32–33,
36, 67, 99, 102, 114, 119, 121–122,
124, 127, 143, 164, 180 *see also*:
unconscious
choice, 8, 26
concept of, 63
elements, 101
evolved, 16, 19, 32, 63, 67, 99, 119,
121
mental state, 36
pre-, 114
process, 106
psychic phenomena, 68
representations, 137
rudimentary, 16, 32, 36, 63, 67, 101,
121, 154
truncated, 36, 180

–unconscious
relationship, 36, 113–114
vision, 25
constant conjunction, 41, 82, 89,
115–116, 119–120, 123–124,
126–127, 130, 138–140, 143, 159
container, xiv, xviii, 20, 30, 34, 36–37,
43, 97, 101–104, 117–118, 127,
135, 137–138, 141, 149, 151, 162,
168–169 *see also*: object
adequate, 34, 52
alpha, 109
break-up of, 107
–contained, 67, 102–103
function, xxi, 83
interaction, 119
model, 97
relationship, xxi, xxiii, 6, 20,
29–30, 36, 40, 54, 61, 63, 80,
83, 97, 100, 103, 117–119,
149, 158, 162, 168–169, 177
good enough, 39
lack of, 40, 55, 66
negative, 31
receptive, 30–31, 102, 162
skin, 174
transformational, 43, 97, 100, 162

depressive, 169, 179 *see also*:
anxiety
feelings, 84, 90
guilt, 161
integration, 15
maternal, 178–179
position, 8, 13, 113, 117–118, 122,
161, 164, 169
dream(ing) (*passim*)
capacity to, 114, 122
collective, 144
concept of, 121
fear of, 35
function of, 57, 97, 124, 126
furniture of, 16, 21, 33, 99, 177
hostility towards, 18
incapability to, 18, 36, 47
life, 106

192 INDEX

narrative, 127, 143
night-time, 108
the patient, xxiv
reality, 16, 33, 106
relational, 109
the session, xxiv
theory of, 15
thoughts, 10, 66, 99–100, 105–106,
109, 112–113, 122–123,
126–127, 129, 131, 141, 146,
174, 177–178
waking, 108–109, 141
-work alpha, xxxi, 12, 98–99, 108,
135, 140, 146, 168
world of, 21

ego, xxiii, 13, 21–23, 35, 67, 114, 161,
164, 173, 176
bad, 19
core, 66
fragments of, 99–100
functions, 16–17, 19, 22, 36, 89, 104,
125, 173
mental equipment, 63
splitting of, 13
super-, xxiii, 21–22, 35, 99–100, 114,
142, 145–146
cruel, 149
murdering, 104
primitive, xxiii, 13, 79, 89, 173
super-, 67, 82, 145, 173, 175–177,
181
Einstein, A., xvii, 48
Etchegoyen, H., 115

fear, xiii–xiv, 11, 23, 30–31, 35, 84,
101, 104, 107, 120, 151, 160, 169
Freud, A., 20
Freud, S., xiii, xviii–xix, xxiii–xxiv,
8–10, 12–13, 16–17, 33, 35, 59,
61–63, 68, 99, 105, 108, 113–114,
122–126, 129–130, 135, 137,
144–145, 155–156, 168, 170
cited works, 4, 12–13, 17, 59, 68,
101, 124

Grassano de Piccolo, E., 176
Green, J., 27
Grotstein, J., xii–xiii
guilt, 6, 71, 74–80, 86, 88–89, 107, 161,
172 *see also*: depressive

hallucination, 31, 34, 43–44, 46–49, 51,
53–56, 99, 106, 109, 137, 159
hate, xiii, 3, 36, 103–105, 108, 113,
135–136, 142, 151, 168, 172, 174
Heimann, P., 14

instinct(ive), 18, 31, 59, 122, 161, 165,
171
energy, 61
epistemophilic, 61, 168
life, 31
introjection, xxii, 22, 29, 31, 33, 79, 97,
106
function, 22
identification, 22
infant, xxii
processes, 66
projective–, 25, 63, 66
re-, 31, 66, 97, 101, 127, 168, 170,
176–177, 181
invariance, 48, 81, 141, 154, 156–158

Jonze, S., 20

Klein, M., xi–xii, xviii–xx, xxii, xxiv,
6–9, 13–21, 27, 29, 32–33, 35, 59,
61, 63, 66, 97, 104–105, 108,
113–114, 117–118, 122, 125, 136,
161, 163–164, 168, 172
cited works, 19, 27–28, 169

Lewin, K., xi
Liberman, D., 176
Lumet, S., 71

Mandelbrot, B., 41, 56
Meltzer, D., 18, 21, 100, 104, 137, 152,
155, 158, 169
Montalcini, R. L., 166

Neborak de Dimant, S., 176

object (*passim*)
  actual, 68, 99, 135
  animate, 46, 81
  autistic, 179
  bad, 19
  bizarre, 21, 62, 99–100, 106, 137
  breast-, 104, 167–169, 176, 179
  containing, 168–169, 172
  evacuation of, 22
  evolving, 106
  external, 21
  good, 19
  hostile, 29, 31, 61
  inanimate, 40, 46, 56, 100, 146, 179
  internal, 101, 173
  living, 41–42, 45, 50, 82, 93, 104,
      106–107
  natural, 57
  part-, 60
  psychoanalytic, 68, 106, 130
  receptive, xiv
  related, 81, 116
  relations, 24, 35, 59–60, 161,
      172–173, 178
    early, 6
    hypothesis, 59
    partial, 63
    primitive, xi
  sensory, 134, 144
  symbolised, 127
  thinking, 66
  total, 114, 161
  transformative, 172
  understanding, 101
    mis-, 101
  whole, 119
oedipal
  complex, 33
  conflict, 125, 140
  myth, 144
  preconception, 63, 125, 164, 180
  precursor, 125
  problems, 141
  relationship, 44

situation, 33, 163
triangle, 146, 163
Oedipus, 62, 124, 128
  complex, 124–125, 129
  conflict, 22, 124, 128, 163
  myth, 61, 63, 125–126, 129–130

paranoid–schizoid position, 8, 13,
    18–19, 117–118, 122, 164
phantasy, 13, 18–19, 23, 125, 161, 164
    see also: unconscious
  absence of, 122
  intrusion of, 102
  omnipotent, 19–20, 28–29, 97, 117
phenomena, xi, xiv, xviii, xx, 7, 15,
    25, 32, 51, 96, 113 *see also*:
    unconscious
  group, xx, 5
  infrasensorial, xx
  observable, 59
  psychic, 68
  psychological, xx
  psychosomatic, 51
Pistiner de Cortiñas, L., 159, 171, 176,
    179–180
principle
  of investigation, 157
  of mental functioning, 16
  pleasure, 17, 29
    –pain, 114
  reality, 16–17, 29, 69, 113
  uncertainty, 48, 74
projection, 22–23, 31, 33, 63, 101, 181
projective *see also*: introjection
  geometry, 134, 154, 158
  identification, xiv, xvi, xxi, 8, 14,
      17, 19–25, 27–31, 33, 36, 40, 51,
      53, 61, 63, 65, 67, 80–81, 84–85,
      92, 97, 100–103, 117–120, 127,
      158, 167–173, 175–178
  medium, 156
  non-, 120
  process, 66
  transformations, 157–158, 176–177,
      181
protomental, xx, 34, 51, 166

194 INDEX

psychic
 birth, 34
 catastrophe, 50
 changes, 108, 116
 correlation, 161
 crisis, 140
 data, 68
 death, 80, 176
 functioning, 14
 intra-, 35–36
 life, 109, 168
 part of the personality, 46
 phenomena, 68
 qualities, 63, 68, 114, 121
 reality, 18, 21, 23, 34, 68, 102, 124,
  129, 135, 137–138, 152,
  154–155, 177, 180–181
 soma–, 34, 51
 transformation, 51
 work, 108

Racker, H., xi, 14
reparation, xxii, 23, 111, 161, 163–164,
 172
repression, 19, 23, 32, 85, 114, 122,
 124
Rickman, J., 4–5
Roitman de Woskoboinik, P., 176
Rosenfeld, H., 6

Segal, H., 6, 22
selected fact (SF), 40–41, 77–78,
 82, 91, 115, 117, 119–120,
 122–124, 131, 138–140, 146,
 162, 164
self, xiii, 172
 -affirmative, 139
 authentic, 31
 -aware, 55
 -esteem, 79
 frenetic, 56
 -generated, 179
 -immune, 177
 -knowledge, 69, 172, 174
 -reflection, xii
Shakespeare, W., 67, 74, 111, 120

Spitz, R., 66
splitting, 13, 17–19, 22, 28, 33, 50, 104,
 115 *see also*: ego
 enforced, 41, 50, 104, 115
 minute, 21
 natural, 19
 static, 115
symbol(-ism), 14–16, 21–22, 30, 32, 53,
 60, 78, 87, 90, 96, 102, 113,
 124–127, 133, 137, 163

transference, 25, 35
 counter-, xi, 14
 linear, 24
 movement, 24–25
 psychotic, 23–24
tropism, xiv, xvi, 51, 60, 160–162,
 165–181
Trotter, W., 4

unconscious(ness), xix, xxiv, 13, 16,
 19, 36, 62, 99, 102, 114, 122, 127,
 143, 154, 156, 164 *see also*:
 conscious
 conflict, 81, 124
 dynamic, 114
 elements, 101
 function, xix
 mental life, 143
 motivations, 73
 phantasy, 18–19, 64, 122, 125, 161
 phenomena, 68
 process, xii, 106
 quality, 114
 representations, 137
 repressed, 114
 thought, 33, 99
  waking, 100

violence, 16, 22–23, 30, 34, 80–81, 85,
 88, 104, 139–141, 176–177, 181
vision *see also*: conscious
 binocular, 7, 9, 25, 32–33, 114,
  137
 hyper-realistic, 102, 106
 monocular, 25

monolithic, 90
panoramic, 11
surrealistic, 21

Wilde, O., 143
world, 1, 19, 21, 40–41, 48, 56, 66, 76,
 130, 146, 159
 animate, 180
 arid, 180
 autistic, 179, 181
 chaotic, 47

external, 17, 32, 134–135, 177
hallucinotic, 178
inanimate, 171, 180
inner, 177
lifeless, 179
motionless, 142
outside, 68, 99, 129
primitive, 30
psychoanalytic, xi
psychotic, 176, 197
toxic, 178